POETIC CLOSURE

A Study of How Poems End

POETIC CLOSURE

A Study of How Poems End

BY

BARBARA HERRNSTEIN SMITH

The University of Chicago Press

CHICAGO LONDON

Library of Congress Catalog Card Number: 68–15034
The University of Chicago Press, Chicago 60637
The University of Chicago Press, Ltd., London W.C. 1

Published 1968. Printed in the United States of America

To J. V. Cunningham

Preface

This study is concerned with how poems end. It grew out of an earlier one that was concerned with how Shakespeare's sonnets both go and end; and although the child has consumed the parent, it testifies to its lineage throughout these pages, where sonnets, Shakespearean and other, will be rather frequently encountered. In my earlier attempts to describe and to some extent account for the strengths and weaknesses of Shakespeare's sonnet endings, I found myself involved at almost every point with more general considerations of poetic structure and with what I finally recognized as a subject in its own right, poetic closure. I also found that, although literary theorists from Aristotle on have been occupied with beginnings, middles, *and* ends, there had not been (aside from a brief and somewhat whimsical essay by I. A. Richards) any treatment of this subject as such. The questions and problems that pushed outward from sonnet endings to lyric closure in general continued to move out toward even broader considerations of closure in all literature, in all art, and finally in all experience. Having bumped into a continent, however, and even having set a flag upon the shore, I realized that I was equipped to explore and chart only a bit of the coastal area. It seemed wise, then, to hold the line at poetic closure. Accordingly, the more general aspects of the problem appear primarily in the introductory chapter, and thereafter as allusions to fiction, art, and music in occasional digressions and illustrative analogies.

Personal limitations defined the scope of the study from the outset, and personal prejudices—or at least particular assumptions—shaped it all along. These assumptions are initially outlined in chapter 1 as some rather dogmatically asserted, but not altogether unfamiliar, notions regarding poetry, the reader's perception of poetic structure, and other matters relating to the general subject of closure. The organization of the chapters that follow was dictated by the basic proposition that closure—the sense of finality, stability, and integrity—is an effect that depends primarily upon the reader's experience of the structure of the entire poem. Thus, chapter 2 examines the relation between closure and various formal structures, chapter 3 that between closure and various thematic structures. Chapter 4 considers the limited but significant extent to which closural effects may be obtained or strenghtened by terminal features in a poem that function more or less independently of its particular structure. Chapter 5 is concerned with a number of related points that follow from the observation that closure is relative in strength, and that various degrees as well as modes of closure may have expressive effects. Two special problems receive particular attention in this final chapter, namely failures of closure and the apparent cultivation of "anti-closure" in modern poetry. The final section returns to some of the definitions and assumptions outlined in chapter 1 as they are implicitly challenged or qualified by some radical developments in the theory and practice of contemporary poetry and art.

I should point out here that the categories used in this study, especially those in chapter 3, are not always the traditional ones and frequently cut across conventional classifications by genre and period. The reason for this is quite simple: since the traditional categories do not usually discriminate the structural features of a poem that are most significant in the reader's experience of closure, to adhere to them would be to obscure the distinctions most interesting for our purposes. My object, in this study, was neither to account for the closural aspects of every poem ever written nor to provide a historical survey of closural features and practices. It was, rather, to explore the general dynamics of the relation between structure and closure in poetry, and to illustrate the points with a consideration of the most familiar and prevalent structural types. I would hope, however, that the exploration was extensive enough, the principles that emerged substantial enough, and the illustrations numerous and representative enough to enable others to understand better the closural aspects of poetry in general and of whatever particular poems interested them.

Not every poem cited here receives equally full attention: a slighty lyric by Herrick may receive as much space as, and much closer consideration than, *Paradise Lost*. My procedure in this regard was to give each example only as much attention as seemed warranted by the point in hand—as much, in other words, as seemed necessary to clarify the point it served to illustrate. The poems cited, moreover, are "representative" only with respect to structural types or closural modes; although examples are drawn from diverse periods, poets, and styles, no attempt was made to achieve historical or geographical "balance." Almost all the poems cited are in English, and probably more of them were written in the sixteenth and seventeenth centuries than in any other period. The bias here reflects, again, my own interests and limitations, but should not compromise the validity of the general points or the usefulness of the particular categories. Readers who are dismayed by the scarcity of allusions to classical, medieval, continental, or non-European poetry will, I believe, find few poems written in these periods or languages with structural or closural features that utterly elude the classifications offered here.

The line between memory and invention is often blurred, and I have surely not cited all those whose work has been of significance to me in this study or whose concepts have been incorporated in it. I would like to mention a few, however, whose works have been of considerably more importance here than is apparent from the explicit references in my text and bibliography. Two recent studies served as heartening examples of what could be done to break through the isolation and incestuousness that have characterized aesthetics for so long: Leonard B. Meyer's *Emotion and Meaning in Music* (Chicago, 1956) and E. H. J. Gombrich's *Art and Illusion* (New York, 1960), both of which bear impressive witness to the relevance of the experimental study of behavior and perception to questions of style and effect in the arts. I owe a special debt to Meyer's work for mediating at many points between my own amateurish knowledge and the technical concepts and terminology of the psychology of perception. I have also appropriated some crucial concepts and terms from B. F. Skinner's *Verbal Behavior* (New York, 1957)—often, I suspect, for purposes that would perplex or dismay their author. The notions and approaches of I. A. Richards, Kenneth Burke, and Yvor Winters will be recognizable enough throughout these pages, but I gratefully acknowledge here my general indebtedness to the work of each of them, particularly to Richards' *Principles of Literary Criticism* (London, 1924), Burke's *Counter-Statement* (Chicago, 1931), and Winters' *In Defense of Reason* (Denver, 1943). This study is dedicated to J. V. Cunningham—a primary source incapable of receiving adequate acknowledgement, for there is hardly a page here that does not carry the impress of his mind and, probably even more than I realize, the echo of his words. I should also mention, however, that not every page carries the approval of his sceptical eye.

I have had, throughout the preparation of this study, the benefit of the interest, learning, and encouragement of my colleages at Brandeis University and Bennington College. I am especially grateful to Catherine O. Foster, Victor Harris, Stanley Edgar Hyman, Harold Kaplan, and Howard Nemerov for their scrutiny of early drafts, for the many hardheaded objections and substantive suggestions they made, and for the genial way in which they made them. I was spared financial expense in connection with this study by grants from the Faculty Facilities Fund and the Huber Foundation at Bennington College, and I was spared considerable time and energy by the skill and attentiveness of Miss Isabel

Sherwood, who prepared the typescript. Finally, I must thank my husband, Thomas H. Smith, for his dependable good sense and good humor while this work was being generated, for the opinions of it that he offered and withheld, and for his respect, which made all the difference.

Acknowledgement is due to those who granted permission to reprint the following copyrighted material:

"From the country of the Yerewas," reprinted from *Primitive Song* by C. M. Bowra by permission of The World Publishing Company and Weidenfeld & Nicolson Ltd.

"i was sitting in mcsorlay's," copyright 1925 by E. E. Cummings; "r-p-o-p-h-e-s-s-a-g-r," copyright 1935 by E. E. Cummings, renewed 1963 by Marion Morehouse Cummings. Reprinted from *Poems 1923–1954* by E. E. Cummings by permission of Harcourt, Brace & World, Inc.

"You wonder why *Drab* sells her love for gold," and "All hastens to its end," from *The Exclusions of a Rhyme* by J. V. Cunningham, reprinted by permission of Swallow Press, Denver, Colorado.

Excerpts from "The Love Song of J. Alfred Prufrock," "Portrait of a Lady," and "Gerontion," reprinted from T. S. Eliot's *Collected Poems 1909–1962* by permission of Harcourt, Brace & World, Inc. Excerpt from "East Coker" in *Four Quartets*, copyright 1943 by T. S. Eliot, reprinted by permission of Harcourt, Brace & World, Inc. and Faber & Faber Ltd.

Excerpt from "Legal Fiction," reprinted from *Collected Poems of William Empson* by permission of Harcourt, Brace & World, Inc.

"Acrobats," by Ian Hamilton Finlay, reprinted by permission of the author and Mr. John Furnival of the Bath Academy of Art.

"Dedication of a Bow: to Serapis" by Kallimachos, from Dudley Fitts, *Poems from the Greek Anthology*. Copyright 1938, 1941, © 1956 by New Directions. Reprinted by permission of New Directions Publishing Corporation.

"Nothing Gold Can Stay," from *Complete Poems of Robert Frost*. Copyright 1923 by Holt, Rinehart and Winston, Inc. Copyright 1951 by Robert Frost. Reprinted by permission of Holt, Rinehart and Winston, Inc. and Jonathan Cape Limited.

"The Straw," from *Collected Poems 1965* by Robert Graves. Copyright © 1955 by Robert Graves. Reprinted by permission of the author and Collins-Knowlton-Wing, Inc.

Excerpt from "At Castle Boterel," reprinted by permission of The Macmillan Company from *Collected Poems* by Thomas Hardy. Copyright 1925 by The Macmillan Company. First published in Great Britain in 1916.

"The Summing-Up," copyright © 1958 by Stanley Kunitz, reprinted from *Selected Poems, 1928–1958* by Stanley Kunitz by permission of Atlantic–Little, Brown and Co.

"The Crack," from *O Taste and See* by Denise Levertov. Copyright © 1964 by Denise Levertov Goodman. Reprinted by permission of New Directions Publishing Corporation.

Excerpt from "The Drinker," reprinted from *For the Union Dead* by Robert Lowell by permission of Farrar, Straus & Giroux, Inc. Copyright © 1960 by Robert Lowell.

"I'll tell you a story About Jack a Nory," from *The Oxford Dictionary of Nursery Rhymes*, edited by Iona and Peter Opie. Reprinted by permission of the Clarendon Press, Oxford.

Excerpt from "Anthem for Doomed Youth," from *The Collected Poems of Wilfred Owen*, edited by C. Day Lewis. Copyright © Chatto & Windus Ltd, 1963. Reprinted by permission of New Directions Publishing Corporation, Chatto & Windus Ltd, and Mr. Harold Owen.

"In a Station of the Metro," from *Personae* by Ezra Pound. Copyright 1926, 1953 by Ezra Pound. Reprinted by permission of New Directions Publishing Corporation and Faber & Faber Ltd.

Excerpt from "By the Pool," reprinted from *The Screens and Other Poems* by I. A. Richards by permission of Harcourt, Brace & World, Inc. and Routledge & Kegan Paul Ltd.

Excerpt from "Many Are Called," reprinted by permission of

The Macmillan Company from *Collected Poems* by E. A. Robinson. Copyright 1921 by E. A. Robinson, renewed 1949 by Ruth Nivison.

"My Papa's Waltz," copyright 1942 by Hearst Magazines, Inc. Reprinted from *The Collected Poems of Theodore Roethke* by permission of Doubleday & Company, Inc.

Excerpts from "Sunday Morning," "Thirteen Ways of Looking at a Blackbird," and "Debris of Life and Mind," reprinted from *The Collected Poems of Wallace Stevens* by permission of Alfred A. Knopf, Inc. and Faber & Faber Ltd.

Excerpt from "A Refusal to Mourn the Death, by Fire, of a Child in London," from *The Collected Poems of Dylan Thomas.* Copyright 1945 by the Trustees of the Estate of Dylan Thomas. Reprinted by permission of New Directions Publishing Corporation, J. M. Dent & Sons Ltd, and the Trustees for the Copyrights of the late Dylan Thomas.

Excerpt from Bartolomeo Vanzetti's "Last Speech to the Court," from "Appendix II" of *The Letters of Sacco and Vanzetti,* edited by Marion Denman Frankfurter and Gardner Jackson. Copyright 1928, 1956 by The Viking Press, Inc. Reprinted by permission of The Viking Press, Inc.

"Sunflowers," from *The Collected Later Poems* of William Carlos Williams, copyright 1950 by William Carlos Williams; "Between Walls" and "This Is Just to Say," from *The Collected Earlier Poems* of William Carlos Williams, copyright 1938, 1951, by William Carlos Williams. Reprinted by permission of New Directions Publishing Corporation and MacGibbon and Kee Ltd.

Excerpts from "John Day, Frontiersman," "To a Young Writer," and "On Teaching the Young," reprinted from *Collected Poems* by Yvor Winters by permission of Swallow Press, Denver, Colorado.

"Down by the Salley Gardens," copyright 1906 by The Macmillan Company, renewed 1934 by William B. Yeats; excerpts from "Among School Children" and "Leda and the Swan," copyright 1928 by The Macmillan Company, renewed 1956 by Georgie

Yeats; excerpts from "The Second Coming" and "The O'Rahilly," copyright 1924 by The Macmillan Company, renewed 1952 by Bertha Georgie Yeats. Reprinted from *Collected Poems* by William Butler Yeats by permission of The Macmillan Company, Mr. M. B. Yeats, and Macmillan & Co. Ltd.

CONTENTS

1 *Introduction*

Done, finished, over. *Consummatum est. La commedia è finita.* The idea of that which is terminated suggests both dread and satisfaction. As Johnson wrote, in the last of the *Idler* essays:

> There are few things not purely evil, of which we can say, without some emotion of uneasiness, "this is the last." Those who never could agree together, shed tears when mutual discontent has determined them to final separation; of a place which has been frequently visited, tho' without pleasure, the last look is taken with heaviness of heart. . . . This secret horrour of the last is inseparable from a thinking being whose life is limited, and to whom death is dreadful.[1]

It may be partly for the same reason, however, that the reverse is also true: there are few things, good or evil, of which we can say without some emotion of uneasiness, "the end will never come." Haunted, perhaps, by the specter of that ultimate arbitrary conclusion, we take particular delight, not in all endings, but in those that are designed. Our most gratifying experiences tend to be not the interminable ones but rather those that conclude.

There is a distinction, however, between concluding and merely

[1] Samuel Johnson, *The Idler and The Adventurer*, eds. W. J. Bate, John M. Bullitt, and L. F. Powell (New York and London, 1963), pp. 314–15.

stopping or ceasing. The ringing of a telephone, the blowing of the wind, the babbling of an infant in its crib: these stop. A poem or a piece of music concludes. We tend to speak of conclusions when a sequence of events has a relatively high degree of structure, when, in other words, we can perceive these events as related to one another by some principle of organization or design that implies the existence of a definite termination point. Under these circumstances, the occurrence of the terminal event is a confirmation of expectations that have been established by the structure of the sequence, and is usually distinctly gratifying. The sense of stable conclusiveness, finality, or "clinch" which we experience at that point is what is referred to here as *closure.*

Closure need not, however, be temporal; that is, it is not always a matter of endings. Indeed, the term has been used most frequently by psychologists to refer to a quality of visually perceived forms, spatial structures which exhibit relatively clear, coherent, and continuous shape. In such forms no particular point is experienced as the *last* one; and although one can speak of closure in works of spatial art it is obviously inappropriate to speak of it there as a quality of finality or conclusiveness. Whether spatially or temporally perceived, a structure appears "closed" when it is experienced as integral: coherent, complete, and stable.

It would seem that in the common land of ordinary events—where many experiences are fragmentary, interrupted, fortuitously connected, and determined by causes beyond our agency or comprehension—we create or seek out "enclosures": structures that are highly organized, separated as if by an implicit frame from a background of relative disorder or randomness, and integral or complete. Not only works of art are thus distinguished, of course; other events and activities, such as games, may exhibit the qualities just described. A game of chess or football has integrity and a relatively high degree of structure; it also concludes and not merely stops.

The sources of our gratification in closure probably lie in the most fundamental aspects of our psychological and physiological organization, an area where speculation is attractive but ignorance keeps pulling us up short. If we refer the satisfaction in closure to what we commonly affirm to be our more general satisfaction in, or search for, order, we have really not said much, for the sources of *that* satisfaction have certainly not been established. Perhaps all we can say, and even this may be too much, is that varying degrees or states of tension seem to be involved in all our experiences, and that the most gratifying ones are those in which whatever tensions are created are also released. Or, to use another familiar set of terms, an experience is gratifying to the extent that those expectations that are aroused are also fulfilled.

We have, however, learned to qualify both these formulations in the recognition that the most direct fulfilment of expectations or immediate release of tensions is not, after all, as gratifying as something a little different. The most direct way to release the tension of being hungry is to eat a square meal, but when we enter a restaurant with healthy appetites and begin by ordering an "appetizer," we obviously have some other route to gratification in mind. We enjoy, it seems, teasing our tensions, deferring the immediate fulfilment of our appetites and expectations. What we gain thereby is a local heightening of tension which, it might be supposed, makes the eventual resolution all the more satisfying. It is also true, however, that the experience of tension is not necessarily unpleasant, but, on the contrary, may be itself a source of pleasure, especially if the promise of eventual resolution is secure. When we hear a piece of music in which the continual presence of structural principles yields the sort of promise I am referring to here, our pleasure derives largely from the tensions created by local deferments of resolution and evasions of expectation. One suspects that poetry affects us in the same fashion, and contemporary literary theorists have certainly made us increasingly aware of the numerous sources of tension in poetry (though they sometimes tend, rather misleadingly, to locate the tensions in the poem rather than in the reader). In any case, it is evident that our experience of a poem is not a series of continual frustrations or disappointments that are resolved only at the conclusion of the work. It is rather that the sense of conclusiveness in the last lines of a poem, like the finality of the last chords of a sonata, seems to confirm retrospectively, as if with a final stamp of approval, the valued qualities of the entire experience we have just sustained.

Further speculation on the general psychological dynamics of closure is tempting (and the temptation will not always be resisted in the pages that follow), but speculation it must remain. Our terms here, such as "tension" and "states of expectation," are likely to appear naïve and become obsolete when the psychology and presumably the physiology of perception are better understood. One point, however, whatever its eventual translation may be, seems secure enough, and it is quite central to the present study: namely, that the sense of closure is a function of the perception of structure.

I A Definition of Poetic Structure

It will be useful to regard the structure of a poem as consisting of the principles by which it is generated or according to which one element follows another. The description of a poem's structure, then, becomes the answer to the question, "What keeps it going?" To think of poetic structure this way, rather than as an organization of, or relationship among, elements, is to emphasize the temporal and dynamic qualities that poetry shares with music. Moreover, it allows the possibility of a corollary question, namely, "What stops it from going?" and immediately suggests the close relationship between poetic structure and closure.

The principles of poetic and musical structure are comparable insofar as both forms of art produce experiences which occur over a period of time and are continuously modified by successive events. Because language, however, has semantic or symbolic as well as physical properties, poetic structure is considerably more complex. A sonata consists only of an organization of sounds, but a sonnet consists of an organization of symbols as well. The conclusion of a poem is, therefore, doubly determined. The sonnet, composed in accordance with a particular meter and rhyme scheme, necessarily concludes at the last syllable of the fourteenth line. It also concludes, however, at the end of a sentence, for it has been composed in accordance with—or at least in reference to—the principles of linguistic discourse.

The consequences of the double nature of language become even more relevant to poetic structure and closure when we consider that a poem is an utterance or, as I shall explain later on (section III), the imitation of an utterance. A sonnet is not merely a syntactically correct organization of linguistic symbols, but it also represents a statement or speech of some kind: an argument, perhaps, or a declaration, or lament. It concludes, therefore, not merely with the completion of a line and a sentence, but with the completion of that utterance: the argument is clinched, the catalogue of praise is exhausted, the lament is brought to some point of acceptable conclusion. Similarly, the narrative poem in heroic couplets concludes not only with a completed couplet, but also with a completed story.

Now it will be noticed that in one respect these descriptions are quite circular: they amount to saying, "The poem will end at the end." The dynamics of that circularity will be the subject of this study. A poem continues to go in a certain way until, at a certain appropriate point, it stops going. What will concern us is what makes that point indeed "appropriate": why, and under what circumstances, the reader has the sense that cessation is also conclusion.

Certain terms that appear repeatedly in the pages that follow are used in a somewhat restricted, though not otherwise unusual, sense. The words "form" and "structure," for example, are often used interchangeably to refer to the general organization of a poem, but I have found it useful to distinguish them. *Structure* is the more general term, and will be defined as the product of all the principles, both formal and thematic, by which a poem is generated: the principles, as I said above, according to which one line (or any other unit, larger or smaller, from a sound to a sentence or a stanza) follows another. *Form,* here, will be simply equivalent to formal structure. It is the product of formal principles of generation only: the systematic repetition or patterning of certain elements.

The division of structural principles into two kinds, formal and thematic, corresponds to a more general division which, because it is inherent in the double nature of language, can be observed in all the elements of a poem. *Formal elements* are defined as those which arise from the physical nature of words, and would include such features as rhyme, alliteration, and syllabic meter. The *thematic elements* of a poem are those which arise from the symbolic or conventional nature of words, and to which only someone familiar with the language could respond; they would include everything from reference to syntax to tone.

The use of some of these terms can be illustrated in the following poem:

> The Heart asks Pleasure—first—
> And then—Excuse from Pain—
> And then—those little Anodynes
> That deaden suffering—
>
> And then—to go to sleep—
> And then—if it should be
> The will of its Inquisitor
> The privilege to die— [2]

The form (or formal structure) may be described as a pattern of alternating weak- and strong-stressed syllables, divided by lines into

[2] *The Complete Poems of Emily Dickinson,* ed. Thomas H. Johnson (Boston, 1960), p. 262.

units of 6–6–8–6, repeated once.[3] When we add that the final sounds of the second and fourth lines in each stanza are near-rhymes, we have mentioned all the principles involved in the formal generation of the poem. Other formal elements appear and even recur in the poem, of course, but none of them systematically enough to be considered part of its formal structure. These, then, may be referred to as *nonstructural elements*. Among the more notable of them here are the repetition of the sounds /ae–e/ in lines 2–6 ("And then," and "That deaden"), the formal parallelism of lines 5 and 6, and the predominance of /i/ among the vowels of the last three lines. These nonstructural elements are of considerable importance in the effect of the poem, but neither their appearance nor recurrence is determined by any systematic principle, and, as we shall see, this fact will affect the reader's experience of them in relation to closure.

The thematic structure of Dickinson's poem is generated by three principles concurrently: (1) a single syntactic sequence of subject, verb, and compound series of predicate nouns and noun phrases; (2) a temporal sequence ("first . . . and then . . . and then . . . ," etc.); and (3) a quantitative sequence with respect to what might be called "degree of sensation" ("pleasure . . . excuse from pain . . . anodynes . . . to sleep . . . to die"). Among the innumerable thematic elements that are significant in the effect of the poem, but not systematic enough to constitute principles of generation, are the following: the appearance of "deaden" in line 4 and its modified recurrence in the last line ("to die"); the modification of syntactic parallelism in lines 3–4 and the suspension of it in lines 6–7; the suggestions of the word "Inquisitor"; and the ironic juxtaposition of "privilege" and "die" in the concluding lines. These, again, would be regarded as nonstructural elements.

[3] Meter is a special problem. My examples in the pages that follow are almost all from English poetry, where meter is based at least partly on stress, and the perception of stress-determined meter does depend upon the recognition of such *thematic* elements as syntax. Nevertheless, meter must be regarded as a *formal* element, for it is the physical property of stress that is patterned to produce it.

A complete description of the poem's structure would include an analysis of the relations between formal and thematic elements: for example, the rhythmic variations and the way in which certain lines (1 and 2) reinforce syntactic parallelism and others (particularly 6) deflect it.[4]

II The Perception of Poetic Structure

Analogies between music and poetry are always suggestive, and particularly so in connection with closure. For one thing, because closure in music is a more familiar concept than poetic closure, allusions to the one will often clarify observations on the other. Moreover, the principles of musical closure have been analyzed and described in great detail, and their general features are understood about as well as anything in musical structure—which means a great deal better than anything in poetic structure.[5] In the pages that follow, I shall draw from time to time upon the possibilities of this analogy. Any extrapolation from music to poetry is, however, limited, for the analogy must always stop short at just the point where poetry becomes, for most purposes, most interesting: that is, where the symbolic rather than the physical properties of language are involved.[6]

[4] Some further comments on this poem will be found below, pp. 111–12.

[5] Cf. Robert Lundin, *An Objective Psychology of Music* (New York, 1953), pp. 70–75; Paul R. Farnsworth, *The Social Psychology of Music* (New York, 1958), pp. 41–43; Leonard B. Meyer, *Emotion and Meaning in Music* (Chicago, 1956), pp. 128–56. Lundin and Farnsworth both discuss the famous "Lipps-Meyer Law," a phenomenon discovered and first investigated in the early 1900's, and described by Farnsworth as "the striking finality effects [that] can be obtained by playing a successive interval (or broken chord or melody) where the ratio of the frequency of one of the tones is to that of the other as 2 or some multiple of 2 is to some other number" (p. 42).

[6] Several studies of prosody have made use of the presumed similarities between poetry and music, among them Sidney Lanier's *The Science of English Verse* (New York, 1907), George R. Stewart's *The Technique of English Verse* (New York, 1930), and Henry Lanz's *The Physical Basis*

What shall concern us for the moment is the fact that, since poetry and music both produce experiences that are temporally organized, the principles of poetic and musical structure are to that extent comparable. The fact that a poem may have spatial extension—that its text is situated on a page, framed by a margin, and arranged typographically in a certain way—may, of course, affect the reader's sense of its structure. But in general it is more accurate and more revealing to regard the text of a poem as analogous to the score of a piece of music. In an essay entitled "On Speaking Verse," Paul Valéry writes:

> A poem, like a piece of music, offers merely a text, which, strictly speaking, is only a kind of recipe; the cook who follows it plays an essential part. To speak of a poem in itself, to judge of a poem in itself, has no real or precise meaning. It is to speak of a potentiality. The poem is an abstraction, a piece of writing that stands waiting, a law that lives only in some human mouth, and that mouth is simply a mouth.[7]

Like musical notation, the printed words of a poem are not so much the symbolic representation of sounds as a conventionalized system of directions for making them. Or, to put it another way, the text of a poem and the score of a piece of music each provide minimum directions for the performance of the work in question. This is most apparent when we think of dramatic literature, for the relation between script and score is clear. What seems to distinguish the text of a lyric from the text of a play (or the score of a concerto) is the fact that, in the latter, a performer mediates between the artist's directions and the audience. We may keep the

---

of Rime (London, 1931). Their common deficiencies are discussed by René Wellek and Austin Warren in *Theory of Literature* (New York, 1949), pp. 169–72, and Lanz's work is considered briefly below (pp. 46–49). The work to which I am indebted for most of the musical allusions that appear here is Leonard B. Meyer's *Emotion and Meaning in Music* (see n. 5), a book that has almost nothing to say about poetry, but a great deal to say about music.

[7] *The Art of Poetry*, trans. Denise Folliot (New York, 1961), p. 162.

analogy alive, however, by considering that when a lyric poem is read, the reader is functioning as both actor (and director or conductor, if you like) and audience; that is, he responds to his own performance of the poem, a performance which he executes according to his interpretation of the directions given to him by the printed text.[8] Meter, for example, is certainly not a property of the text itself, but only of its performance; one cannot respond to the meter of a poem without "hearing" it performed, either by another reader or by one's self, vocally or subvocally.[9]

The analogy of text to score can take us further than I intend to go just now. For the moment, I wish only to point out some of the implications for this study which may be drawn from the fact that, when we read a poem, what we respond to is not primarily the static spatial array of marks on a page, but the very process of our own performance. It is the experience of this process which is organized by the structure of the poem, and it is that experience which is concluded at the end of it.

One of the most important implications is that the reader's experience is not only continuous over a period of time, but continuously changes in response to succeeding events. As we read, structural principles, both formal and thematic, are gradually deployed and perceived; and as these principles make themselves known, we are engaged in a steady process of readjustment and retrospective patterning.

Part of this process can be illustrated if we take a look at those alphabetical series which used to (and perhaps still do) appear on I.Q. tests. The problem is to continue a series of which only the

[8] We might also remember that a lyric was originally only the verbal part of a performance which was made up of words and music together. When directions for performing the music came to be codified in a score, directions for performing the lyrics were codified in a text. Cf. Bruce Pattison, *Music and Poetry of the English Renaissance* (London, 1948), pp. 20–38.

[9] How remote the performance is from actual physical production is beside the point, as are the neurological locus and form of the sounds heard by the "inner ear." In any case, it must take at least as long to read a poem as to recite it, and the physical properties of each word must be given their appropriate value.

first few units are given. For example, if we are given the series

A B A B A B A______,

and we see that it seems to be generated on the principle of alternating *A* and *B*, we can continue it by writing *B* in the blank. Or, given the series

A B C D E______,

we would probably assume that it was generated in accordance with the conventional sequence of letters in the Roman alphabet, and continue it with *F*. These two examples correspond, respectively, to the perception of formal and thematic principles of generation in poetry. In the first, the perception of an alternating pattern does not depend upon any knowledge of the symbolic or conventional nature of the letters. Someone knowing only the Hebrew or Greek alphabet could see the pattern as well as an American. The letters are patterned with respect to their form only, and could be replaced by:

In the second example, however, the principle of the series could be perceived only by someone familiar with the conventional sequence. The formal properties of the letters will give him no clue as to the pattern. It would be as if we asked him to complete the series:

Now it is clear that when a series is laid out before us on a page, we can examine the relations between the units easily enough. What would happen, however, if they were given to us not in spatial, but in temporal, sequence? Let us say the examination is oral, and the examiner reads the letters to us one by one. First we hear

A.

This gives us no information at all, except insofar as familiarity with such tests would lead us to expect a letter, rather than a number or a word or a bell, to follow. Next we hear

B.

At this point, familiarity with the alphabet may lead us to expect C, but we might remember that other principles of generation could be involved. When we hear, as the third item, another

A.

we immediately readjust our expectation of an alphabetical sequence and begin to assume that a pattern of alternation is to follow. If the series is, indeed, alternate A and B, each succeeding unit, as it is offered, will reinforce our assumption of that pattern, and the series will become more and more predictable. We might remember, however, that until the series is announced as *concluded,* we cannot be sure of the pattern. The examiner might continue, for example, so that the series was

A
B
A
B
C
D
C
D
E
F
E
F, etc.

or

A
B
A
C
A

D
A
E
A
F, etc.

In each case, when our expectation was foiled (at the first C in each example), we would readjust not only our expectations concerning the future items, but also our perception of the preceding ones. The latter response is what I referred to above as "retrospective patterning."

If we are actually taking such an examination, the occurrence of that first disruptive C would probably affect us in a special way. We might feel annoyed, or flustered, or perhaps "threatened," for the order which we had begun to assume would be destroyed and (because no new order would yet have emerged) we would be at the edge of a very minor chaos. If, on the other hand, we had faith in the competence and good will of the examiner and also in our own powers of perception, this disruption of our expectations might be felt as exciting or challenging. We would know that the old order was dead, but we would anticipate the new one with interest.

The processes involved in the perception of such series as described above are very much the same as those involved in the perception of structural patterns in both music and literature. In all of them, the experience of patterns and principles of generation is dynamic and continuous. Poetic structure is, in a sense, an inference which we draw from the evidence of a series of events. As we read the poem, it is a hypothesis whose probability is tested as we move from line to line and adjusted in response to what we find there. And, as the illustrations suggest, the conclusion of a poem has special status in the process, for it is only at that point that the total pattern—the structural principles which we have been testing—is revealed.

This does not mean that we are emotionally gratified only at the end of a poem or a piece of music. To begin with, we need only consult our own experiences to know that this is not so. Secondly, poems consist of more than their structures. Finally, the pleasure which we take in perceiving completed patterns is not the only emotion involved in the process I have been describing. As I pointed out above, every disruption of our expectations causes some kind of emotion, and, as the analogy might have suggested, the emotion is not unpleasant if we are confident of the presence of design in the total pattern. As we read a poem we are continuously subjected to small surprises and disappointments as the developing lines evade or contradict our expectations. But far from annoying us, this toying with and teasing of our expectations is a major source of our "excitement"—that is, our pleasure—in literature. If the surprises and disappointments are not finally justified, so to speak, by the total design, then to that extent the poem is a poor one. If, on the other hand, there have been no surprises or disappointments, if all our expectations have been gratified, then the poem has been as predictable—and as interesting—as someone's reciting the alphabet. Art inhabits the country between chaos and cliché.

III Poetry and Speech

We often distinguish literature from nonliterary discourse by observing that each uses language in a different way. We may say, for example, that whereas the primary function of language is practical, poetry exploits those properties of words that are irrelevant to the business of pragmatic communication. This is not inaccurate, but it should be added that the literary use of language still relies, for its effects, upon its relation to nonliterary discourse. Our responses to poetry depend upon and are modified by our previous experiences with nonpoetic language. A poem is not merely a verbal artifact, an aesthetically engaging organization of linguistic elements; for those elements are also organized syntactically, according to the same principles that determine their selection and sequence in ordinary discourse, and even the most syntactically dissolute contemporary poem affects us at least partly through the symbolic or conventional properties of words.

The distinction between the literary and nonliterary use of language may, however, be made in other terms that are more revealing, especially for a study of closure. Specifically, we may conceive of a poem as the imitation or representation of an utterance. This is not to say that a poem is a false or merely "emotive" form of speech. It is an imitation in the same sense that a play is the imitation or representation of an action. Everything the poet "says" may be true, but his saying of it is not. It is *as* an utterance that the poem is a fiction, a pretense.[10]

The point may be further clarified if we recognize that the poem is *ahistorical,* that it does not "occur" in the same sense as does the nonfictive utterance. Every speech is spoken by someone, sometime, somewhere, to someone else. It is spoken, moreover, under the pressure of a particular occasion, as a response to immediate events, internal or external, and with the intention of affecting its audience in some manner. Every utterance, in other words, occurs within a specific context of circumstances and motives. When a poem occurs, however, it is unmoored from such a context, isolated from the circumstances and motives that might have occasioned it.

[10] Although in this section I continue to speak specifically of poetry, the distinction offered here separates not verse from prose but fictive from nonfictive speech. Novels are also imitations of discourse: the narrative itself, not only the events narrated, is "fictional." As many critics and theorists have noted and lamented, we do not have in English a pair of terms that allows us to refer conveniently to poetry and "prose fiction" as distinct from other more or less literary uses of language. Thus we find ourselves obliged to speak of "imaginative literature" or "poetry in the broadest sense" or some such *ad hoc* class when our subject is what I refer to here as fictive or mimetic speech. If we retain the term "poetry" for this subject, it must be with the significance suggested in Ben Jonson's insistence that ". . . hee is call'd a Poet, not hee which writeth in measure only; but that fayneth and formeth a fable, and writes things like the Truth." ("Timber: or, Discoveries," *Ben Jonson,* ed. C. H. Herford, Percy and Evelyn Simpson [Oxford, 1954], VIII, 635.)

When we read a poem or hear it read to us, we are confronted by the performance of an act of speech, not the act itself. It is not "the speaker" who is speaking; we are not the mistress, urn, or nightingale whom he addresses; the rival, here being cursed, is long since dead; the lover's pain, here feelingly expressed, is long since quieted. Or, of course, that mistress, urn, rival, pain—indeed, that speaker—may never have existed at all in the historical world.

Even when the poem is occasioned by the poet's actual experiences and is most nearly a transcription of his individual "voice," it remains, as a poem, only a *possible* utterance, what the poet *might* say. Although the revelation and articulation of that possibility may be one source of the poet's most compelling claim upon our interests and emotions, nevertheless the claim is not the same as that made upon us by one who addresses us directly, his discourse directly shaped by the pressures of an immediate or "historical" occasion. Both the poet, in composing the poem, and we, in responding to it, are aware of the distinction, and it controls both the form of his discourse and the nature of our response.

It has often been remarked that the tragic events in tragedies do not affect us as do the tragic events in our lives or in the lives of those we know or hear about. Similarly, the grief of Tennyson at Hallam's death and the exuberance of Spenser's prenuptial exclamations and imperatives (e.g., "Ring ye the bels, ye yung men of the towne,/And leaue your wonted labors for this day" [11]) do not move us, in their poems, in quite the same way as they would were Tennyson or Spenser actually speaking to us. We not only know that the references in the *Epithalamion* to an ongoing wedding procession are fictional; we also know to how great an extent the selection and organization of language in "the groom's" speech have been shaped by considerations quite other than his wedding-day emotions—considerations, that is, which arose specifically from the fact that his speech was a poem.

It should be recognized, furthermore, that a poem is not merely

[11] "Epithalamion," *The Poetical Works of Edmund Spenser*, ed. J. C. Smith and E. de Selincourt (London, 1957), p. 582.

the record of an utterance that occurred in the past, as would be the transcription or text of an oration. For the poem, *as an utterance,* had no initial historical occurrence. It is, was, and always will be the script for its own performance; like a play, it "occurs" only when it is enacted.

I stated earlier that a poem is not merely a verbal or linguistic artifact. And yet, to a certain extent, that is precisely what it is. The point to be emphasized, however, is that poetry is a *representational* art and that each poem is the representation of an act of speech. For the poem to have its characteristic effect, the representation must be sufficiently "realistic." That is, the literary artifact must create the illusion of being a historical utterance precisely to the extent that a play must create the illusion of being a historical action, which is to say *not completely:* the illusion is not to function as a deception. Coleridge has, of course, been here before us, but "the willing suspension of disbelief" is granted with a continually operating reservation. If we are unwilling to respond to the poem as a *possible* utterance, one substantial source of its value and effect is lost to us. If, on the other hand, we respond to it as if it were a historical utterance, another substantial source of its value and effect is lost. We might wonder, for example, if the spectator in a theater who rushes on the stage to disarm the villain is any more naïvely and improperly deluded than the reader who believes, when he is reading Donne's "Holy Sonnets," that he is eavesdropping on the poet's private meditation.

Language, in poetry, is used mimetically. It is used, moreover, in a *characteristic* mimetic manner to suggest as vividly as possible (or necessary) that very historical context which it does not, in fact, possess. That is, the poem represents not merely the words of an utterance, but a *total* act of speech. We hear frequently of the "heresy of paraphrase" in connection with poetry. Our response to any speech, however, not only to a poem, is controlled by more than its paraphrasable sense. The speaker's particular diction and syntax, his emphases, pauses, and repetitions (and, when he is speaking aloud to us, the modulations of his voice, his facial expressions and other gestures) all become incorporated in our perception of his meanings and motives. We respond not only to what he is saying but to how he is saying it and, thereby, to what is making him say it: his emotions, his intentions, and all those most subtle and delicate qualifications of paraphrasable sense which the total act of speech may reveal.

The poem, however, must carry its context on its own back. No clues to meaning are provided by the environment in which the poem is read or heard: there is nothing but the reader, his own experiences, and the particular linguistic structure before him. (An "expressive" reading will, of course, imitate the sort of vocal modulations that occur in actual speech, but the reading remains interpretive; that is, the performer interprets, in what he hopes is a proper way, the implicit directions provided by that linguistic structure.) That context does, nevertheless, spring into existence as he reads, and its effective existence is the mark of the characteristic art and achievement of the poet. For all those properties of language which in nonliterary discourse may—incidentally, as it were—help to inform us of the speaker's meaning and motives, are, in poetry, specifically controlled and organized to that end.

The mimetic character of poetic language is most obvious in a "dramatic monologue" such as Browning's "My Last Duchess," where details of the Duke's speech identify the speaker, audience, and situation quite precisely, and reveal the Duke's motives and personality as well. In most lyrics, however, the context is not, and need not be, realized with such particularity. In Petrarchan love poetry, for example, the situation is so conventionalized—the languishing lover and the obdurately chaste, cruel, or monogamous lady—that little of it need be made explicit in any particular poem. In Wordsworth's sonnet, "Composed upon Westminster Bridge," the occasion is sufficiently indicated by the title, and the speaker needs no identity other than that suggested by his reactions.[12] The

[12] It should be noted that titles frequently serve precisely this purpose in poems; they do not describe or define the contents of the poem so much as set it up. One may regard titles as among the linguistic resources of the poet or as more or less "external" clues to context, along with dates of composition, epigraph quotations, and perhaps the poet's very name.

poem is, nevertheless, mimetic, for it offers us not the record of what was said "upon Westminster Bridge, September 3, 1802," but rather the representation of what might have been said.

No matter how much or how little of a specific context is suggested or made explicit in the poem, we always experience it as an act within a scene. Our response to the poem, including our sense of its closure, will depend therefore upon our identification of the sort of act and scene it represents. The identification depends, in turn, upon our own prior experiences with utterances and their contexts. As we read the poem, our expectations concerning the probable direction of its development and the nature of its conclusion are determined partly by the particular structural principles that begin to emerge, but also by our experiences with an incalculable number of verbal situations: acts and scenes, utterances and contexts.

The significance of this relation between poetry and discourse for the study of closure is evident. It implies, for example, that our sense of the "appropriateness" of a poem's conclusion at a particular point or in a particular manner will frequently arise from our identification of the poem with a certain kind of utterance that tends to conclude at such a point or in such a manner. If the poem suggests a sermon (by developing through a series of moral observations delivered with a certain vocabulary and tone), we are likely to expect its conclusion to be a gnomic summary or cautionary remark of some kind. The possibility is illustrated in Shakespeare's Sonnet 129 ("Th' expense of spirit in a waste of shame is lust/In action. . . ."), which concludes with:

> All this the world well knows, yet none knows well
> To shun the heaven that leads men to this hell.[13]

Herrick's epigram, "Upon a child that dyed," obviously imitates a mortuary inscription: "Here she lies, a pretty bud . . . ," it begins.

[13] All texts of Shakespeare's sonnets in this volume are from my own edition of them, to be published in 1968.

And it concludes with the conventional epitaph's address to the passer-by:

> Give her strewings; but not stir
> the earth, that lightly covers her.[14]

As we read a poem, we identify not only the act (the kind of utterance) it represents, but also the scene: a presumable context for that utterance, including the speaker's situation and motives and sometimes a particular audience. This sort of identification is equally significant for closure because once again it will affect our expectations concerning the probable development and conclusion of the poem and thereby our sense of the appropriateness of the conclusion that does appear. As we shall see, closure is frequently secured with reference not so much to the discursive structure of the poem as to the context it implies. A conclusion that might otherwise appear improbable, illogical, or in some way unstable, will appear proper, "logical" in the broad sense, and conclusive when referred to the speaker's presumed motives, situation, or audience. The conclusion would have, as we say, "dramatic" propriety.

This, and other points touched upon in the last few paragraphs, receive further consideration, elaboration, and illustration in chapter 3. Another aspect of the relation—or, in this instance, the distinction—between poetry and discourse is introduced in the following section and developed in chapter 2.

IV Poetry, Form, and Integrity

The traditional distinction between poetry and verse is, with some

[14] *The Complete Poetry of Robert Herrick*, ed. J. Max Patrick (Garden City, N.Y., 1963), p. 169. Here we might say that the poem imitates an inscription imitating an utterance.

qualifications, a useful one. *Poetry* is properly discriminated from either a nonmimetic use of language or from other mimetic arts; *verse* is properly discriminated from prose. As Sir Philip Sidney observed, however, although "it is not riming and versing that maketh a Poet," still, "the Senate of Poets hath chosen verse as their fittest rayment . . ., not speaking (table talke fashion or like men in a dreame) words as they chanceably fall from the mouth, but peyzing [i.e., weighing] each sillable of each worde by iust proportion according to the dignitie of the subiect." [15] Verse, in other words, while not a defining characteristic of poetry, is conventionally associated with mimetic discourse, and is thus an identifying characteristic. What I should like to consider here are some of the implications for a study of closure that follow from that identifying distinction between poetic and discursive form.

In "that numbrous kind of writing called verse," language is organized according to some formal principle, not as in most discursive speech, where the distribution of formal elements is more or less random: "words as they chanceably fall from the mouth." More broadly, poetic form may be defined as the kind of structure produced by a patterning of the formal properties of language according to some principle of organization and/or repetition. We recognize, of course, that prose is not without form in this sense, and that a selective use of formal repetition (alliteration and parallelism, for example) may be as much a resource of rhetorical effects for the prose writer as for the "versifier." Prosc, morcover, may be rhythmic, for the sources of our experience of rhythm in language are always the same, namely the repeated occurrence of a particular pattern of the distribution of formal linguistic elements (particularly, in English verse and prose, the distribution of major stresses and junctures). We will, then, obtain a sense of rhythm in prose when, for example, a number of parallel clauses of approximately equal length occur in succession. Rhythm is clearly perceptible in the following passage from Sir

[15] "An Apologie for Poetrie," *Elizabethan Critical Essays*, ed. G. Gregory Smith (London, 1950), I, 160.

Thomas Browne's *Religio Medici,* where alliteration also contributes to the effect:

> . . . but I that have examined the parts of man, and know upon what tender filaments that Fabrick hangs, doe wonder that we are not alwayes so; and considering the thousand dores that lead to death doe thanke my God that we can die but once.[16]

It is not difficult to find passages of this sort in highly rhetorical prose, and we are perhaps only too familiar with efforts to provide them with a typographical lineation that emphasizes their rhythm and suggests the formal structure of free verse. Seldon Rodman, in his *New Anthology of Modern Poetry,* offered Bartolomeo Vanzetti's last speech to the court as just that:

> I have talk a great deal of myself
> but I even forgot to name Sacco.
> Sacco too is a worker,
> from his boyhood a skilled worker, lover of work
> with a good job and pay,
> a bank account, a good and lovely wife,
> two beautiful children and a neat little home
> at the verge of a wood, near a brook. . . .[17]

It is very much to the point that many readers find something almost irrationally irritating about having prose thus set up, as if something is being claimed for the piece illegitimately. It is not a matter of sentimentality nor of sow's ears and silk purses, but rather that we are being asked to respond in a fashion that we sense as inappropriate. What makes us uneasy with Rodman's transcription is not so much that it does not work as that it works too well. We would feel something of the same uneasiness had

[16] *The Works of Sir Thomas Browne,* ed. Geoffrey Keynes (Chicago, 1964), I, 54–55.
[17] (New York, 1938), p. 191.

Browne's essay continued to exhibit a comparable degree of rhythmic constancy for its duration. We would become distracted, unsure of our responses. The essay, in other words, like Vanzetti's speech, would begin to sound like poetry.

There are two points to be made here. One returns us to matters discussed in the previous section and need not be elaborated. It is simply the fact that as soon as we perceive that a verbal sequence has a sustained rhythm, that it is formally structured according to a continuously operating principle of organization, we know that we are in the presence of poetry and we respond to it accordingly. We respond to it, that is, as mimetic ahistorical discourse, expecting certain effects from it and not others, granting certain conventions to it and not others. All our experiences with language and literature, from the time we are small children, condition that discrimination. Consequently, when Vanzetti's eminently "historical" speech is set before us with typographical "meter," our sense of how to respond is understandably confused.

The second point brings us closer to our concerns in this section. There are numerous rhythmic passages in Browne's essay, but the rhythm of one passage is not related to the rhythm of the next (except, incidentally, as a consequence of the habits of Browne's personal style), and no over-all principle of formal structure is maintained through the entire piece. In a poem, however, it is precisely the designed presence of such over-all principles that allows us to speak of "poetic form," and it is the presence of such principles that is most significant for poetic closure.

In the following chapter I shall be concerned with the specific closural resources of the major kinds of poetic form, and in chapter 4, with the closural effects of less structural uses of formal repetition. Here, however, I should like to touch briefly upon a more general problem, namely the relation of the formal distinction between verse and prose to the idea of integrity or completeness.

We may think of *integrity* as, in one sense, the property of a system of which the parts are more obviously related to each other than to anything outside that system. It is evidently by virtue of its structure that a work of art has integrity in this sense. A passage of music frames itself, so to speak, by being more highly organized than anything else in the environment of sound or silence.[18] It has, compared to that environment, relatively clear shape and coherence. Similarly, a painting is framed not so much by the piece of wood around its borders as by the borders implied by its own internal structure. In general, any highly structured system will tend to be perceived as a figure against a ground. It will draw attention to itself, focusing and, in effect, organizing our responses. Coleridge apparently had this effect of meter in mind when he wrote of "the perpetual and distinct attention to each part, which an exact correspondent recurrence of accent and sound are calculated to excite." [19]

I suggested above that one of the most significant effects of meter (or, more broadly, of principles of formal structure) is simply to inform the reader that he is being confronted by poetry and not by anything else. Putting this somewhat differently now, we might say that the constant presence of meter in the poem continues to maintain a clear distinction between poetic and non-poetic discourse. Meter serves, in other words, as a frame for the poem, separating it from a "ground" of less highly structured speech and sound. When the public reading of a poem is interrupted by the reader so that he can comment on a passage, we know, quite independently of the break in thematic coherence, when he stopped reading and started "speaking." The framing effect of meter is also illustrated by the sort of "aural illusion" created by a poem-within-a-poem, comparable to the optical illusions used by psychologists to illustrate the circumstances under which a visual figure and ground switch places. In the third act of *Hamlet*, for example, the players' lines are in rhyming couplets.

[18] In the perception of shapes, a completely homogeneous environment (such as silence or space) has the same effect as random stimulation (such as noise or disorderly visual events): both become the background when a highly structured stimulus is introduced into the perceptual field.

[19] *Biographia Literaria*, ed. J. Shawcross (Oxford, 1965), II, 10.

Here the blank verse of the play itself, otherwise the "figure," becomes a more discursive ground against which the rhyming iambics sound, appropriately, more like "poetry." [20] Rhymed iambics themselves become the more discursive ground when, in Book IV of Keats's *Endymion,* the Indian Maiden's strophic song occurs.

My point here is that one of the most significant ways in which form contributes to our sense of the integrity of a poem is by, in effect, drawing an enclosing line around it, distinctly and continuously separating it from less highly structured and nonmimetic discourse. As Sidney points out:

> The poet neuer maketh any circles about your imagination to coniure you to beleeue for true what he writes. . . . What childe is there that, coming to a Play, and seeing *Thebes* written in great Letters vpon an olde doore, doth beleeue that it is *Thebes?* [21]

And what child is there who, hearing his mother recite nursery rhymes, believes that she is addressing him otherwise? Meter is the stage of the theater in which the poem, the representation of an act of speech, is performed. It is the arena of art, the curtain that rises and falls as well as the music that accompanies the entire performance.

Although integrity, in the sense of internal coherence and distinct identity, is obviously a factor in the experience of poetic closure, closure usually implies another more common sense of integrity also, namely *completeness.* Even a poetic fragment has coherence and a distinct identity: a few lines of metrical verse are clearly perceptible as such, as are a few bars of music. Compared to an environment of ordinary sounds, the mere repetition of a single

[20] The "player's speech" in Act II, scene 2, is in blank verse, but it occurs in a context (or against a ground) of prose.

[21] "An Apologie for Poetrie," I, 184–85.

piano chord three times in succession will have "form" and, in a restricted sense, integrity. It will not, however, have closure.[22] Moreover, it is questionable whether, or in what sense, we could speak of that form as being whole or complete.

Integrity in the sense of wholeness is a difficult concept to discuss, especially in connection with art, where the term has acquired strong honorific value. One might expect the sense of closure to be a consequence of the presence and perception of wholeness, but, as I shall suggest and explain in the chapters that follow, it may actually be the other way around. That is, it may be that we acknowledge a poem as whole or complete when, for various *other* reasons, we experience at its conclusion the sense of closure.

The concept of completeness itself is tricky. Consider the following figure:

C

Is it complete? Well, that depends. In a context of circles, it is not complete:

O O O C

In a context of Roman letters, however, it is:

C O W C O O

Our sense of the completeness of a form, in other words, often depends upon the class of forms with which we identify it. We

[22] That is, not unless the third chord is sounded with greater force, or after a longer pause, or is otherwise distinguished. (See "terminal modification," p. 53, below.)

will know that a sonnet is complete *as such* only if we know what sonnets are.

It is true that the perception of completeness may, under certain circumstances, be independent of convention or class-identification. A form such as a simple geometric figure seems complete when the structural principle that apparently generated it has, so to speak, played itself out. When we construct a circle with a compass, at a certain point the pencil has nowhere else to go. If we continue to move it according to the initial principle, we will merely retrace the circle we have already "completed." In certain poetic forms, such as the rondeau, closure may be secured through a structural principle analogous to that of the circle; and, in general, whenever a poetic form repeats at its conclusion a formal unit with which it began, closure will be thereby strengthened. Formal structure in these instances, however, is "circular" only in the loosest sense and never more than by analogy to geometric circularity. To mention only the most obvious distinction, one is perceived spatially and the other temporally. We cannot ever really "return" to the beginning point in a poem or piece of music; we can only repeat it. And, as will be illustrated later, it is the repetition, not the "return," that is the source of closural effects in such poems.

A more common source of the sense of formal completeness, in poetry and elsewhere, is, in fact, that use of repetition that we refer to as symmetry. If the following figure seems complete, it is probably by virtue of its bilateral symmetry:

It would certainly seem incomplete if only this much were given:

The sense of incompleteness here arises from the fact that the principle that generated one part of the figure was repeated to a sufficient extent to lead us to expect its total repetition. Symmetry of a comparable sort strengthens our sense of the integrity of certain stanza forms: a quatrain, for example, with octosyllabic lines rhyming *abab*.

It must be recognized, however, that few generative principles yield unambiguously complete forms, either in themselves or when repeated. Indeed, given any form generated by an infinitely repeatable or extensible principle, we cannot say if it is a whole or only part of a more extensive whole. The same is true if the form is composed of infinitely repeatable whole units, as here:

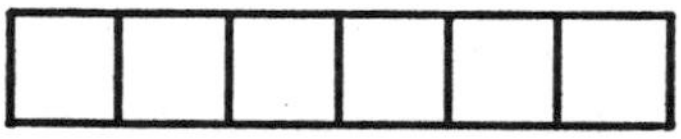

It will appear incomplete, of course, if one of the units is incomplete:

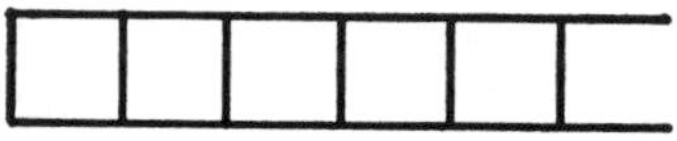

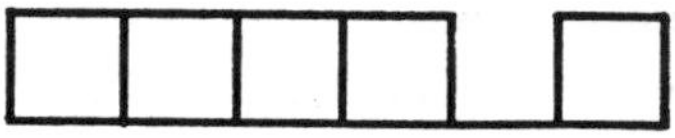

but a sequence of four squares is neither more nor less "whole" than a sequence of five or fifty. Similarly, regarded exclusively as a *formal* structure, ninety-eight lines of blank verse are neither more nor less complete than ninety-nine or a hundred. Moreover, paradoxical as it may seem, an "incomplete" terminal line, one that is significantly shorter than the others in the poem, will often, for reasons I shall elaborate in the following chapter, have stronger closural force than a normal line in that position.

The relation of poetic form to closure is, then, not a simple one. To the extent that principles of formal structure contribute to the internal coherence of a poem and maintain its distinct identity, they evidently strengthen the reader's sense of integrity and closure. As I have been suggesting, however, it is usually difficult and often impossible to say what makes a poem *complete* in terms of formal structure alone, and the notion of formal "integrity" in this sense may indeed be chimerical. We always experience a poem not only as an organization of formal elements but also as an utterance, and our sense of its ultimate integrity, completeness, and closural adequacy is complexly determined by both aspects.

V Style and Conventions

I have made an assumption in the preceding sections which is axiomatic to this study: namely that, other things being equal, we expect to find what we have found before. One implication of this psychological tendency was suggested in section III: as we read a poem, we tend to identify its structure with patterns of discourse familiar to us from nonliterary experience. Poems, however, are not only like other kinds of speech; they are also like other poems. Consequently, our expectations regarding any particular poem will be at least partly determined by our previous experience with poetry—poetry in general, the poetry of that period or style, and the poetry of that writer.

What makes poems more like other poems than like other forms of discourse are those characteristics which we call poetic conventions. These characteristics are, however, ultimately derived from the formal and thematic elements of discursive language; we speak of them as *conventions* only when they occur more systematically and with greater frequency than in ordinary speech. A poetic convention could, in fact, be described as a consistent or systematic deviation from the conventions of discursive speech, and a poetic *style* could be described as a particular combination of such deviations.

As I said above, the power of poetry always depends upon its relation to the language of discourse. This is one reason why styles change and one set of conventions is replaced by another. When a poetic style becomes too familiar or rigidly predictable, the reader's expectations are too completely controlled by, and satisfied in terms of, strictly literary conventions. In other words, when a poem becomes a closed system, it has nothing to say and nothing to reveal but the operation of its own laws. Its style has become a cliché and it is time for a poetic revolution, for a renewal of the relation between poetic style and speech.[23]

Poetic conventions, styles, and even revolutions are significant in the study of closure for several reasons. One is simply that closure is often strengthened by convention: the reader's sense of finality will be reinforced by the appearance, at the conclusion of a poem, of certain formal and thematic elements which typically appear at the conclusion of poems in that style. One of the most common features of primitive songs, for example, is the reiteration of the last line:

> From the country of the Yerewas the moon rose;
> It came near; it was very cold,
> I sat down, oh, I sat down,
> *I sat down, oh, I sat down.*[24]

To the Andaman Islander, whose poet composed this song, the repetition will be something of a signal—or like a sign reading, "All songs end here." It can have this particular effect only for the reader or listener familiar with this kind of conclusion from other poems. If it affects the Western reader in this way, it is partly because he is familiar with the device from ballads, folk songs, and nursery rhymes.

It is also true, however, that a certain conclusion is likely to *become* conventional because it is, to begin with, effective in

[23] It is noteworthy that most of the major revolutions in English poetry have raised the banner of "Back to the language of real life!" One cannot, however, thus account for all stylistic trends, for poetry must meet a double obligation: to life and to art. That is, poetic speech must retain its relation to discursive speech but must not become identical with it. When the stylistic revolution has developed too far in that direction, so that poetic speech begins to lose its distinction, there will be a counter-revolution—and this time under the banner of "Back to the decorum of Art!"

[24] C. M. Bowra, *Primitive Song* (Cleveland, 1962), p. 279. (Italics are in text.)

creating a sense of closure. The device which I just mentioned—the reiterated last line—is not "merely" conventional, for its power arises from one of the most fundamental and universal facts of literary experience: that is, the effects of repetition.[25] The device is, as I suggested, most common in poetry which retains its connection to primitive or naïve sources, and only in such poetry can we speak of it as a convention. It reappears, however, in the most sophisticated Western poetry—but it occurs there with far less simplicity and directness. We might say, then, that the poetic convention of one style is the poetic resource of all styles, and no "convention" is ever wholly lost.[26]

As styles change, poetic conventions do not quite disappear, but they do fall back from prominence into the common sea of poetic devices. Consequently, we can speak of fashions in poetic closure as in any other aspect of style. Certain conclusions which are common in one period are rare in another, or radically modified. The antithetical summaries, for example, which provide the concluding lines of many sixteenth-century poems—

> Oh farewell, life; delightful death, farewell!
> I die in heaven, yet live in darksome hell.[27]

—would be as alien in a modern poem as a pavan in a modern dance.

The changing fashions in poetic closure are obviously related to more general developments in literary history. As the general features of style change, and particularly as new kinds of structures appear, the older forms of closure are likely not to be effective. The reasons for this will be examined in the following two chapters, where we shall see that certain endings which are appropriate for

[25] The dynamics of various forms of repetition and their relation to closure are analyzed below, pp. 42–44, 48–49, and 155–66.

[26] *Assonance* is the resource, for example, of which *rhyme* is the convention.

[27] George Gascoigne, "Deep Desire Sung this Song"; text in *Poetry of the English Renaissance*, ed. J. William Hebel and Hoyt H. Hudson (New York, 1957), p. 89.

one kind of structure may be completely inappropriate for another kind. And, as we might expect, in periods of stylistic revolution or transition there may be a lag between one development and another: a poet introducing a new structure, for example, may carry over inappropriate devices of closure from an older style. This possibility will be considered in chapter 5, among other problems, failures, and anomalies of poetic closure. I shall also be concerned, in that chapter, with another factor in the fashions of poetic closure: that is, the effects of social history on the contemporary reader's and writer's attitudes toward, and expectations of, poetic art. Some of the unusual features of modern poetic closure (such as apparent anti-closure) will be considered in relation to both literary and extra-literary developments.

My final point regarding styles and conventions is to minimize their importance in a study of this kind. Devices of closure are neither more nor less resistant to historical change than any other poetic device, from meter to metaphor. It would be possible, I imagine, to make a *historical* study of closure: to trace in succeeding literary generations the emergence, prevalence, decline, and disappearance of various kinds of poetic conclusions, as one would various kinds of meter or figurative language. I would point out, however, that all these poetic devices are effective by virtue of our psychological construction and particularly our responses to language; and these, in turn, apparently remain constant under extremely diverse circumstances, historical and other.[28] I shall, in the following two chapters, be describing *kinds* of closure, not *styles* in

[28] It may be supposed that conventions of closure which depend upon unique features of a particular language or society could not cross linguistic or cultural borders. Since I do not cross many linguistic or cultural borders myself, I cannot judge their significance—if such conventions exist—for this study. It is true that the sense of closure is often lost in translation; but that is an entirely different matter and presents no problem for us here. (The same general principles of closure are found in the poetry of all European languages; it is only that the formal elements which create closure in a particular poem are often not readily duplicated in another language.) The question I am concerned with in this note is whether or not we can assume a universal psychology of closure—and I can only answer that I do not know, but that I am assuming it anyway. I might add that recent studies in comparative

closure, and my examples will be drawn from English poetry usually without regard to chronology. I shall, however, make historical and stylistic observations which, as they come up, seem necessary, relevant, or interesting. And, in the final chapter, where I shall be particularly concerned with styles in modern poetry, I shall attempt to review some of the most significant historical aspects of closure.

VI Closure and Stability

The perception of poetic structure is a dynamic process: structural principles produce a state of expectation continuously modified by successive events. Expectation itself, however, is continuously maintained, and in general we expect the principles to continue operating as they have operated.[29] Now, it is clear that a poem cannot continue indefinitely; at some point the state of expecta-

---

linguistics suggest that such an assumption is not unwarranted (see esp. *Universals of Language*, ed. Joseph H. Greenberg [Cambridge, Mass., 1963]); and from what I have read of the translated and transliterated poetry of non-European languages, the assumption seems justified. But I do not trust the translations for this purpose, since the translator could very well—though unwittingly—introduce (just because he felt the need of them) devices of closure which were not in the original. I can only hope, then, that what I have to say of poetic closure will be as true of Hopi and Hindustani as it seems to be of English, Latin, German, French, Italian, and Spanish poetry.

[29] Cf. the Gestaltist "law of good continuation," formulated as follows by Leonard B. Meyer: "A shape or pattern will, other things being equal, tend to be continued in its initial mode of operation" (*Emotion and Meaning in Music*, p. 92). Gestalt psychologists have been particularly concerned with describing the dynamics, and attempting to establish the laws, of the perception of structure. In what follows, here and later, I shall be incorporating some of their observations, if not explanations or more general theories. It is difficult to pinpoint references, since not only the concepts but also the terminology of the Gestalt school are now the common property of psychologists and laymen alike. I am most indebted, however, to the formulations of Kurt Koffka in *Principles of Gestalt Psychology* (New York, 1935), to their extrapolations for music in Meyer's study, and to their extrapolations for visual art in E. H. J. Gombrich's *Art and Illusion* (New York, 1960).

tion must be modified so that we are prepared not for continuation but for cessation. Closure, then, may be regarded as a modification of structure that makes *stasis*, or the absence of further continuation, the most probable succeeding event. Closure allows the reader to be satisfied by the failure of continuation or, put another way, it creates in the reader the expectation of nothing.

That expectation of nothing, the sense of ultimate composure we apparently value in our experience of a work of art, is variously referred to as stability, resolution, or equilibrium. It is obviously a function or effect of closure, but its particular sources are worth some attention here, for they are frequently misunderstood. E. M. W. Tillyard, speaking of Milton's "Epitaphium Damonis," attributes the "failure" of the poem to the fact that "it reveals a troubled, disunited mind," and he offers the following generalization, familiar in one form or another, to support his point: "A quite successful poem dealing with painful experience will not reveal a troubled state of mind: it will derive its success precisely from expressing a state of mind that has found equilibrium after and in spite of sorrow." [30] Tillyard mentions "Lycidas" and Coleridge's Dejection Ode as among such successful poems, and adds that in the "Epitaphium," as in Meredith's *Modern Love*, "the pains that made up the experiences described have not been resolved: however moving and interesting, both poems suffer from this unsurmountable defect."

As our recollection of numerous contrary examples assures us, however, Tillyard is mistaken in insisting that a successful poem cannot "reveal a troubled disunited mind," or that it is successful only if that mind has found some ultimate equilibrium. His mistake consists of *misplacing* the required equilibrium, in putting it in the mind of the poet rather than in the poem or, better yet, in the mind of the reader. For it is not the described experience of the poet that must be "resolved," but the actual experience of the reader.

Although we apparently demand resolution, equilibrium, or sta-

[30] *Milton* (New York, 1930), p. 99.

bility of a work of art, we object when a poem or play is static: we want "drama" in our dramas, and "development" in poems, novels, and musical compositions. The demands are not contradictory, of course, but we must emphasize that the stability is an ultimate state—that is, a final one. If we think of it as "the expectation of nothing," clearly such a state would be desirable only at the *end* of a poem or piece of music.

The writer wishes to maintain our interest in his play, novel, or poem continuously throughout the duration of its performance, and he does this by sustaining our continuous expectation of further development: that is, by providing constant sources of instability. The formula of introduction-complication-climax-resolution, most familiar to us in connection with dramatic structure, has its counterpart in any temporally organized work of art, from short story to sonata. In each, the sense of stability is continuously evaded until the end: disguises are undisclosed, entrances are promised, revelations are deferred, tonic chords are avoided. In contrapuntal music, such as madrigal or fugue, one melodic progression is introduced before the previous one is completed, so that there is not full cadence until the very end.

The writer also wishes, however, that we have no further expectations at the end of the play, novel, or poem, no "loose ends" to be accounted for, no promises that go begging. The novelist or playwright is likely to end his work at a point when either nothing could follow (as when the hero dies) or everything that could follow is predictable (as when the hero and heroine get married).[31] The poet ends his work at some comparable point of stability, but unless (as sometimes happens) the poem follows a temporal sequence, this point will not be something we could call "the end of the story." It will, however, be a point of stability that is either determined by or accommodates the poem's formal and thematic principles of structure.

Although stability implies composure and the absence of further

[31] Needless to say, this is an oversimplification. I shall develop the point and defend the principle in a later discussion (pp. 117–20).

expectations, this does not mean that our experience of the work ceases abruptly at the last word. On the contrary, at that point we should be able to re-experience the entire work, not now as a succession of events, but as an integral design. The point may be clarified if we consider that we cannot speak of the "end" of a painting or piece of sculpture, although, as the Gestalt psychologists demonstrate, the concept of stability applies readily to visually perceived structures. Presumably, then, the notion of "*ultimate* stability" would have a different meaning here. It has been suggested, however, that the observer's experience of a work of "spatial art" is also temporal, in that it takes time for his visual and perhaps kinesthetic responses to play themselves out or to reach the point where the parts of the design are appreciated in relation to the whole.[32] In both painting and poetry, then, the "ultimate stability" of the work refers not to a point at which the observer's or reader's experience is "finished," but to a point at which, without residual expectations, he can experience the structure of the work as, at once, both dynamic and whole.

We may now summarize some of the observations made here and in the preceding sections regarding the functions of poetic closure. Closure occurs when the concluding portion of a poem creates in the reader a sense of appropriate cessation. It announces and justifies the absence of further development; it reinforces the feeling of finality, completion, and composure which we value in all works of art; and it gives ultimate unity and coherence to the reader's experience of the poem by providing a point from which all the preceding elements may be viewed comprehensively and their relations grasped as part of a significant design. Recalling the conclusion of *To the Lighthouse*, we might say that closure is the final brush stroke on Lily Briscoe's canvas, which integrates, clarifies, and completes all the disparate lines and colors of the painting and reveals the ultimate principle and cause of their existence.

[32] Cf. Etienne Souriau, "Time in the Plastic Arts," *The Journal of Aesthetics and Art Criticism*, 7 (1949): 294–307.

Closure and Stability

And therefore it is easie to observe, that in all Metricall compositions, . . . the force of the whole piece, is for the most part left to the shutting up; the whole frame of the Poem is a beating out of a piece of gold, but the last clause is as the impression of the stamp, and that is it that makes it currant.

[John Donne, *Sermons*]

2 *Formal Structure and Closure*

I Introduction

Repetition is the fundamental phenomenon of poetic form, as the latter term is used in this study. All the principles that have been or may be used to generate formal structure in poetry are describable in terms of the repetition of either a certain physical feature of language—as in rhyme and alliteration—or a relationship among such features—as in stress patterns and syllable counts. The fundamental unit of poetic form is the line, not (as it is sometimes suggested) the "foot." For one thing, poetic form can exist without feet altogether, as in syllabic verse and much free verse. More important, however, is the fact that formal structure is perceived as a relationship among elements, and a foot is thus not formally significant until it has been repeated or perceived in relation to some other foot—that is, not until it functions in a line.[1]

Since repetition is important not only in poetic structure but

[1] Similarly, one cannot speak of a *tone* as musically significant until it is perceived in relation to another tone. For this reason the *phrase* is commonly regarded as the fundamental unit of melodic structure. Bruce Pattison (*Music and Poetry of the English Renaissance* [London, 1948], p. 76) discusses the correspondence of the poetic line to the musical phrase.

also in closure, it will demand our attention all through this study. One must recognize, however, that "repetition" is not always the same phenomenon: there are several ways in which it can function in poetry, and each of them affects closure differently. First, not all repetition is, like meter, structural or perceived as systematic. It is often what we may call "occasional," as in the following lines:

> *Come forth, come forth,* the gentle Spring,
> And carry the glad newes, I bring . . .[2]

Second, a repetition may be separated by other material (as in a refrain) or not (as in the example above.) Repetition may, moreover, involve formal or thematic elements, or both. The recurrence of the initial phrase, "Ask me no more," in Carew's familiar "Song" is both formal and thematic. The series of questions in the octave of Shakespeare's seventy-sixth sonnet ("Why is my verse so barren of new pride . . . ?/Why with the time do I not glance aside . . . ?/Why write I still all one, ever the same . . . ?") constitutes a thematic repetition but, aside from the word "why," not a formal one. Finally, formal and thematic repetition may reinforce or conflict with one another, as we see in the relation of the word "all" to the stresses in this couplet:

> All love, all liking, all delight
> Lies drown'd with us in endlesse night.[3]

Not only does each kind of repetition affect structure and closure differently, but the most important kind—the systematic repetition which creates meter, rhyme pattern, and stanzaic form—is itself a complex event with multiple effects. Each of the varieties of repetition will be met again in later discussions, and the effects

[2] Ben Jonson, "Song" from *Chloridia;* text from *Poems of Ben Jonson,* ed. George Burke Johnston (Cambridge, Mass., 1955), p. 300.

[3] "Corinna's going a Maying," *The Complete Poetry of Robert Herrick,* ed. J. Max Patrick (Garden City, N.Y., 1963), p. 100.

of systematic repetition will be initially outlined in this section. The point to be emphasized now is only that the variety and complexity exist, and that they will make it impossible to formulate any single or simple principle to express the relation of repetition to either poetic structure or closure.

Since the experience of closure is the complex product of both formal and thematic elements, it is difficult to examine the effects of either one independently of the effects of the other in any given poem. To gauge the closural force of its formal structure, for example, we would have to strain out all the forces for closure that arise from the poem's thematic elements, to ignore the fulfilment of syntactic expectations and of any others that affect us through the poem's relation to the conventions of discursive speech. Rather than attempt to shut off our reactions to meaning, we may consider the sources of closural effect in some "poems" that have no meaning, that consist of nothing but form: nonsense-poems, in other words, composed of groups of words having no thematic relation but arranged in accord with some purely formal principle. The following group was selected at random from the column heads of a dictionary and arranged to produce a "quatrain" of four eight-syllable lines:

abduct chess epitome hut
limited infer teach wit source
homogenize sailboat rainfall
vain hiatus merger seeming (1)

If one reads these lines in sequence with a slight pause at the end of each, the degree of order represented by the octosyllabic groups will not be overwhelming, but it will become increasingly perceptible. At some point, probably by the third line, this rhythmic unit will be sufficiently strong to make any subsequent line of radically shorter length—let us say three syllables—appear anomalous. Can we say that the last line of the sequence creates any sense of closure? We may observe, to begin with, that although it is "complete," it is not any more so than each of the preceding three lines. Moreover, if the sequence were presented aloud to a listener for the first time, he would have no more reason to expect it to end at *that* point than after any other eight-syllable sequence. If he read it aloud to himself, he would probably be inclined to give an emphatic inflection to the last word, but only because he *saw* that it went no further; for we tend to impose closure on what is known, independently, to be the terminal point of a sequence. If we hear a bell tolling the hours and know from a watch that it is ten o'clock, the tenth tone will be heard as slightly louder or longer.[4]

On the other hand, certain characteristics of the quatrain do make our experience of the fourth line different, and suggest some of the conditions that strengthen or weaken closure. The last line would, for example, be more stable than any of the preceding ones. The general rule is that to the extent that stimuli possess similar features they form groups and are perceived as unified, coherent, and stable structures.[5] Consequently, as the metrical principle which generates the lines becomes more apparent, the metrical character of each succeeding line becomes more secure and the

[4] This tendency would probably be regarded by Gestalt psychologists as illustrating the operation of the "Law of Prägnanz," which states that "psychological organization will always be as 'good' as the prevailing conditions allow" (Kurt Koffka, *Principles of Gestalt Psychology* [New York, 1935], p. 110), meaning that, wherever possible, we tend to perceive groups of stimuli as combining to form simple, coherent and stable wholes. Since the principles formulated by these psychologists will be referred to on several occasions in the following pages, it may be appropriate to point out here that they were originally designed to account for the perception of visual phenomena, but that their extension to other sense modalities has been justified by later experiments (cf. Floyd H. Allport, *Theories of Perception and the Concept of Structure* [New York, 1955], p. 119).

[5] The "laws of organization," as formulated by Max Wertheimer, designate the conditions which maximize our tendency to respond to groups of individual stimuli as unified "percepts." These conditions include proximity and similarity. (Max Wertheimer, "Laws of Organization in Perceptual Forms," in *A Source Book of Gestalt Psychology*, ed. Willis D. Ellis [New York, 1939], pp. 71–88.)

collection of lines as a whole becomes more stable. (Indeed, because the mind strives to perceive order, the very randomness of the thematic elements may function as a sort of negative principle: that is, to the degree that thematic randomness is more expected in each line, the fourth line will be more "comprehensible," in a sense, and thus more acceptable and stable than the first. As we shall see in a moment, however, the randomness eventually has another more significant effect.)

It is clear, however, that if the eight-syllable lines continued without variation and with no further approach to thematic significance, the reader would become increasingly irritated, bored, or oppressed. What we have encountered here is one aspect of the complex effect of systematic repetition: while such repetition tends to give stability to the structure of which it is a part, the further it is extended the more desperate becomes our desire for variation or conclusion. This latter effect is comparable to what Gestalt psychologists call "saturation,"[6] and since it will concern us frequently in the pages that follow, I will appropriate their term for convenient reference. In connection with the saturating effects of musical repetition, Leonard Meyer points out that the listener's reaction will depend upon the degree to which he perceives the repetition as "meaningful."[7] What we may say here is that, to the extent that the generation of eight-syllable lines is perceived as a principle of form, the repetitions will be stabilizing and gratifying; but that, to the extent that what is being generated is otherwise meaningless and without apparent direction or purpose, the repetitions will produce boredom, fatigue, impatience, or flight—but not closure.

What we have observed up to this point suggests that though systematic repetition strengthens the formal coherence and stability of a poem, its extension does not determine a point of closure and may, indeed, produce anti-closural effects. The formal structure of the quatrain was, however, minimal, and we may ask what

[6] See, e.g., Koffka, *Principles of Gestalt Psychology*, pp., 410–14.
[7] *Emotion and Meaning in Music* (Chicago, 1956), pp. 135–38.

would happen if we approximated poetic meter more closely by changing and arranging the words to emphasize an iambic stress pattern, as follows:[8]

abduct infer epitome
homogenize hiatus bare
unlimited parade ablaze
engrave dissatisfy consist (2)

To the extent that the added principle produces a rhythmic effect that is more secure than in example 1, the qualities of terminal stability and completeness here are stronger. But a listener would still have no reason to believe that further lines are not forthcoming; and if the reader finds himself emphasizing the final word by changing its pitch, force, or duration, it is not because of the formal structure but because of the information conveyed by the typographical segregation of the lines: knowing that the sequence terminates at a certain point, he will impose on that point the characteristics which strengthen or are associated with closure.

What we find, in fact, is that by adding another principle of generation—another systematic repetition—what we have strengthened is not closure but the expectation of further lines or the *desire* for closure. And, as it turns out, meter is a force for closure only when it ceases to function as a pure systematic repetition. If, for example, all the lines of a poem are decasyllabic, no one line of ten syllables is more "complete" in that respect than any other, and, other things being equal, each line will strengthen the expectation of a succeeding decasyllabic line. Consequently, if the poet wishes to disturb the reader's complacent expectation of continuation (either for closure or for any other reason), one of the most effective devices he could use would be simply a longer or

[8] By choosing predominantly polysyllabic words and assuming only that they would be given their normal pronunciations, one insures that the stress pattern will be as independent as possible of syntax and sense.

shorter line. Thus the strength of closure at the conclusion of a Spenserian stanza is increased by the alexandrine line.

Another way in which meter can be exploited to strengthen closure is as a return to a norm after a deviation. In the following poem by Herrick, one of the many factors which combine to make the eighth line closural is the fact that it returns to a strict iambic pattern after the most deviant line in the poem:

I dare not ask a kisse;
  I dare not beg a smile;
Lest having that, or this,
  I might grow proud the while.

No, no, the utmost share
  Of my desire, shall be
Onely to kisse that Aire,
  That lately kissed thee.[9]

As we approach more closely to typical poetic meters, then, it becomes increasingly clear that systematic repetition, in itself, is not a closural force, but that the expectations it produces can be exploited for closural effects. In a final look at nonsense-verse, let us consider what happens when we add one more formal principle—"the jingling sound of like endings":

abduct infer epitome
homogenize organically
unlimited degree parade
foresee dissatisfy repaid (3)

The additional principle has evidently sharpened the formal integrity of each line and strengthened the cohesiveness of the quatrain as a whole. Again, the conditions for closure have in

[9] "To Electra," *Complete Poetry of Robert Herrick*, p. 306. *Kissed* is, of course, disyllabic.

certain respects multiplied—but can we say that with the conclusion of this sequence we have a significantly stronger sense of completeness and finality than in the previous examples? I think we can, but that it arises from a new source: not from the addition of rhyme as such, but from the association with conventional poetry which the rhyme encourages.

There is, we should note, apparently nothing in this arrangement that would enable a listener to predict the number of lines to follow any better here than in the two previous sequences. But the appearance of the rhyme in the second line will not only sharpen his perception of the formal principles at work; it will also suggest the form of a conventional verse couplet. The first two lines, then, will be perceived as a unit and, given any metrically complete third line (no matter what its terminal sound), the listener's expectation of *a fourth line* will be much greater here than in any of the preceding examples. That is, the couplet unit, by introducing a numerical limit (not of four lines, of course, but of groups of two; other couplets could follow, but any even-numbered line would be more conclusive than an odd-numbered line), significantly enhances the finality (lastness) [10] of the last line.

My point here has not been to emphasize the role of the reader's literary experience in creating the sense of closure. (That factor will be considered in the following section, in connection with the sonnet.) It has been, rather, to suggest again that the fulfilling of formal expectations is never a sufficient condition for the experience of closure. If the reader's literary experience had not condi-

[10] The nature of this study goes far toward exhausting the language of its terms for "end," of which there are many. I want to keep certain near-synonyms distinct, however, so that the major assertions will not look like tautologies. *Complete*, *stable*, and *final* (and other words like *resolved*, etc.) are all commonly used as synonyms for concluded, but here they are used to refer to the attributes or causes of the experience of conclusiveness. *Finality*, in particular, is often used as equivalent to *closure*, especially in studies of music. Here, however, it means only the quality of lastness—that which defines the terminal point of any sequence, whether or not that sequence is felt to be stable, complete or resolved.

tioned him to respond to this quatrain in terms of couplets, the existence of rhyme would have brought him no further toward the sense of closure here than in the conclusions of the previous examples. It was not his literary experience as such that made the difference, but that experience as one of the many other factors which can effectively interact with form to create closure.

But does not rhyme itself constitute one of the most effective closural devices in poetry? The question might better be rephrased as follows: is there anything in the nature of rhyme that makes its closural effect any different from or more significant than that of any other systematic repetition? It has been suggested that end-rhymes in poetry correspond to the most typical and effective source of closure in music, that is, the return to the tonic.[11] The occurrence of the key tone at the conclusion of a piece of music, it is said, is not only analogous to rhyme but represents the same psychological phenomenon, the satisfaction for the listener arising, in each, from his expectation of a particular sound.

This theory has much to recommend it, but, as it turns out, the correspondence is neither so exact nor so simple. For one thing, it involves questionable assumptions about the nature of musical tonality. More important for this study, it involves a distortion or oversimplification of the facts of speech and poetry. The musical and linguistic problems are, for the most part, too technical for discussion here, but a few of them can be roughly indicated. The "return to the tonic," for example, does not always consist of the *recurrence* of a key tone. That is, a key tone may sound final even though it has not occurred earlier in the melody. (The reasons for this arise from the whole nature of tonality in music, a phenomenon to which nothing in speech or poetry is finally comparable.[12])

[11] Henry Lanz, *The Physical Basis of Rime* (London, 1931), p. 56 and *passim.*

[12] A melody in the key of C will be "resolved" on C, even though the tone has not been sounded earlier. Nothing like a key, however, is implied by the sounds of speech, even as they are organized in poetry. Lanz suggests that the organization of vowel sounds in a poem produces the equivalent of the tonal system in a piece of music (pp. 9–62). A tonal system, however, is the product

But rhyme, by definition, requires that a particular sound have occurred at least once before. Consider the following couplet with which Jonson opens his volume of *Epigrammes:*

To the Reader

Pray thee, take care, that tak'st my booke in hand,
To reade it well: that is, to understand.[13]

The sense of closure here is strengthened, but not created, by the presence of rhyme. It is clear that without the rhyme the couplet would be "flat." Indeed, we probably would not call it a couplet, and because isolated unrhymed distichs are extremely uncommon in English poetry, we might not recognize it as a poem. Part of the closural effect of the rhyme, then, arises from its satisfaction of expectations having nothing to do with the formal structure of the lines. An unrhymed distich is not necessarily unclosed, however, as numerous epigrams in *The Greek Anthology* testify. And in Jonson's poem, if one substituted "sympathize" for "understand," the lines would still have a perceptible meter, and their thematic integrity would itself be a considerable force for closure. What the rhyme provides, in fact, is an additional "grouping" factor, a

---

of a fixed relation among frequencies (pitches), whereas vowels are distinguished not by their absolute frequencies but by the pattern of their relative frequencies and resonances ("formants"). (See Colin Cherry, *On Human Communication* [Cambridge, Mass., 1957], pp. 147–56, and George A. Miller, *Language and Communication* [New York, 1951], pp. 33–41.) It is not my purpose here to engage in a full-scale discussion of, or argument with, Lanz's theory of rhyme. His study was an altogether admirable and painstaking attempt to account for the formal (or what he called "musical") elements of poetry in terms of the then contemporary theories of music, acoustics, and linguistics. It has, however, become the victim of recent developments, changes, and refinements of theory and method in all these fields, and it would be pointless as well as ungenerous to indict him for every oversimplification or unwarranted assumption. I have, therefore, merely presented my own observations and conclusions without indicating, at every point, how they differ from his.

[13] *Poems*, p. 7.

similarity between two otherwise related units that binds them even more closely as a single perceptual form.[14]

One cannot say that the second rhyme-word in Jonson's couplet has fulfilled an expectation set up by the first because there is nothing in the lines to create such an expectation (always excepting the effect of the reader's previous experience with English distichs). To be sure, the meter, by establishing a norm, does set up a system of expectations—but with respect to the meter alone. Nothing in the formal structure of an iambic pentameter line leads us to expect that its last sound will be repeated at the end of the next iambic pentameter line. If it did, the reading of blank verse would be an endless series of frustrations or disappointments. The expectation arises only when the principle of rhyme has been perceived as such, and it thus takes at least one couplet (or rhyme) to create the expectation of another.

What all this points to is that rhyme usually affects us in the same way and for the same reasons as does any other systematic repetition, and is thus no more related to "the return to the tonic" than are stress patterns or syllable counts. None of these formal principles can in itself produce the sense of closure. A systematic repetition is, on the contrary, a force for continuation that must be overcome if closure is to occur. Rhyme strengthens closure in the isolated couplet, but it is not functioning there as a principle of systematic repetition. There it affects us by providing an additional grouping element that enhances the formal integrity of the couplet. To the degree that the "return to the tonic" owes its effect in music to the full articulation of an implied form, rhyme may be compared to it. (This was not, however, the grounds for Lanz's theory.) But even when this is granted, the comparison must consist largely of pointing out dissimilarities and exceptions; for

[14] According to Wertheimer's "laws of organization" or of "grouping" (see n. 5, above), the most effective factors for strengthening the cohesive forces among perceptual elements are their similarity, proximity, and contiguity. Couplet-rhyme obviously exhibits the first two of these, and any rhyme exhibits the first.

poetry does not depend upon rhyme to the same extent that music depends upon tonality,[15] and the usual effect of end-rhyme is contrary to the effect of sounding a key note.

What we must emphasize here is that rhyme is neither the *sine qua non* of poetic closure nor a sufficient condition for its occurrence. Poems may have closure without end-rhyme, and the appearance of end-rhyme does not guarantee closure. The first of these points will be illustrated in sections V and VI of this chapter in connection with blank verse and free verse, the second in section IV in connection with rhymed couplets.

We have observed that insofar as formal structure is the product of systematic repetition it is not in itself a sufficient condition for closure. It may be objected, however, that the nonsense quatrains which gave rise to this observation hardly exhaust the possibilities of poetic form. Are there not, in real poetry, formal structures which in themselves create the sense of closure at their conclusions? Is there no poem in which a termination point is implied by the very principles that generate its formal structure?

First of all, we must carefully distinguish between the sense of completeness conferred upon any structure by our perception of its formal symmetry and the actual *determination* of completeness by a given formal principle. Thus a poem consisting of a single quatrain rhyming *abab* will appear formally complete, but so will a poem consisting of two or more such quatrains; for the symmetrical pattern is itself infinitely repeatable, and no matter how many units of the pattern are presented to us, we will be able to perceive the total structure as symmetrical.

But what about such elaborately predetermined forms as the rondeau or the sestina? Is it not true that the sestina is obliged to conclude when the possible serial orders of the six key words have been exhausted? But we may ask, in turn, for whom this obligation

[15] Lanz was interested in maintaining just the reverse. The final chapter of his book (*The Physical Basis of Rime*, pp. 302–42) in fact constitutes a "defense of rime," in which he devotes much energy to demonstrating the inferiority, inadequacy, and cultural threat of "free," i.e., unrhymed, verse.

is binding. For the poet, if he accepts it—but he may write double and triple sestinas, repeating the original principle until his ingenuity, inspiration, and interest are exhausted.[16] The point, however, is not that formal rules may be violated or modified, but that, as far as the reader is concerned, the formal limits imposed by a convention are by no means implied by the generating principles of any particular poem. They may, of course, affect the reader insofar as they *are* conventions and his familiarity with them conditions his expectations and responses. And certain conventional terminations may have closural effects because they exhibit special devices that modify the formal principles by which the poem is generated (e.g., in the Spenserian stanza, as noted above). Both these effects, that of familiarity and that of "terminal modification," will be discussed in the following section. What we must emphasize at this point is that there is no formal principle which in itself can prevent a poem from continuing indefinitely. What we shall consider in the rest of this chapter is by what means—given that rule—the poet prevents the reader from expecting unlimited continuation.

II Closure and Formal Conventions
The English Sonnet

The sonnet is one of the most highly determined formal structures in Western poetry and is probably the most familiar single form in the history of our literature. It is also one of the few forms with a

[16] And even then, recognizing the need for a special closural device, he may modify the original principle to secure it. Many poets, for example, following Arnaut Daniel's original model, conclude their sestinas with a triplet in which appear all six end-words. See, e.g., Sidney's "Yee Gote-heard Gods" (*The Poems of Sir Philip Sidney*, ed. William A. Ringler, Jr. [Oxford, 1962], p. 111) and the sestina that concludes "August" in *The Shepheardes Calendar* (*The Poetical Works of Edmund Spenser*, ed. J. C. Smith and E. de Selincourt [London, 1957], p. 450).

predetermined length. In other highly conventional forms, such as *terza rima* and rhyme royale, the stanzaic structure is rigidly prescribed but the number of stanzas is not limited by any rule. The sonnet, however, is obliged to conclude not only in a fixed way but at a fixed point. Still, as I suggested above, the poet's self-imposed obligations are not binding on the reader. Each sonnet must convince the reader of its conclusiveness, and the question we are asking here is whether there is anything in its formal structure alone which will so convince him.

Now it has often been observed that the terminal rhyming couplet of the English sonnet allows the poet to end it with striking resolution, finality, punch, pointedness, and so forth. It is also true, however, that many sonnets are poorly concluded, their endings limp or flat. No matter how perfectly constructed the poem may be with respect to form, if its thematic structure is inadequately concluded, the terminal couplet will not do the job by itself. We may still ask how much of a job it does and how it does it—realizing that to speak of its epigrammatic force, or rounding-off or knitting-up powers, is only to restate the fact, but not to explain it.

There is good reason to maintain that a rhymed couplet, when it corresponds to a syntactically complete utterance, is, in itself, an effectively closed form. Nevertheless, the sense of closure produced by a sonnet ending does not arise so much from the independent effectiveness of the rhymed couplet as from its effectiveness in relation to the formal structure that precedes it. In order to appreciate this relationship, it will be necessary to distinguish its effect from that of the reader's possible familiarity with sonnet conventions, and that is not a simple matter. We may begin, however, by considering a reader's experience of the formal structure of Shakespeare's twenty-first sonnet:

> So is it not with me as with that Muse
> Stirred by a painted beauty to his verse,
> Who heaven itself for ornament doth use

And every fair with his fair doth rehearse,
Making a couplement of proud compare
With sun and moon, with earth and sea's rich gems,
With April's first-born flowers, and all things rare
That heaven's air in this huge rondure hems.
O let me, true in love, but truly write,
And then believe me: my love is as fair
As any mother's child, though not so bright
As those gold candles fixed in heaven's air.
  Let them say more that like of hearsay well;
  I will not praise that purpose not to sell.

Let us imagine that a reader with a wide and long-standing knowledge of English literature has finished reperusing the first twenty of Shakespeare's sonnets and has before him this one—its position centered on the page, its lines numbered in the margin, and its couplet indented. Clearly his experience of its formal structure will be different from that of a person who, having no previous acquaintance with sonnets, is having it read aloud to him for the first time. Without going over the same ground as was covered already in connection with nonsense-verses, I think we can assume that the naïve listener (if he has some acquaintance with poetry and is not insensitive) will have the metrical principles fairly secure by at least the fourth line, and by the eighth line he will have a sense of the quatrain rhyme scheme. A more sophisticated listener might at that point be conscious of the "sonnet-ness" of what he was hearing, and when the thematic development of the ninth line suggested the familiar "turn" of the sonnet, he would be almost certain that a sestet—a third quatrain and rhymed couplet—were to follow.[17] For the naïve listener, however,

[17] Perhaps I should make it clear that when I speak of the naïve or sophisticated listener's or reader's "sense," "recognition," and "certainty" of these formal principles, I do not mean to imply that he verbalizes them as such, even to himself. What I am distinguishing is not the precision of his technical vocabulary but the relative strength of his responses and expectations. A three-year-old child, even if he cannot speak, can respond to a nursery rhyme with "recognitions" and "certainties" and even "surprises" concerning its rhythmic structure.

the thematic turn, even if he perceived it as such, could not tell him anything about the form of the next six lincs. Indeed, he would have no reason to expect, at that point (the beginning of the ninth line), that he was going to hear anything other than quatrains follow; and he would have no way of knowing from the formal structure of what he has heard how many of them to expect.

By the end of the twelfth line, where the sophisticated listener has virtually preconstructed the form of the concluding couplet, the naïve listener is just as likely to be expecting another quatrain. But now we observe something quite interesting: although each of these two listeners will be experiencing the final couplet in an entirely different way—or at least from an entirely different set of expectations—the effect of the couplet will be, in *both* cases, to strengthen the sense of closure. For the sophisticated listener, it will reinforce his conditioned expectation of conclusion; for the naïve reader, *it will qualify his expectation of a certain kind of continuation.* (In other words, if the last two lines had not rhymed, they would have appeared to be the beginning of a fourth quatrain: *abab, cdcd, efef, gh . . .* [*gh*?].)

As I pointed out earlier, one of the most effective ways to indicate the conclusion of a poem generated by an indefinitely extensible principle is simply to modify that principle at the end of the poem. It then becomes a series running AAA . . . *x*, where the occurrence of *x* in connection with other (thematic and nonstructural) elements suggesting conclusion will be much more effective for closure than one more A. What I would suggest, then, is that we regard the English sonnet as a stanzaic form,[18] generated by quatrains, where the device of "terminal modification" has become incorporated as a convention. If the couplet of an English sonnet has notable closural force it is largely because *any* terminal modification of form will strengthen closure. Similarly, the rondeau incorporates, as a convention, the terminal repetition of an initial element, a device which (as we shall see) *always* tends to have a

18 Typographical arrangement often emphasizes the possibility, of course.

closural effect. We may conclude that although the reader's sense of closure at the end of a highly conventional form will be increased by his familiarity with that form, it does not depend exclusively upon it.

Another question, however, is raised by this point. Can the reader's familiarity with a conventional conclusion *decrease* its closural effectiveness? Can it be said, for example, that since terminal modification operates by qualifying the reader's expectation, a sophisticated reader who *expects* a change cannot be affected by this device? What I would answer at this point is that in responding to a poem we may be affected as both a naïve and a sophisticated reader, and that these responses do not cancel each other out, but are compounded. The problem is fundamentally the same as that suggested by a comparison of a first reading and a rereading of the same poem. The more general form of the question (and, in this form, it is relevant to music as well as literature) is whether the system of expectations operating during an initial reading or hearing is the same in subsequent readings or hearings. To what extent is our response to a poem, novel, play, or piece of music modified by our previous experience, our knowledge of "what is going to happen"?

The answer suggested by our actual experiences with literature and music is that, although this modification is inevitable, it is much less important than one might otherwise suppose. Conformity to exact expectations rather than satisfaction of one among several may, of course, become a source of pleasure to the extent that a work is remembered exactly.[19] Moreover, in reading a familiar work, one may experience a heightening of tension as one approaches the passages remembered as especially gratifying.[20] Finally, as we have noted before, one tends to impose closure on any

[19] Meyer discusses some of these effects in connection with music, *Emotion and Meaning in Music*, pp. 59–60, 90.

[20] On the other hand, these passages may have been especially gratifying because tension had been heightened, even initially, by structural elements in the work.

point that is known independently to be terminal. Even when all this is granted, however, the more general quality of our responses must be described as remarkably similar from one reading or hearing to the next. We might say that one tends to suppress what one knows for the sake of the pleasure of not knowing. It is also likely that the specific knowledge of any particular work can never be secure or complete enough to overcome the systems of expectation created by the structure of that work. And we must also remember that these structural expectations are themselves strengthened by innumerable extraliterary experiences—particularly those with the language of everyday discourse—and these experiences will continue to condition our expectations no matter how familiar we may become with a particular poem.

The first quatrain of Shakespeare's seventy-third sonnet, for example, contains two subtle surprises, one thematic and one formal:

> That time of year thou mayst in me behold
> When yellow leaves, *or none, or few,* do hang
> Upon those boughs which shake against the cold,
> *Bare ruined choirs,* where late the sweet birds sang.

Our experience with the logical conventions of discourse makes the series "yellow leaves, *or few, or none*" much more probable than the present series; and I think that the affective quality of the line which results from this nonlogical sequence is still available at the hundredth reading of the sonnet. Similarly, even though one has the quatrain absolutely fixed in one's memory, the deviation from the iambic norm at the beginning of the fourth line will continue to be experienced as an expressive deviation during any particular reading of the poem—a reading, that is, in which one allows oneself to respond to the poem as a total structure.

Or, to take another kind of example: when we see a performance of *Oedipus Rex,* no matter how well we know not only the plot but the exact sequence of scenes and lines, we will have some feeling like "hope" at the conclusion of the third ode—as if perhaps *this* time Oedipus will turn out to be not the son of Laius, but a demigod.

To return to the question of the effect of familiarity upon the reader's experience, we may now restate as a principle the suggestion offered earlier: neither conventions as such nor any foreknowledge of the details of a poem can successfully decrease the sense of closure produced by the structure of the work itself. Each reading is, in a sense, a new and unique experience, the quality of which continues to depend as much upon the relation of the poem's structure to *all* our experiences as upon our previous experience with that poem or others like it in form.[21]

III Stanzaic Forms

The systematic repetition of formal elements is fundamentally a force for continuation, and closure is, of course, always weakened by the expectation of continuation. What we shall consider in this section is how, in a poem generated through a succession of formally identical stanzas, the poet can secure the reader's acceptance of the last stanza as, indeed, terminal. One way has already been suggested in connection with the sonnet: through terminal modification or, in stanzaic poems, through some change in the form of the last stanza so that it is not actually identical to the

[21] Nothing could be further from my purpose than to imply that when we read, we are responding only to "the poem itself." On the contrary, I will wish to emphasize throughout this study how deeply our responses to any particular poem are affected by all our previous experiences—with the world at large, with everyday language, with literature in general, and with poems of related styles. As Iago said, "You know what you know." My point is that knowledge does not operate as a collection of discrete items of information, but as a complexly interrelated system of conditioned expectations and dispositions. How they align themselves on any particular occasion and which of them will be prepotent will depend upon all the features of that occasion.

preceding ones. The change need not be a radical one to be effective in this respect, and there are other devices for strengthening closure that are particularly appropriate to stanzaic forms.

It will be instructive to begin with a glance at the characteristics of strophic verse when it is still closely allied to its musical origins. As Bruce Pattison demonstrates, there is every reason to believe that Tudor lyrics were almost universally intended to be sung and that, as he puts it, they "passed straight from poet to composer." [22] In an air, the strophic divisions of the lyric corresponded to a musical division, the same tune being repeated for each successive stanza. To the extent that any literary element was repeated from stanza to stanza, the coincidence of phrasing in words and music would be maximized, and the expressive power of the music most readily exploited. When successive stanzas are very different in syntax or with respect to other thematic elements, the music which is most appropriate for one stanza is likely to be less appropriate for the others. One may observe with what care Campion composed his lyrics so that the same musical phrase would be suitable for corresponding lines in each stanza, [23] and it is not surprising that in so many of Wyatt's lyrics each stanza opens with identical lines and concludes with an identical refrain.

It is also true, however, that perfect repetition is, both musically and verbally, not only the least interesting, informative, or emotionally expressive structure, but also an anti-closural force. The musical solution to this problem will be obvious to anyone who has heard a rendition of Elizabethan songs: the performer indicates the end of the piece by slowing down the tempo, by prolonging or repeating the last phrase or word, or by increasing or decreasing the force of his delivery. The relation between musical

[22] *Music and Poetry of the English Renaissance*, p. 35. I am indebted throughout the following discussion to Pattison's study, esp. pp. 76–88. Cf. also Albert Wellek, "The Relationship between Music and Poetry," *The Journal of Aesthetics and Art Criticism*, II (Winter, 1962): 149–56, esp. p. 155.

[23] See, e.g., "My sweetest Lesbia," *The Works of Thomas Campion*, ed. Percival Vivian (Oxford, 1909), p. 6.

and literary closure in these songs is complicated by the fact that lyrics could be composed to allow for effective musical conclusions,[24] or the composer (or performer) could make an otherwise weak lyric conclusion more effective by musical modification.[25]

[24] See, e.g., Jonson's "Her Triumph" (*Poems*, pp. 115–16), where the last line of the last stanza—"O so white! O so soft! O so sweet is she!"—can be effectively adapted to all the devices of musical closure mentioned above.

[25] Cf. Wyatt's lyric No. 113 (*Collected Poems of Sir Thomas Wyatt*, ed. Kenneth Muir [Cambridge, Mass., 1960], pp. 102–3):

And wylt thow leve me thus?
Say nay, say nay, ffor shame,
To save the from the Blame
Of all my greffe and grame;
And wylt thow leve me thus?
    Say nay, Say nay!

And wylt thow leve me thus,
That hathe lovyd the so long,
In welthe and woo among?
And ys thy hart so strong
As for to leve me thus?
    Say nay, Say nay!

And wylt thow leve me thus,
That hathe gevyn the my hart,
Never for to Depart,
Nother for payn nor smart;
And wylt thow leve me thus?
    Say nay, Say nay!

And wylt thow leve me thus
And have nomore Pyttye
Of hym that lovythe the?
Helas thy cruellte!
And wylt thow leve me thus?
    Say nay, Say nay!

There is little in the final stanza to suggest finality or otherwise to distinguish it from the preceding three, and, like many of Wyatt's lyrics, it could be accused of lacking both development and closure. It is likely, however, that the line, "Helas thy cruellte!" was intended to receive special emphasis in its musical rendition—with a break, perhaps, and a relatively long pause preceding the last two lines. These, in turn, would have been sung with a tempo and force, and probably additional repetition, that would have expressive power and also effectively distinguish them from the earlier refrains.

The point, however, is that where lyrics were intended for musical rendition, stanzaic form was the most effective structure the poet could use, and he could count on the devices of musical modification to provide or strengthen the needed closure.

Where lyrics were no longer designed for or written in conjunction with music, stanzaic divisions might still be retained as an effective formal structure and the poet would have the advantage of his freedom from certain musical demands, such as thematic repetition in succeeding stanzas. But he would also be obliged to find verbal resources that would compensate for what he had lost in the expressive power of music. Most important from our point of view would be the loss of musical modification to single closure and, consequently, the greater degree of verbal modification required in the last stanza. Later we will consider the more complex structure and closure of a stanzaic poem not designed for music. If we look first, however, at a few of Wyatt's songs, we can identify some of the purely verbal resources that were available to any lyricist.

The device which Wyatt used with greatest success and subtlety was the terminal modification of the refrain. The simplest modification may be seen in the following lyric:

> Fforget not yet the tryde entent
> Of suche a truthe as I haue ment,
> My gret travayle so gladly spent
>   Fforget not yet.
>
> Fforget not yet when fyrst began
> The wery lyffe ye know syns whan,
> The sute, the seruys none tell can.
>   Fforgett not yett.
>
> Fforget not yet the gret assays,
> The cruell wrong, the skornfull ways,
> The paynfull pacyence in denays,
>   Fforgett not yet.

Fforget not yet, forget not thys,
How long ago hathe ben and ys
The mynd that neuer ment amys,
Fforget not yet.

Fforget not then thyn owne aprovyd
The whyche so long hathe the so lovyd,
Whose stedfast faythe yet neuer movyd,
Fforget not thys.[26]

The slight change from "Fforget not yet" to "Fforget not thys" clearly strengthens the sense of closure in the final stanza; it is not, however, the only closural device in the poem. For one thing, the final stanza amounts to a summary of the first three, as the phrase "Fforget not *then*" might lead one to expect. This phrase signals the approaching conclusion both formally and thematically: formally, by modifying the phrase which had begun all the previous stanzas, and thematically, by preparing the reader for a more or less logical conclusion. Also, the fact that the last refrain had been anticipated in line 13 gives its recurrence much the effect of an additional rhyme.

Although many of Wyatt's refrains are, like that of the poem quoted in footnote 25, completely repetitive, a good number of them become a more complex structural element through minor modifications from stanza to stanza. As we can observe in the following list of refrains, the modification tends to be much more striking in the concluding stanza:[27]

57: . . . Yet rew vpon my pain.
. . . To rew vpon my pain.
. . . But rew vpon my pain.
. . . Reioyse not at my pain.

[26] No. 130, *ibid.*, p. 121.
[27] The poems are cited by their number in Muir's edition; they appear on pages 43, 51, 55, and 73.

67: . . . But onlye liff and libertie.
. . . Lacking my liff for libertie.
. . . And all for lack of libertie.
. . . And losse of liff for libertie.
. . . Graunt me but liff and libertie.
. . . My deth, or liff with libertie.

72: . . . For to content your cruelnes. (2)
. . . And to content your cruelnes.
. . . For to content your cruelnes.
. . . For to repent your cruelnes.

91: . . . Most wretched harte why arte thow nott ded?
. . . And he is wretched that wens hym so.
. . . Most wretched harte why arte thou nott ded?
. . . For he is wretched that wenys hym so.
. . . Moost wretched hert, why art thou not ded?
. . . And he is wretched that wens him soo.
. . . Most wretched herte why art thou not ded?
. . . Sayeth he is wretched that wens him soo.
. . . Moost wretched hert why art thou not dede?
. . . For he is wretched that wens him soo.
. . . Vnhappy thenne why art thou not dede?
. . . Sins vnhap cannot kil me soo.

It is evident, even with only the refrains before us, that the terminal modifications usually involve thematic elements that are in themselves significant in signaling closure. The allusion to death, for example, in 67, is typical; and a refrain which answers a running question, as in 91, will obviously have a closural effect.[28] Thematic devices are, in fact, among the most valuable resources the poet has at his disposal to strengthen closure, and they will be discussed at length in the following two chapters. Here we may take the occasion to observe how a thematic device works in one

[28] Cf. No. 111 (*ibid.*, p. 100), where the first five stanzas have the refrain, "It is possyble?" and the sixth concludes, "All ys possyble."

poem in which the refrains are not completely identical, but where an additional source of closure is clearly needed to distinguish the final stanza. The song "Hevyn and erth and all that here me plain" [29] contains nine quatrains, the last line in each concluding with a repetition, as in "*Mercy, madame, alas, I dy, I dy!*" (line 4) and "To here my plaint, dere hert, awake, awake!" (line 8). The poem is not notable for its thematic development, each stanza urging the lady in different terms to show the lover some charitable affection. The last stanza, however, identifies itself clearly by its final line: "Cruell, vnkynd! I say farewell, farewell!"

Thematic elements may also be used to signal closure even where the form of the refrain remains identical throughout. Some of Wyatt's most subtle effects are achieved by allowing a refrain to remain constant but altering its significance in succeeding stanzas through the material that precedes it, as in the following poem:

In eternum I was ons determed
For to have lovid and my minde affermed,
That with my herte it shuld be confermed
    In eternum.

Forthwith I founde the thing that I myght like,
And sought with loue to warme her hert alike,
For, as me thought, I shulde not se the like
    In eternum.

To trase this daunse I put my self in prese;
Vayne hope ded lede and bad I should not cese
To serue, to suffer, and still to hold my pease
    In eternum.

With this furst rule I fordred me apase,
That, as me thought, my trowghthe had taken place
With full assurans to stond in her grace
    In eternum.

[29] No. 73, *ibid.*, p. 56.

It was not long or I by proofe had found
That feble bilding is on feble grounde;
For in her herte this worde ded never sounde,
    In eternum.

In eternum then from my herte I kest
That I had furst determined for the best;
Nowe in the place another thought doeth rest,
    In eternum.[30]

The wit and also the pathos of this song arise largely from the ingenuity with which the poet rings the changes on the phrase, "In eternum," which seems to be repeated almost compulsively. It is as if the poet is saying: "I cannot get it out of my head that love implies some sort of permanence. Well, now I know better; but, in my own way, I shall continue to demonstrate its relevance." The closural effect of the last stanza is a product of several thematic elements, as reflected in the word "then," which here indicates both temporal succession and logical conclusion. As a signal for approaching termination, its effect is also heightened by the occurrence of the key phrase, "In eternum," just before it, which suggests that a general or summary observation is to follow.

Before we leave Wyatt's lyrics we should note his use of what may appear to be the simplest, even the most naïve, of closural devices in strophic verse, namely the repetition, with very slight modification, of the entire first stanza at the conclusion of the poem. In two of Wyatt's songs[31] the return to the opening stanza serves as a frame for what might be considered the "song proper." The framing stanzas announce that a song will be sung and then that it just has been sung. The advantage here is clear: the song itself need possess only the frailest thematic structure; closure is insured. As we shall see later, one of the most effective ways to close a poem is simply to announce that one is doing so. As it

[30] No. 71, *ibid.*, p. 54.
[31] No. 51 (*ibid.*, p. 37) and No. 66 (p. 49).

happens, one of these two poems, "My lute awake," is among Wyatt's most tightly "plotted" lyrics, and we may look at it more closely as an example of closure through framing stanzas:

My lute awake! perfourme the last
Labor that thou and I shall wast,
  And end that I have now begon;
For when this song is sung and past,
  My lute be still, for I have done.

As to be herd where ere is none,
As lede to grave in marbill stone,
  My song may perse her hert as sone;
Should we then sigh, or syng, or mone?
  No, no, my lute, for I have done.

The Rokkes do not so cruelly
Repulse the waves continuelly,
  As she my suyte and affection,
So that I ame past remedy:
  Whereby my lute and I have done.

Prowd of the spoyll that thou hast gott
Of simple hertes thorough loves shot,
  By whome, vnkynd, thou hast theim wone,
Thinck not he haith his bow forgot,
  All tho my lute and I have done.

Vengeaunce shall fall on thy disdain,
That makest but game on ernest pain;
  Thinck not alone vnder the sonne
Vnquyt to cause thy lovers plain,
  All tho my lute and I have done.

Perchaunce the lye wethered and old,
The wynter nyghtes that are so cold,
  Playnyng in vain vnto the mone;

Thy wisshes then dare not be told;
  Care then who lyst, for I have done.

And then may chaunce the to repent
The tyme that thou hast lost and spent
  To cause thy lovers sigh and swoune;
Then shalt thou knowe beaultie but lent,
  And wisshe and want as I have done.

Now cease, my lute, this is the last
Labour that thou and I shall wast,
  And ended is that we begon;
Now is this song boeth sung and past;
  My lute be still, for I have done.[32]

Here the first stanza announces not only that a song is to follow, but that its performance will constitute a sort of ceremonial declaration of dis-engagement. What the poet has at stake is, as so often in Wyatt, his pride and his sense of emotional independence or self-sufficiency. The song itself develops from lamentation to bitterness and eventually, in lines 26–29, to that tone of remote, disinterested, and chilling compassion that would just suit the poet's motive. In the stanza before the last, however, the strains of bitterness and lamentation threaten again. The last stanza, by returning to the situation at the beginning, serves not only to announce the song's conclusion but also allows the poet to reassert his emotional distance and control.

The closural force of the final stanza here is heightened not only by the effect of the framing stanzas but also by another device similar to one we have already encountered in connection with meter: that is, as a return to a norm after a deviation. Here, the norm in question is that phrase, "I have done," which occurs at the conclusion of each stanza. In every instance, with the one exception to be noted, "done" means *finished.* In line 35, however, it is used as a substitute verb, referring to "wisshe and want."

[32] No. 66, *ibid.*, pp. 49–51.

Consequently, when the phrase appears at the conclusion of the next (and final) stanza with its normal meaning, its closural force is doubled: not only is it a stabilizing return to the norm after a deviation, but also, through the now emphasized meaning of *finished,* it is a thematic heightening of the sense of finality.

As this lyric suggests, the repetition of the first stanza of a poem as its conclusion is not necessarily a simple formal device. It will be useful, however, to consider some of the simpler components of its effect. To begin with, at the most primitive level, it is effective because, as in music, it reproduces a familiar group of sounds. This is not in itself a sufficient condition for closure, but its force is strengthened by the fact that the first stanza constituted an integral formal structure in its own right. Consequently, any part of it, when it reappears, will cause the reader to expect the rest to follow; and when it does follow, closure will be strengthened. (Any minor deviation from exact repetition will only heighten the reader's tension; it will not destroy the system of expectations.)

Second, the repetition of an entire stanza is not only a formal repetition but a thematic one as well: it is the reassertion of an utterance. Depending on the thematic structure of the stanzas that intervene, the reassertion may take on various logical qualities, any number of which can be effectively "conclusive." In Wyatt's three-part poem, "Lo, what it is to love," each part closes with the stanza that opened it. The first of these begins as follows:

Lo, what it is to love!
Lerne ye that list to prove
    At me, I say,
    No ways that may
The grownd of grieff remove.
    My liff alweie
    That doeth decaye:
Lo, what it is to love! [33]

[33] No. 87, *ibid.*, p. 68.

Four stanzas follow, in which love is described by the woes it entails and is defined as a state of general misfortune. The final stanza repeats the first one exactly, but whereas the first could be rephrased, "Ah, love! No one can tell me that it isn't a grief, as I shall shortly prove," the last stanza, using precisely the same words, would be rephrased, "You see? I have just proved that love is a grief, and no one can say otherwise." The thematic structure of the intervening stanzas turned an introduction into a summary and conclusion.[34]

Finally, the terminal repetition of an initial stanza is effective in strengthening closure not only directly, in the ways just described, but also indirectly, in weakening the expectation of continuation. By returning to the original point of departure, it suggests that there is no place else to go and, consequently, that the journey has been completed.

We observed earlier that the special problem of strophic verse intended for musical rendition is that the repetitive structure which is most effective with respect to musical demands is least effective with respect to closure. When the poet is no longer designing his stanzas for music, he is likely to use a more complex and cohesive thematic structure, and this type of structure will provide correspondingly stronger closural effects. Although this is not the place to launch a general discussion of the relation of thematic structure to closure, we can conclude this section with a look at one stanzaic poem in which the relation is clear.

Vertue.

Sweet day, so cool, so calm, so bright,
The bridall of the earth and skie:

[34] The repeated stanza itself contains the framing repetition, "Lo, what it is to love!" We might say that as a first line it asserts its significance, and as a last line its emotional force. It is comparable in this respect to a repeated exclamation, such as "How sad. How sad!" See B. F. Skinner, *Verbal Behavior* (New York, 1957), p. 221, for an interesting analysis of the dynamics of this sort of repetition.

The dew shall weep thy fall to night;
For thou must die.

Sweet rose, whose hue angrie and brave
Bids the rash gazer wipe his eye:
Thy root is ever in its grave,
And thou must die.

Sweet spring, full of sweet dayes and roses,
A box where sweets compacted lie;
My musick shows ye have your closes,
And all must die.

Onely a sweet and vertuous soul,
Like season'd timber, never gives;
But though the whole world turn to coal,
Then chiefly lives.[35]

The formal structure of Herbert's poem is obviously related to that of the song-lyric, but its metrical subtlety, if nothing else, would make musical interpretation not only difficult but largely superfluous. The repetition of "sweet," for example, or the parallel syntactic patterns in each of the first three stanzas, might suggest the kind of repetition in corresponding lines that we saw in Wyatt's lyrics. The lines in Herbert's poem, however, are far from corresponding rhythmically, and it would be difficult to compose a tune that would be equally appropriate to each stanza. The rhythmic differences among the first lines in each stanza, for example, are very great, as even the crudest scansion reveals:

Sweet dáy,/ so cóol,/ so cálm,/ so bríght . . .
Sweet róse,/ whose húe/ ángrie and bráve . . .
Sweet spríng,/ fúll of sweet dáyes / and róses . . .
Ónely a swéet / and vértuous sóul. . . .

[35] *The Works of George Herbert*, ed. F. E. Hutchinson (Oxford, 1959), p. 87.

Also, the thematic relations among the stanzas are not the "variations on a theme" so typical of true song-lyrics. Here there is a concise but complex logical development, moving from examples to generalization in the first three stanzas and to opposition in the last one. The third stanza does not so much repeat the thematic elements of the first two as *contain* them, as the spring contains the days and roses; and the logical generalization (" . . . all must die") is thus reinforced by the formal grouping.

Indeed, what gives this poem so much of its power is the fact that so many elements in its formal and thematic structure conspire to bring about closure at the conclusion of the *third* stanza. The fourth stanza, however, is hardly anticlimatic; on the contrary, it has the effect, entirely appropriate to its theme, of a revelation—that which is known beyond what can be demonstrated logically. At the conclusion of the third stanza, "Vertue" is comparable to such a poem as Herrick's "To Daffodills," the last stanza of which is as follows:

> We have short time to stay, as you.
> We have as short a Spring;
> As quick a growth to meet Decay,
> *As you, or any thing.*
> *We die,*
> As your hours doe, and drie
> Away,
> Like to the Summers raine;
> Or as the pearles of Mornings dew
> Ne'r to be found againe.[36]

The point of Herbert's poem, however, is to deny the Anacreontic conclusion represented in the passage here italicized. The third stanza of "Vertue," then, offers a false conclusion, and though its closural force is an important part of its effect, that force must be overcome in the final stanza—and so it is.

[36] *Complete Poetry*, p. 171.

To begin with, we note that Herbert once again "contains" and thus accounts for all the preceding stanzas—here in the phrase "the whole world." Also, he concludes with a striking modification of the refrain-like fourth line. The triple recurrence of the phrase "must die" had given it something of the quality of a systematic repetition, and to that extent had made it a force for continuation. Consequently, the radical change at the conclusion of the fourth stanza causes an abrupt reversal of the reader's expectation of further development. The same is true for all the other formal and thematic modifications in the fourth stanza, including the rhythmic changes and new syntactic structure. Most effective in this respect is the new rhyme-sound in the second line. As a deviation from the expected /aj/ of *skie, eye,* and *lie,* it creates a momentary breakdown of the formal structure established through the first three stanzas, and consequently causes a heightening of tension which is resolved only at the last word, "lives." This word not only allows a relaxation of tension by providing the resolving rhyme for "gives," but also, as a radical modification of the "refrain," constitutes a strong force for noncontinuation. Finally, as the contrary of "die," it carries out and completes the thematic opposition implied by everything else in the fourth stanza. The sense of finality and stability in the last stanza, then, is clinched by the number of closural forces that converge upon the terminating word, and the poem concludes in the triumph and security of faith. "My musick shows ye have your closes. . . ."

IV The Rhymed Couplet

The relation of closure to the rhymed couplet will depend upon the relation of the couplet to the formal structure of the entire poem. The dynamics of closure will be one thing when the couplet *is* the poem (as in Jonson's epigram, discussed on pages 47–48) and another thing when the couplet is only one of a series (as in the heroic couplets of Marlowe's *Hero and Leander*) or only part of the more complex rhyme pattern of a stanzaic form (such as the sonnet, ottava rima, or rhyme royale). How the couplet functions in any particular poem will be a product of two factors: the force for continuation created by any systematic repetition, and the force for closure created by the articulation of a complete formal structure. These are, of course, opposing forces, and since the couplet produces both,[37] it can be used either to maintain or to arrest the reader's expectation of continuation.

We have already seen, in connection with the sonnet, how the couplet can be used to arrest the reader's expectation of further development in a stanzaic form. How it can maintain this expectation may be illustrated by the following passage from the beginning of Marvell's "The Nymph complaining for the death of her Faun":

> The wanton Troopers riding by
> Have shot my Faun and it will dye.
> Ungentle men! They cannot thrive
> To kill thee. Thou neer didst alive
> Them any harm: alas nor cou'd
> Thy death yet do them any good.
> I'me sure I never wisht them ill;
> Nor do I for all this; nor will:
> But if my simple Pray'rs may yet
> Prevail with Heaven to forget
> Thy murder, I will Joyn my Tears
> Rather than fail. But, O my fears!
> It cannot dye so. Heavens King
> Keeps register of every thing:
> And nothing may we use in vain.
> Ev'n Beasts must be with justice slain;
> Else Men are made their *Deodands*.

[37] Except in the two-line poem, where it does not exhibit systematic repetition.

Though they should wash their guilty hands
In this warm life-blood, which doth part
From thine, and wound me to the Heart,
Yet could they not be clean: their Stain
Is dy'd in such a Purple Grain.
There is not such another in
The World, to offer for their Sin.[38]

The couplet-rhymes in this passage have, in certain respects, the same effect as the iambic stress pattern; and the alternation of weak- and strong-stressed syllables, which creates a system of tension and resolution maintained throughout the poem, is comparable to the alternation of pre-rhyme and rhyme [39] in the couplets. (Although the exact sound of successive rhyme-pairs varies, the pattern of tension and resolution is constant.) Like the weak-stressed syllable, each pre-rhyme creates the expectation of its counterpart and, like the iambic line, each couplet creates the expectation of another. The resolution provided by each rhyme is no greater than that produced by each strong stress or each fourth strong stress, and none is great enough, in itself, to create closure.[40]

The tendency of the couplet to strengthen closure is in this passage subordinated to its effects as a force for continuation. Closure, moreover, is suppressed in various ways: by frequent enjambment between one rhyme and the next pre-rhyme (lines 4–5, 10–11, 18–19), by the ending of sentences and major clauses in the middle of a line (lines 3, 4, 5, 11, 12, 13, 21), and generally by ensuring that syntactic resolution does not reinforce the resolution of rhyme. When, at the conclusion of the poem, closure is desired, the tendency of the couplet to strengthen it is exploited by reversing these devices.

[38] *The Poems and Letters of Andrew Marvell,* ed. H. M. Margoliouth (Oxford, 1952), I, 22.

[39] For convenience, I will refer to the first of two rhyming sounds as the "pre-rhyme," and to the second simply as the "rhyme."

[40] See the discussion of rhyme and closure above, pp. 46–49.

The power of couplets to work for continuation, then, obviously increases to the degree that they are not "end-stopped." But what if they *are* end-stopped? How can formal continuity be maintained in a poem that is generated by a principle which tends to produce closure every two lines? And what can provide the sense of *final* closure at its conclusion? Although it may seem paradoxical, the "closed couplet" [41] may be just as strong a force for formal continuity as the open couplet, and in certain respects, even stronger. It functions, however, in a slightly different way. What we must recognize is that all those conditions which produce closure in the individual couplet also increase the integrity of the couplet as a formal unit, so that it tends to function within the poem as a single, though complex, formal element. Thus a succession of closed couplets will have all the characteristics of *any systematic repetition of formal elements,* including the most important characteristic analyzed in section I, namely, its effectiveness in maintaining the reader's expectation of continuation.

What all this means is that, in closing itself, the couplet does not necessarily close the structure of which it is a part. Consider the following two chains, which provide an interesting, if limited, analogy:

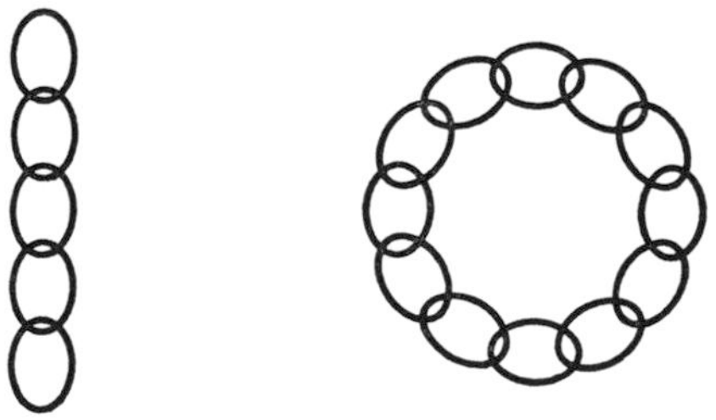

a b

[41] The term "closed couplet," especially when used in connection with neoclassical verse, usually refers to more than end-stopping, i.e., the coincidence of syntactic and metrical pauses. The couplets of Pope, for example, have characteristic rhetorical features, such as balance, antithesis, parallelism, and alliteration, which clearly strengthen their self-containment. These devices

In each chain, the individual links are closed; but whereas chain *b*, as a whole structure, is closed, chain *a* is not, and there is nothing to prevent us from adding links to it indefinitely.

To turn from analogy to example, let us consider the following passage from the beginning of Blake's "Auguries of Innocence": [42]

A robin redbreast in a cage
Puts all Heaven in a rage.
A dove-house fill'd with doves and pigeons
Shudders Hell thro' all its regions.
A dog starv'd at his master's gate
Predicts the ruin of the State.
A horse misus'd upon the road
Calls to Heaven for human blood.
Each outcry of the hunted hare
A fibre from the brain does tear.
A skylark wounded in the wing,
A cherubim does cease to sing.

The combination of closed couplets and didactic or prophetic material may seem to have the effect of generating a list of detachable aphorisms. To the extent that this is true, we might say that the thematic development of the poem is as end-stopped as its formal structure. Nevertheless, the tendency of the couplets to form atomized units is ultimately counteracted by several other forces, both formal and thematic. In each succeeding couplet, its apparent tendency to close itself (and the series) is increasingly overpowered by the momentum of repetition—a repetition which, moreover, involves not only the formal structure of each couplet (its meter and rhyme), and the obvious thematic elements, but also the syntactic pattern and its relation to the form. (Each

---

will be discussed in later sections, but here we need only note that, to the extent that they reinforce closure in individual couplets, they simply enhance the effects described in the following paragraphs.

[42] *The Poetical Works of William Blake*, ed. John Sampson (Oxford, 1961), pp. 171–75. I have omitted the opening quatrain.

couplet, for example, divides exactly into subject and predicate.) Far from allowing one to "relax" at the conclusion of each unit, this series builds an increasingly strong state of tension. Just enough relief is provided, however, to keep the tension from obliterating every other effect, without arresting the momentum. It is provided by slight modifications of the meter, or of the syntactic pattern, or of other elements that had previously been part of the repetitive system. The fifth couplet, for example, changes the first word from "a" to "each" and places the predicate verb at the end rather than at the beginning of the second line.

These deviations are required because the greatest danger to formal continuity created by the closed couplet is not that of premature closure but of "saturation," or, in more familiar terms, of boredom and fatigue. In this respect, as in others, a series of closed couplets is no different from any other principle of systematic repetition. When a stimulus continues to be repeated exactly over a considerable period of time, our expectation of further repetition ultimately must contend with our desire for closure or at least for change. Up to a certain point, this produces a heightening of tension; but after that, it is as if the nerves "give up" and simply fail to respond altogether. Something like this happens when we are obliged to remain unoccupied for a long time in a room with a loudly ticking clock. At first our irritation will increase steadily; but after a while the ticks no longer compel attention and they become absorbed in the generally homogeneous climate of sound around us.

I am not concerned here with the psychological dynamics of such a process, [43] but I think it suggests why systematic repetition in poetry cannot be extended too long without variation. Meter,

[43] It may involve something comparable to sensory adaptation or neural fatigue, or something more fundamental or more complex than either of these. See Charles E. Osgood, *Method and Theory in Experimental Psychology* (New York, 1953), pp. 77–82, for a summary of recent research in sensory adaptation. D. O. Hebb discusses mental and neural fatigue and the effects of monotony in *The Organization of Behavior* (New York, 1949), pp. 208, 211–15, 224–27.

for example, not only becomes oppressive when it is too regular, but may, like the ticking clock, ultimately become "imperceptible." We will not, to be sure, feel that we are suddenly reading prose; but the power of the meter either to compel our attention or to organize our expectations and responses will gradually diminish in strength. It also suggests that to the extent that rhymed couplets function as a form of systematic repetition, they not only tend to strengthen formal continuity (and thus counteract their own closural effects), but they eventually tend to produce other reactions (those that are implied by the term "saturation") that are at odds with both closure and continuity. What we can observe in the lines from Blake's poems is that the variations necessary to prevent these saturating effects can be introduced without modifying the form of the closed couplet as such. In other words, "perfect" closed couplets can be generated indefinitely without weakening the poem's formal continuity and also without producing saturation.

Given that a succession of closed couplets does not necessarily create closure with respect to the total structure of the poem, it remains to consider how closure *is* created at the conclusion of such a poem. The problem is not a new one, and some of the solutions have been discussed before. First, as in stanzaic forms, a series of closed couplets can be effectively concluded through terminal modification. The couplets can, for example, be replaced by some other formal unit, such as a quatrain rhyming *abab*. In "Auguries of Innocence," the couplet rhymes are retained to the end of the poem, but in the last eight lines (lines 125–32) the usual two-line syntactic group is replaced by two four-line groups, and other formal modifications appear:

> We are led to believe a lie
> When we see not thro' the eye,
> Which was born in a night, to perish in a night,
> When the Soul slept in beams of light.
> God appears, and God is Light,

To those poor souls who dwell in Night;
But does a Human Form display
To those who dwell in realms of Day.

The metrically anomalous third line and the bunching of rhymes in lines 3 to 6 have the additional effect of disturbing the expectations previously established. The slight heightening of tension thus created is finally resolved in the last couplet, which, because it appears as a re-establishment of the metrical norm, has its independent closural effect strengthened.

The more usual solution to the problem of terminal closure in a closed-couplet poem is provided by its thematic structure, and this is evidently involved in the conclusion of "Auguries of Innocence." The number of ways in which thematic elements can strengthen closure is almost incalculable, and we must once again defer their discussion to later chapters. We may conclude this section, however, with a brief glance at the final lines of another poem in closed couplets, quite different from Blake's:

Then cease, bright Nymph! to mourn thy ravish'd Hair
Which adds new Glory to the shining Sphere!
Not all the Tresses that fair Head can boast
Shall draw such Envy as the Lock you lost.
For, after all the Murders of your Eye,
When after Millions slain, your self shall die;
When those fair Suns shall sett, as sett they must,
And all those Tresses shall be laid in Dust;
This Lock, the Muse shall consecrate to Fame,
And mid'st the Stars inscribe *Belinda*'s Name! [44]

As in the concluding lines of "Auguries of Innocence," part of the effect here is created by the heightening of tension just before the final couplet, so that the independent tendency of the couplet to

[44] "The Rape of the Lock," Canto V, ll. 141–50, *The Poems of Alexander Pope*, ed. John Butt (New Haven, 1963), pp. 241–42.

strengthen closure is reinforced. Here, however, the effect is achieved not by metrical deviations but by the syntactic suspension in lines 5 to 8, the resolution of which in the last couplet is comparable to the restoration of the metrical norm in Blake's poem. There are several other ways in which closure is strengthened at the conclusion of *The Rape of the Lock*, and I will not attempt to present an exhaustive analysis here—especially since many of the thematic devices, to be appreciated, require the further discussion that will appear in later sections. We may notice, however, that the passage opens with the words, "Then cease . . . !" which more or less announce the approaching conclusion; that the major themes of the poem are drawn together in the final lines; that the key word, "lock," appears in the last couplet; and, finally, that the general sense of the passage is to suggest an ultimate state of permanence.

V Blank Verse

As we move from the sonnet to stanzaic forms and couplets, to blank verse, and finally to free verse, we are tracing a line which runs from the greatest to the least degree of formal determination. As we progress, it becomes increasingly difficult to account for closure through the analysis of strictly formal aspects of structure; for, in general, as the number of formal principles decreases, closural effects increasingly depend upon the thematic features of the poem.

When one thinks of the most familiar blank verse poems—*Paradise Lost* and *The Prelude*, for example—it is clear that the effectiveness of their conclusions has very little to do with their formal structures. The five lines with which *Paradise Lost* concludes—

> Some natural tears they dropp'd, but wip'd them soon;
> The World was all before them, where to choose

> Thir place of rest, and Providence thir guide:
> They hand in hand with wand'ring steps and slow,
> Through *Eden* took thir solitary way.[45]

—bring the poem to its end with that quality of poised repose that is so characteristic of Milton's poetic conclusions. Speaking of the poem's readers, Dr. Johnson observed, "None ever wished it longer than it is," and one may agree without accepting the implication of tedium. We do not wish it longer, we could not even imagine it longer, because no poem has ever justified its conclusion better. It is not my purpose here, however, to dwell upon the marvels of Milton's poetic architecture, but only to point out that, powerful as the conclusion of *Paradise Lost* is, that power has everything to do with the poem's thematic structure and almost nothing to do with its formal structure—with the fact, that is, that it is written in blank verse.[46]

A sonnet, like the well-wrought urn to which Donne compared it, gives its shape to whatever it contains. Stanzaic forms are like blocks: a tower of any height may be constructed of them, but its shape will still be defined and limited by the shape of the blocks. Although the blank-verse line, like the rhymed couplet, is in some respects a kind of minimal stanza, it is not a completely self-determined unit of formal structure. A poem may consist of a single Spenserian stanza or a single couplet, but the single blank-verse line has almost no functional identity. Or to put it another way, the effect of its form depends upon its repeated extension. Blank verse may be best compared, perhaps, to an inexhaustible

[45] Book XII, ll. 645–49; *John Milton: Complete Poems and Major Prose,* ed. Merritt Y. Hughes (New York, 1957), pp. 468–69.

[46] The qualification—"*almost* nothing"—will concern us later, but it is perhaps necessary at this point to recall that in this study "formal structure" has a restricted meaning. For example, the complex system of correspondences and contrasts which bring together Heaven and Hell, history and myth, and psychology and theology in *Paradise Lost* would be considered here as part of the poem's thematic structure. Assonance, polysyllabic words, metrical variations, etc., are formal elements, but nonstructural.

spool of tape: it will measure any bolt of material, but cannot, in itself, determine the shape or length of that material.[47] It has no self-generated cut-off point, and it will stop measuring only when the material itself is ended.

It is true, of course, that a formally rigorous blank-verse poem must conclude at the end of a decasyllabic line. But since there are so many decasyllabic line-ends in the poem, this hardly provides much closural force. On the contrary, the kind of systematic repetition by which blank verse is generated is a particularly strong force for continuation: any given blank-verse line will cause the reader to expect another one. What, then, will distinguish the end of a blank-verse poem? Is there any way in which the sense of finality can be strengthened apart from thematic closure?

The most effective, if not the most subtle, way is illustrated in Shakespeare's plays, where closure was a practical necessity as well as a poetic desideratum. Since there was no curtain to tell the audience that a scene had concluded, the playwright had to provide this information through some turn of the actors' speech. Shakespeare would eventually find several ways to incorporate such a turn of speech without straining verisimilitude, but even in his later plays he frequently employed the most obvious device of terminal modification: that is, he concluded the last speech in a scene with a rhymed couplet.[48]

> . . . The play's the thing
> Wherein I'll catch the conscience of the King. *Exit.*
> [*Hamlet*, Act II, scene 2, lines 633–34.]

> Let me, if not by birth, have lands by wit;

[47] There is, however, the negative limit of length, in that a blank-verse poem must not be too short. In terms of the analogy, it would be like using a yardstick to measure a microbe: the material must not come to an end before the unit of measure has been reached.

[48] See Federick W. Ness, *The Use of Rhyme in Shakespeare's Plays* (New Haven, 1941), pp. 25–94, for further remarks on the functions, frequency, and general characteristics of Shakespeare's dramatic couplets.

All with me's meet that I can fashion fit. *Exit.*
[*King Lear*, Act I, scene 2, lines 199–200.]

. . . That thou, residing here, go'st yet with me,
And I, hence fleeting, here remain with thee.
Away! *Exeunt.*
[*Antony and Cleopatra*, Act I, scene 3, lines 103–5.]

Prospero my lord shall know what I have done.
So, King, so safely on to seek thy son. *Exeunt.*
[*The Tempest*, Act II, scene 1, lines 326–27.] [49]

Insofar as the device became conventional, the couplet might function as a recognized signal, pure and simple. As we saw earlier in connection with the sonnet, however, a convention usually has independent force; in the scene-end also, the couplet would be effective not only as a closed formal unit but by arresting the listener's expectation of continuation—here, the expectation of continuing blank-verse lines.[50]

Blank verse is most easily closed, then, when it ceases to be blank verse. There is another way, however, in which the characteristics of the form itself can be exploited to strengthen closure. Though the closural effect in this case is modest compared to others we have discussed, it will be entirely adequate when it appears in conjunction with the numerous other forces for closure that are likely to be present in a blank-verse poem. Although it occurs in Shakespeare's later plays, the special conditions of dramatic poetry would complicate the analysis of this device in any particular passage. Consequently, we shall return to *Paradise Lost* for an example.

[49] Texts of the plays, here and elsewhere in this study, are from *The Complete Works of Shakespeare*, ed. George Lyman Kittredge (Boston, 1936).

[50] Ness remarks that the couplet was never used systematically enough in the plays to constitute a purely conventional prompting device (*The Use of Rhyme in Shakespeare's Plays*, p. 62).

The device I am referring to is analogous to the final cadence of a fugue, a madrigal, or any similarly counterpointed polyphonic work. In such pieces, continuation is maintained and strengthened by preventing the component melodies from reaching a final cadence at the same time. Conversely, the conclusion of the piece coincides with the simultaneous cadence or the appearance of the tonic in all the melodic lines. A corresponding effect can be seen in one of Milton's blank verse "paragraphs." [51] Although these paragraphs average about ten to fifteen lines each and thus give something of the appearance of stanzas, they are in no way comparable to formal strophes, for they have no fixed length and are determined entirely by divisions in the thematic material of the poem: a speech, the description of a certain scene, a portion of narrative summary, and so forth. Nevertheless, Milton often uses the paragraph as if it were a stanza by giving it a formal coherence and integrity that corresponds to and emphasizes the thematic integrity of the passage. Consider the following lines from the conclusion of Book XI (Michael is commenting on Adam's groping interpretation of the first rainbow):

> To whom th' Arch-Angel. Dext'rously thou aim'st;
> So willingly doth God remit his Ire,
> Though late repenting him of Man deprav'd,
> Griev'd at his heart, when looking down he saw
> The whole Earth fill'd with violence, and all flesh
> Corrupting each thir way; yet those remov'd,
> Such grace shall one just Man find in his sight,
> That he relents, not to blot out mankind,
> And makes a Cov'nant never to destroy
> The Earth again by flood, nor let the Sea

[51] James Whaler, in his study of *Paradise Lost* (*Counterpoint and Symbol: An Inquiry into the Rhythm of Milton's Epic Style* [Copenhagen, 1956]), presents a remarkably convincing analysis of Milton's metrical "fugues." The devices he examines are more numerous and subtle than those described here, though the latter are included among them.

Surpass his bounds, nor Rain to drown the World
With man therein or Beast; but when he brings
Over the Earth a Cloud, will therein set
His triple-color'd Bow, whereon to look
And call to mind his Cov'nant: Day and Night,
Seed-time and Harvest, Heat and hoary Frost
Shall hold thir course, till fire purge all things new,
Both Heav'n and Earth, wherein the just shall dwell.[52]

Although not every line is, strictly speaking, enjambed, at no point before the end of the speech does a line-end correspond to a full stop. The major syntactic breaks—colons and semicolons—invariably fall in the middle of a line, so that there is no full rest until the very last line. What we are describing here is also comparable to the devices noted on page 72, where they were used to inhibit the closural force of rhymed couplets. In both instances, the prevention of coincidence between formal and thematic (i.e., syntactic) elements has the effect of strengthening the reader's expectation of continuation and, ultimately, of strengthening the force of closure when the coincidence is allowed to occur.

In reading the passage aloud, either the force of the meter or the force of the syntax will propel one forward continuously, and only at the end can the reader's voice have the inflection appropriate to the end of an utterance. Also, the numerous stress deviations and variable caesura decrease the stabilizing force of the metrical norm without, however, destroying its power to sustain the expectation of regularity. In other words, since the metrical norm continuously eludes but never completely escapes us, we continue to pursue it. And we find it, of course, in the final line, which is not only the least deviant in the passage but also has a caesura in the most "normal" position—after the second strong stress. The ultimate effect of all these suspensions, variations, and deviations is to create a formal structure which maintains the reader's expectations of continuation while building up and finally satisfying his expec-

[52] *John Milton: Complete Poems and Major Prose,* p. 453.

tation of closure. The effect itself is not extraordinary; we have seen it before in the sonnet and in stanzaic poems. What is remarkable is that it can be achieved with a succession of blank-verse lines—a formal structure which is apparently so unpromising for closural effects.

VI Free Verse

If, as I have been suggesting, the formal resources of closure decrease as the form of the poem is increasingly undetermined, it is clear that the closural resources of free verse are minimal. This is not to say, however, that the formal structure of free verse is negligible or that it offers *no* such resources. Generalization is particularly hazardous here because it is difficult to produce or discover a definition of "free verse" that embraces all its acknowledged varieties, that can be stated in positive terms which do not amount merely to a celebration of artistic liberation, and that allows us to distinguish it from, rather than simply oppose it to, other more conventional forms. Although an adequate discussion of the relation of free verse to general propositions regarding poetic form would take us far afield of our present concerns, even those concerns require that we give it some attention here—especially since considerable controversy and a certain amount of obscurantism surrounds these matters.

We may begin with the question raised by Graham Hough in his generally valuable and often enlightening essay on free verse: "What," he asks, "makes a free verse line a line at all?" And he replies: "It is only a line because it is a rhythmical unit, and it is only a rhythmical unit because it is a unit of sense." [53] We must object, however, not only because lines of free-verse poems are often not units of sense, but because a unit of sense is not inherently rhythmic. It is experienced as rhythmic only insofar as it participates in a pattern of similar units. All discursive prose

[53] "Free Verse," *Image and Experience: Reflections on a Literary Revolution* (Lincoln, Neb., 1960), p. 103.

consists of units of sense (or syntax), but discourse is rhythmic only when successive syntactic units also correspond formally: in other words, when certain formal features such as stress distribution are repeated If, then, the free-verse line *is* experienced as a rhythmic unit, it must be because it exhibits formal features that are repeated in successive lines.

Hough's definition of the free-verse line is not sufficient. Nor can that definition be the basis of an absolute distinction between free verse and conventional forms, although that is precisely his contention. "In traditional verse," he continues, "this is not so. The line has a length and shape independent of sense or syntax—the length or shape we describe when we call it an Alexandrine or an octosyllable." It may be doubted, however, whether the integrity of a line of metrical verse can indeed be maintained independent of sense or syntax. The meter of the poem can be *described* without reference to either, but the metrical principle cannot be rhythmically effective unless the integrity of the formal unit (that is, the line) is also, in fact, frequently reinforced by syntactic integrity. It is no accident of literary history that the lines of conventional verse tend to correspond to well-defined syntactic units. It is, rather, a consequence of the fundamental structure and perception of language: the fact that the distribution of stresses and pauses (the features of language that are most commonly the basis of rhythm) are themselves, in any meaningful sequence of words, a function of syntax and sense.

No absolute distinction may be made between the sources of rhythm in free verse and metrical poetry, and none need be made between the nature of "the line" in each. In both, the sense of rhythm is created by the continual approximation of the actual distribution of the formal features of the poem to a pattern that is defined for the reader by that very approximation or conformity; and in both, the line is a unit of that pattern. The iambic-ness of an iambic line is not an a priori rule stored in the reader's sensorium, but his own perception of and response to a pattern of stresses and pauses that emerges as he reads. Similarly, the rhythm of a free-verse poem, as it is reflected in and reinforced by its lineation, is experienced as an expectation of the recurrence of certain distribution patterns of formal features—not exclusively or necessarily patterns of stress, however.

Although the line in a free-verse poem is not a constant pattern, it usually reflects a limit of variability. In the following poem, for example, the number of syllables in each lines varies between four and eight, and the number of major stresses between two and four:

Sunflowers

There's a sort of
multibranched sunflower
blooms hereabouts
when the leaves begin
first to fall. Their
heads lean in the rain
about an old man who,
stumbling a little,
solicitously carries in
his tomatoes from
the fallen vines, green
in one blanket and, in
the other shining reds.[54]

These limits are confined enough to establish a principle that corresponds to the metrical "norm" of a conventional poem: it is experienced as an iambic norm would be, as a *probability* of occurrence that creates a rhythm and controls the reader's expectations. What the reader expects here, from line to line, is not a fixed number of syllables or pattern of stresses, but that certain limits of variability will not be exceeded. We must add, however, that limits may operate with respect not only to variability but also to constancy. In a sonnet, for example, we expect that rhyme words will not be identical; that is, we expect certain changes as well as repetitions. Thus the fact that, with one exception, no two suc-

[54] *The Collected Later Poems of William Carlos Williams* (Norfolk, Conn., 1963), p. 258.

ceeding lines in "Sunflowers" contain exactly the same number of syllables or distribution of stresses is to be considered a limit: it operates as a formal principle by affecting our expectations—not of regularity, but of change.

The distinction between metrical verse and free verse is a relative, not an absolute, one: it lies in the *range* of the formal features of language that are patterned in each, and in the *extent* to which the principles of formal generation in each are limited in variability. Free verse obviously cannot be "scanned" by the same methods we apply to metrical poetry, but that does not mean that no formal principles are operating in it. What it does mean is that traditional scansion, since it is concerned primarily with the distribution of relative stress-values, does not discriminate other linguistic features, such as pitch levels, the relative value of junctures, assonance, internal rhyme, and simple word-repetition, that are frequently more significant than stress in creating the formal structure and rhythmic effects of free verse.

It is also obvious that the distribution patterns in conventionally metrical poetry are more narrowly determined than those of free verse. In the former, the patterns are generated by strictly—usually numerically—determined principles, which, by convention, admit of only slight deviations and variations. In free verse, on the other hand, the distribution patterns are not only less strictly determined but often involve features of language, such as intonational cadence, which, though repeatable, are inherently nonquantifiable. A close conformity to numerically generated principles is not necessary for the creation and perception of rhythmic effects, however. Our ears will do the measuring even when our fingers can not, and the pleasures of rhythmic constancy—the sense of pattern, coherence, design, or control—are substantial enough so that, in our own efforts to "keep the beat," we will tolerate and, as necessary, compensate for, a fairly wide degree of variability or deviation.

Lineation has the same functions in free verse as in metrical poetry. Hough, however, mentions "the vulgar suspicion that much free verse is really prose, distinguished from other prose merely by courtesy and typography," and adds that he sometimes shares the position.[55] We should recognize that there is, nothing illegitimate in the free-verse poet's exploitation of courtesy and typography—that is, convention and lineation—to help define the formal structure of his poem and control the reader's perception of its rhythm. Since we have, indeed, been conditioned by convention to expect rhythm whenever we are confronted by what looks like poetry, we might as well courteously accept the implied invitation to read the poem as rhythmically as possible. The same sequence of words, printed as prose, would invite a quite different reading. Lineation, moreover, not only tells the reader that he should expect rhythm, but also tells him how to pace his performance so as best to perceive the rhythm *designed* to emerge from it. Certainly we hear a different structure of sounds in Williams' "Sunflowers" when we read it not as prose but following the instructions implied by the lineation: slowly enough to permit the physical qualities of the words to reveal themselves, pausing at the ends of lines, stressing certain stresses—all in such a way as to make as prominent as possible the potential rhythmic parallelism of successive lines.

While it is evident that certain varieties of free verse could not flourish in a culture without printing or at least writing, it is just as evident that not all free verse depends upon typography for its form or the determination of its lines. Few readers would have trouble recognizing the rhythm of, and providing proper lineation for, the following sequence of words: "Twenty-eight young men bathe by the shore, twenty-eight young men and all so friendly; twenty-eight years of womanly life and all so lonesome." As for those poems, including many by Williams, that do rely upon typographical lineation for clues to formal structure, we might as well concede that they exist. We need not concede, however, that their status as verse has been thereby compromised, not as long as the conventions operate and the clues function appropriately.[56]

[55] *Image and Experience*, p. 105.

[56] Hough offers Ezra Pound's brief poem, "The Study in Aesthetics," as further evidence for his suspicion that "Much free verse is really prose," and

While the formal principles of free verse may vary considerably within an individual poem and from poem to poem, and although they are not usually amenable to simple or economical description, these principles are not so unique, "organic," or ineffable as to resist description altogether. To take a single and, at that, rather simple example, we may consider more closely the passage from Whitman's "Song of Myself," part of which was printed above as prose:

Twenty-eight young men bathe by the shore,
Twenty-eight young men and all so friendly;
Twenty-eight years of womanly life and all so lonesome.

She owns the fine house by the rise of the bank,
She hides, handsome and richly drest aft the blinds of the window.[57]

---

comments as follows: "I don't want to break this butterfly on a wheel, but there does not really seem to be any reason at all why this should be regarded as verse; *except that it is small and self-contained, and there is no particular precedent in English for printing small pieces of this kind in prose,* and it is therefore easier to promote them to the status of verse." (*Ibid.*, p. 106, italics mine.) We might notice that although he does not appreciate its force, Hough is actually referring here (in the italicized passage) to precisely the reason why much free verse is *not* really prose. Certain "small and self-contained" pieces are, as he says, not usually printed as prose. The sort of piece he has in mind, however (and which is exemplified in Pound's poem), is not merely small and self-contained; it is also what I described on pp. 15–19 as mimetic or ahistorical. Moreover, the fact that such pieces—that is, relatively short, noncontextual ("self-contained") representations of personal utterance—are usually printed as verse is not merely, as he implies, a matter of convention. It also reflects the fact that these pieces (which we commonly refer to as lyric poems) are composed rhythmically, with formal features that serve to identify them, to frame and distinguish them from nonfictive, historical utterances. The "precedent" to which Hough alludes not only makes it easy to promote such pieces to the status of verse, but also makes it proper to claim for them the status of poetry.

[57] *Leaves of Grass: Comprehensive Reader's Edition*, eds. Harold W. Blodgett and Sculley Bradley (New York, 1965), p. 38.

Although the lines here are not determined by any conventional principle of stress pattern, syllable count, or rhyme, they are evidently determined at least by syntactic groupings. That is not enough to make them rhythmic, of course, for, as I mentioned earlier, a syntactic unit is not a rhythmic one unless it participates in a sequence of such units that also exhibits formal correspondences. Whitman's characteristic use of parallelism and simple repetition, however, obviously creates just this sort of correspondence in succeeding lines. Moreover, stress patterns and syllable counts, though not repeated exactly, are more highly controlled here than in most discursive prose, and initial word or phrase repetitions are regular enough and sustained long enough to create effects similar to those created by end-rhyme: that is, they *define* a line, not at its end but at its beginning. We should also note that syntactic parallelism creates patterns of intonational cadence which again are not repeated exactly in succeeding lines but recur frequently enough to have rhythmic effects.

These general observations may be indicated with a bit more particularity.[58] To begin with, we notice the fairly close correspondence between the first two lines:

(1) Twenty-eight young men / báthe by the shóre,
(2) Twenty-eight young men / and áll so friéndly;

The third line is a cumulative parallel, corresponding to the whole of the first line and the final phrase of the second:

(3) Twenty-eight years / of wómanly lífe /
and áll so lónesome.

[58] Since the scanning of free verse is an unprofitable pursuit, I will not attempt to indicate all stress values here with the conventional marks. In most instances, though different readers may pace, pause, and stress in slightly different ways, the correspondences are so gross that marks would be superfluous in any case. I do attempt, however, to make the rhythmic parallels as graphic as possible and, at a few points, I thought it might clarify matters if I indicated major (and unambiguously so) stresses. Slashes, by the way, do not mark "feet" or caesuras here, but they separate functional rhythmic units.

Twenty-eight young men / báthe by the shóre /
[and áll so friéndly;]

The fourth line again corresponds fairly closely to the first (and thus also to the second, but to a slighter extent):

(4) She owns / the fíne hóuse / by the / ríse of the bánk,
Twenty-eight / yóung mén / / báthe by the shóre;

The fifth line does not correspond, as a whole, to any of the previous ones, but almost every phrase within it corresponds to a phrase that had occurred earlier in the same position in the line:

(5) She hídes / handsome / and ríchly drést /
aft the blínds of the / wíndow.
[She ówns] / / [of wómanly lífe] /
[by the ríse of the] / [friéndly;]

(*Handsome* here has no exact rhythmic parallel in that position, but the echo of *lonesome* may function as a rhythmic reinforcement.)

The patterns here are obviously subtle and complex, but more so in the description than in the perception of them. It is not the neatness of the analysis that persuades the reader of the presence of rhythmic effects, but the evidence of his own ears: our analytic methods are considerably less discriminating than our nervous systems, which, indeed, not only discriminate but also integrate. The rhythmic force of the patterns described here may, however, be tested by the application of the very notion often used to discredit free-verse rhythms. In the third line of this passage the reader will find himself drawing out the word *years* so as to make the rhythmic parallelism as prominent as possible: that is, he will give to *years* a time value approximately equal to *young men* in the two previous lines. Were this conventional verse, we would be told that counterpoint or tension was thereby created by the conflicting demands of "meter" and "meaning" and, perhaps, that this "deviation from the norm" was expressive, emphasizing the length of those *years*. The point, however, is that although there are no narrowly defined metrical principles here, a *controlling* principle is nevertheless operative and perceptible—and perceptible enough to make deviations significant, expressively or otherwise.

Turning more directly now to the specific concerns of this study, we may consider the implications of the preceding discussion. The most important of these is that, to the extent that the formal principles of free verse control the reader's expectations and that effective modifications are thus possible, the formal structure of free-verse poems offers closural resources comparable to those of conventionally metrical poetry.

As we have seen in previous sections of this chapter, one of the most common and substantial sources of closural effects in poetry is the terminal modification of a formal principle. In a form such as the Spenserian stanza, where the norm is narrowly defined, the mere addition of a single foot to the last line will have closural force. However, since the limits of variability in free verse tend to be wide, the modification, to be effective, must be a rather radical one, significantly more so than any earlier variations in the poem. In Whitman's poetry, where lines are characteristically quite long, terminal modification frequently takes the form of an unusually short final line. Closure in the following poem (of which only the last thirteen lines are given here) obviously depends heavily upon thematic elements: the grammatical resolution of a lengthy periodic sentence, for example, and the finality of the speaker's ultimate gesture, especially as it is emphasized by the contrast of the preceding lines: ". . . as day brightened, I rose from the chill ground. . . ." Closure here is also strengthened formally, however, by the abruptly shorter terminal line:

Vigil of silence, love and death, vigil for you my son and my
  soldier,
As onward silently stars aloft, eastward new ones upward stole,

Vigil final for you brave boy, (I could not save you, swift was your death,
I faithfully loved you and cared for you living, I think we shall surely meet again,)
Till at latest lingering of the night, indeed just as the dawn appear'd,
My comrade I wrapt in his blanket, envelop'd well his form,
Folded the blanket well, tucking it carefully over head and carefully under feet,
And there and then and bathed by the rising sun, my son in his grave, in his rude-dug grave I deposited,
Ending my vigil strange with that, vigil of night and battle-field dim,
Vigil for boy of responding kisses, (never again on earth responding,)
Vigil for comrade swiftly slain, vigil I never forget, how as day brighten'd,
I rose from the chill ground and folded my soldier well in his blanket,
And buried him where he fell.[59]

The closural power of the structural modification here is obvious enough, though we might remark that it is strengthened by other formal elements as well: the strong assonance in the penultimate line (*rose, folded, soldier*), the alliterative pattern in the final two lines (*folded, well, blanket: buried, where, fell*), and the fact that the last line concludes with a rhyme-word (*well: fell*). All of these features, by strengthening the reader's sense of terminal control and coherence, contribute to the closural force of the poem's conclusion.

Another closural resource available to the free-verse poet is the terminal occurence of the "norm" in its most regular form, particularly when preceded by notable deviations from it: in other

[59] "Vigil Strange I Kept on the Field One Night," *Leaves of Grass*, pp. 303–5.

words, when an implicit norm has been eluded, as in the passage from *Paradise Lost* discussed at the end of the previous section. Since the norm, in free verse as well as in metrical poetry, is, by definition, the most probable distribution pattern, it is also the most stable one when it occurs, and its closural effect is directly related to that fact. In Williams' "Sunflowers," closure again depends primarily upon thematic structure: the completion of the sentence, especially after the syntactic suspension heightened both by enjambment and by the expectation of a counterpart to ". . . green/in one basket and, . . ." Closure is also strengthened formally, however, by the unusual regularity of stress alternation in the final line. Although the earlier lines vary in syllable number and stress distribution, their limits establish, as the most probable pattern, a line of six syllables and three major stresses. The reader's effort to maintain rhythmic constancy encounters the least resistance in the final line; tension is relaxed as the syllables fall neatly into a pattern of three iambic feet.

My point here has been that insofar as the formal structure of free verse is comparable to that of metrical poetry the closural resources of form may be effectively exploited by free-verse poets. As one moves from more to less highly determined forms, however, closural effects become increasingly dependent upon thematic structure and special nonstructural devices. Moreover, although the distinction between free and fixed forms can often be expressed as the difference between degrees of variability, this difference is often radical, and its effect on closure must be acknowledged. While our expectations, in a free-verse poem, are controlled by probabilities and confined by limits of variability, we obviously cannot predict the specific occurrence of formal elements with the same degree of confidence as in fixed forms. Consequently, the closural effects that can arise from modifications of formal structure do indeed remain minimal in free verse.

A final word on the quality of closure in contemporary free verse will conclude this section and chapter. Although, as I have been suggesting, closure may be secured in free verse through formal and thematic devices, the sense of closure in much modern poetry is not very strong, and there is good reason to suppose it is often not intended to be. The anti-closural tendencies of modern poetry (and modern art in general) will be considered at some length in the final chapter of this study. Here, however, we may glance at the following poem, which will be recognized as a not uncharacteristic example:

The Crack

While snow fell carelessly
floating indifferent in eddies of
rooftop air, circling the black
chimney-cowls,

a spring night entered
my mind through the tight-closed window,
wearing

a loose Russian shirt of
light silk.
        For this, then,

that slanting
line was left, that crack, the pane
never replaced.[60]

Although the thematic structure of Miss Levertov's poem may be granted as complete, and closural effects here are not negligible, the reader is left with a mildly elegiac impression, a hovering half-question never to be answered, something like: "Ah! Is that possible? No, perhaps, but it can seem that way. But what if . . . ?" and so on. The poem, in other words, exhibits the sort of conclusion that one finds in thousands of similar contemporary poems: a conclusion that, without sounding arbitrary, manages to avoid sounding conclusive.

[60] Denise Levertov, *O Taste and See* (New York, 1964), p. 28.

3 Thematic Structure and Closure

I Introduction

In a brief essay entitled "How Does A Poem Know When It Is Finished?," [1] I. A. Richards answers this leading and loaded question by proposing that ". . . a poem begins by creating a linguistic problem whose solution by language will be the attainment of its end" (p. 168). A poem, he implies, is a closed system; unlike ordinary utterances, it is developed and concluded by principles that are independent of the poet's or reader's experiences, circumstances, or motives. "Well organized poems," he writes, "can be studied as places where transactions between words take place" (p. 169); and it is clear from later passages that he means to suggest that the structure and termination of a poem are determined *exclusively* by these intraverbal transactions. "It is this [i.e., 'the degree of . . . mutual enablement and control' among its words]—not any actions or agonies, and wishes or hopes or endeavors on the part of the poet or his readers—that settles what the poem may be and when and how (and whether) it is finished" (p. 171). The development of a poem, Richards maintains, is analogous to that of an embryo: each grows organically through the mutual interaction of its parts toward a form predetermined at its inception (pp. 164–65).

[1] *Parts and Wholes,* ed. Daniel Lerner (New York, 1963), pp. 163–74.

It is not my intention to argue with Richards' notion of poems as organisms or with the general view of either poetry or closure implied by his essay. I draw attention to his comments, however, first because they appear in an essay which is, to my knowledge, the only place in modern criticism where the question of poetic closure as such is raised, and second, in order to emphasize the very different conception of the relation between poetic and nonpoetic speech to be found in this study and particularly in this chapter. We may agree with Richards that a poem is not to be read as the direct biographical expression of the poet's experiences, and that the pressures of personal and literary history can never entirely account for a poem's particular existence and form. We may also agree that certain intraverbal relations have a great deal more to do with the structure and integrity of a poem than of a nonpoetic utterance. It does not follow, however, that a poem is a self-contained and self-generating system, or that a distinction may be made in these terms between the principles which generate and conclude poems and those which generate and conclude ordinary utterances.

First of all, a poem cannot be regarded as totally independent of the poet's and reader's extrinsic experiences—not if we recognize that our experiences include *language itself*, and that it is upon our past linguistic experiences that poetry depends for its most characteristic effects. Moreover, a poem does not, like the proposition systems of mathematical logic, make its own rules; it adopts and adapts the rules (i.e., the conventions) of nonliterary discourse, so that the principles which generate and conclude the one are conspicuously reflected in those of the other.

This relation between poetic and nonpoetic discourse will be of crucial importance in the discussions of thematic structure that follow. *Thematic* elements were defined earlier as those arising from the symbolic properties of language. As used here, "symbolic" is more or less equivalent to "conventional." That is, the thematic elements of language are effective by reason of the way they are used by the members of a linguistic community. Consequently, the effect of thematic elements (and thematic structure) in poetry depends upon the reader's responses to language as conditioned by his participation in this community. To speak of a poem as a possible utterance (rather than, as Richards would have it, an independent linguistic system) is to emphasize the fact that it is a sequence of words that depends for its effect upon the reader's assumption of its relation to ordinary discourse. That assumption will tend to organize his expectations regarding the poem's thematic structure and will determine to a considerable extent his sense of "how (and whether) it is finished."

This by no means implies that a poem must conclude when, and in the way that, a comparable nonliterary utterance would conclude. For one thing, the conclusions of ordinary utterances are themselves complexly and variously determined. Second, these conclusions are not always "determined": not every linguistic sequence implies its own termination point. Finally, and most important, although poems resemble nonliterary utterances and imitate their structures, they are ultimately something else in both intention and effect. Richards is correct, of course, in maintaining that the linguistic structure of poetry is different from that of everyday speech. The distinction, however, does not lie in the *self-determination* of the one as opposed to the external determination of the other. It lies in the fact that poems are not samples, but *represention*s, of speech.

II Paratactic Structure

In discussing stanzaic forms we observed that when a poem is intended for musical rendition its structure—both formal and thematic—will tend to be simple and repetitive. Indeed, thematic repetition is a characteristic structural principle in most song lyrics, particularly in primitive and naïve styles. When repetition is the fundamental principle of thematic generation, the resulting structure will tend to be *paratactic;* that is, the coherence of the poem will not be dependent on the sequential arrangement of its major thematic units. In a nonparatactic structure (where, for example, the principle of generation is logical or temporal), the dislocation or omission of any element will tend to make the sequence as a whole incomprehensible, or will radically change its effect. In paratactic structure, however (where the principle of generation does not cause any one element to "follow" from another), thematic units can be omitted, added, or exchanged without destroying the coherence or effect of the poem's thematic structure.

Paratactic structure appears frequently in nursery rhymes, traditional lullabies, and in those folk songs which seem to contain, between their fixed opening and close, an almost infinitely expandable and contractable number of verses. In the Lomax anthology, for example, the familiar song "Billy Boy" is printed with twenty-three verses, most of which are rarely heard in performance.[2] They consist of questions like "Can she fry a dish of meat? Can she make a loaf of bread? Can she feed a sucking pig?" and their rhyming answers. Although the opening and closing verses have thematic characteristics appropriate to their positions in the sequence, the central verses may be omitted or rearranged without affecting the thematic coherence of the whole song, and verses which provide additional variations on the common theme may be interpolated almost indefinitely: "Can she drive a four-shift car? Does she have a Ph.D.?" and so forth.

"Variations on a theme" is one of the two most obvious forms that paratactic structure may take. The other one is the "list," and it should be said immediately that they are often hard to distinguish from each other and often combined in one poem. "Variations on a theme" is, in a sense, the thematic counterpart of formal repetition. (To the extent that thematic repetition is exact, it becomes simply formal repetition.) The list, however, has no counterpart in formal structure, and its generating principle is of

[2] *American Ballads and Folk Songs,* collected and compiled by John A. Lomax and Alan Lomax (New York, 1934), pp. 320–22.

an entirely symbolic or conceptual nature. Although (as in "Billy Boy") it is often combined with thematic and formal repetitions, it need not be—as we see in Surrey's "The Happy Life":

> Martial, the things that do attain
> The happy life be these, I find:
> The riches left, not got with pain;
> The fruitful ground, the quiet mind:
>
> The equal friend, no grudge nor strife;
> No charge of rule nor governance;
> Without disease, the healthful life;
> The household of continuance:
>
> The mean diet, no delicate fare;
> True wisdom join'd with simpleness;
> The night dischargéd of all care,
> Where wine and wit may not oppress:
>
> The faithful wife, without debate;
> Such sleeps as may beguile the night:
> Contented with thine own estate
> Ne wish for death, ne fear his might.[3]

I mentioned above that although the central stanzas of "Billy Boy" are more or less interchangeable, the opening and closing stanzas are fixed and have thematic characteristics appropriate to their respective positions. The same is true of the opening and closing lines of Surrey's poem, and we are thereby introduced to the fundamental problem of closure in this section: namely, that a generating principle that produces a paratactic structure cannot in itself determine a concluding point. Consequently, the reader will have no idea from the poem's structure how or when it will conclude. Closure may be secured, however, in various ways, one of which is illustrated by the fixed opening and closing verses of

[3] Henry Howard, Earl of Surrey; text in *Silver Poets of the Sixteenth Century*, ed. Gerald Bullett (London, 1960), p. 139.

folk songs and the clearly "introductory" and "concluding" lines of Surrey's poem. In both, the paratactic structure is enclosed by a "frame," the closural effect of which is amusingly revealed in this nursery rhyme:

> I'll tell you a story
> About Jack a Nory,
> And now my story's begun;
> I'll tell you another
> About Jack and his brother,
> And now my story is done.[4]

The closural dynamics of the "frame" will be examined more closely later; here we need only consider the effect of the concluding lines of Surrey's poem. They acquire closural force most obviously through their generalizing quality: they seem to sum up all that has been said, and in a sense return to the opening lines. Closure is also secured simply through the allusion to death, which

[4] *The Oxford Dictionary of Nursery Rhymes*, eds. Iona and Peter Opie (Oxford, 1951), p. 233. John Skelton exploits the effect with disarming ingenuousness in "The Tunning of Elinor Rumming"—a poem some six hundred lines long, consisting of a rambling descriptive catalogue of a rural alehouse, its proprietress, its customers, their appearance and business transactions. The poem opens and concludes as follows:

> Tell you I chill
> If that ye will
> A while be still,
> Of a comely Jill
> That dwelt on a hill:
> . . . .
> For my fingers itch,
> I have written too mich
> Of this mad mumming
> Of Elinor Rumming!
> Thus endeth the geste
> Of this worthy feast.

(*The Complete Poems of John Skelton*, ed. Philip Henderson [London, 1931], pp. 99–118.)

is one of the most common and effective nonstructural devices. Allusions to any of the "natural" stopping places of our lives and experiences—sleep, death, winter, and so forth—tend to give closural force when they appear as terminal features in a poem; and even the second line of the final stanza here ("Such sleeps as may beguile the night") effectively prepares us for the approaching conclusion.

The characteristics of Surrey's last stanza hardly exhaust the possibilities for providing closure in a paratactic poem. What I have wished to emphasize at this point is only the fact that special terminal features are needed if the conclusion is not to appear arbitrary. Just as Billy and his mother could have extended their dialogue interminably with questions and answers concerning the young lady's accomplishments, so Surrey (or his reader) could have extended the list of solid comforts to include much more. To be sure, part of the significance of this list is its brevity: "This is all it takes, when you get right down to it, to be happy." The fact remains, however, that nothing in the generating principle itself could determine when the list would be completed.

Although paratactic sequence is one of the most primitive forms of thematic structure, it may be used in a highly civilized and urbane poem, as we have just seen.[5] The quality of naïveté suggested by this structure has in fact been exploited by poets when certain effects are wanted, such as forthrightness, honesty, or simplicity. A particularly expressive example of this is found in Ralegh's "The Lie," which we may consider both for its structure and its closure:

> Goe soule the bodies guest
>   vpon a thankelesse arrant,
> Feare not to touch the best
>   the truth shall be thy warrant:

[5] This is even more evident in the epigram by Martial (10. 47) of which Surrey's lines are the translation.

Goe since I needs must die,
  and giue the world the lie.

Say to the Court it glowes,
  and shines like rotten wood,
Say to the Church it showes
  whats good, and doth no good.
If Church and Court reply,
  then giue them both the lie.

Tell Potentates they liue
  acting by others action,
Not loued vnlesse they giue,
  not strong but by affection.
If Potentates reply,
  giue Potentates the lie.

Tell men of high condition,
  that mannage the estate,
Their purpose is ambition,
  their practise onely hate:
And if they once reply,
  then giue them all the lie.

Tell them that braue it most.
  they beg for more by spending,
Who in their greatest cost
  like nothing but commending.
And if they make replie,
  then giue them all the lie.

Tell zeale it wants deuotion
  tell love it is but lust
Tell time it meets but motion,
  tell flesh it is but dust.
And wish them not replie
  for thou must giue the lie.

Tell age it daily wasteth,
  tell honour how it alters.
Tell beauty how she blasteth
  tell fauour how it falters
And as they shall reply,
  giue euery one the lie.

Tell wit how much it wrangles
  in tickle points of nycenesse,
Tell wisedome she entangles
  her selfe in ouer wisenesse.
And when they doe reply
  straight giue them both the lie.

Tell Phisicke of her boldnes,
  tell skill it is preuention:
Tell charity of coldnes,
  tell law it is contention,
And as they doe reply
  so giue them still the lie.

Tell fortune of her blindnesse,
  tell nature of decay,
Tell friendship of vnkindnesse,
  tell iustice of delay.
And if they will reply,
  then giue them all the lie.

Tell Arts they haue no soundnesse,
  but vary by esteeming,
Tell schooles they want profoundnes
  and stand too much on seeming.
If Arts and schooles reply,
  giue arts and schooles the lie.

Tell faith its fled the Citie,
  tell how the country erreth,
Tell manhood shakes off pittie,

tell vertue least preferreth.
And if they doe reply,
spare not to giue the lie.

So when thou hast as I,
commanded thee, done blabbing,
Because to giue the lie,
deserues no lesse then stabbing,
Stab at thee he that will,
no stab thy soule can kill.[6]

As in so many poems of the English moral tradition, the indictment here gains power from its naïve structure. As Ralegh hammers out his all-encompassing and uncompromising "*vanitas, vanitas*," the apparent simplicity (or absence) of development is itself reinforcing his point and tone: "I have no time for elegance and obvious rhetoric; I am telling the truth, pure and simple—this is the way it is."

Although this is clearly an unsingable poem, stanzas 2 to 12 exhibit many of the characteristics we observed earlier in Wyatt's lyrics: the varied repetitions, for example, in syntax, in rhyme-words, in the opening lines of each stanza, and in their refrain-like conclusions. Although omitting any of the central stanzas would, in a sense, narrow the comprehensiveness of Ralegh's *contemptus mundi,* a reader coming to the poem for the first time would not be aware of their omission as such. Also, although a cumulative effect of the repeated unflinching absolutes makes each succeeding stanza more powerful than the one before, the effect would be no different if the order of stanzas 2 to 12 was changed. Finally, although the intended and achieved effect of the central stanzas is to give the reader the feeling that *everything* has been included, other stanzas like the fifth (lines 25–30) could be interpolated almost indefinitely.

[6] *The Poems of Sir Walter Ralegh,* ed. Agnes M. C. Latham (Cambridge, Mass., 1962), pp. 45–47.

Ralegh has, then, appropriated the naïve catalogue structure to strengthen the force and sharpen the tone of a poem which, though it is savage, is not primitive. We may also observe how he evades the limitations and solves the poetic problems that are entailed by the repetitiveness of such a structure. To begin with, the objects of the soul's indictment (i.e., the "items" of the catalogue) are specified in a number of different ways, sometimes figuratively, as in the more or less personified abstractions (zeal, love, age, honor, fortune, etc.) or in the synedoches (the court, the church, schools, etc.), and sometimes literally (potentates, men of high condition, "them that brave it most," etc.). All, however—ideas, institutions, disciplines, and men—are given not only equal treatment by the soul, but also what might be called equal ontological status. The result is twofold: first, it is emphasized that with respect to the soul's values and scrutiny, they cannot be distinguished; and second, while the monotony of thematic repetition is relieved, its force is retained. The refrains are similarly varied with comparable results. If they had been repeated exactly from stanza to stanza, they would ultimately have more the effect of formal than thematic repetition, which is to say that their moral significance would gradually fade. As it is, even though each refrain is never wholly a surprise, the variations prevent us from predicting its exact form, and for this reason the concluding couplets retain their astringent power.

If the structure of the central stanzas of "The Lie" is paratactic, clearly the poem as a whole is not, as we see when we consider the opening and closing stanzas. The poem opens with a directive to the soul which summarizes the nature of its mission, to "giue the world the lie." The final stanza projects the completed mission and its probable consequence, and sustains the conceit which is, in part, the thematic generating principle of the poem. The disembodied soul, throughout the poem, is given the more or less human characteristics of mobility and speech. In the concluding stanza the implicit personification is extended even further: to give someone the lie—to call him a liar—is, in the social code of the age, to insult him in such a way as to risk at least the challenge of a duel. Ralegh extends the personification just far enough to raise this possibility and then confronts it, so to speak, with the "literal" fact of the soul's immortality. As "the bodies guest," the soul is not only a temporary resident, a mobile transient, but also, unlike the body itself, it is invulnerable to the world's attacks or reprisals. The truth may be its "warrant," but immortality is its shield.

The closural effect of this last stanza is thus strengthened by the fact that the generating conceit is not only brought to an explicit termination point ("when thou hast . . . done blabbing") but completed with an implicit return to the beginning. Ralegh need not contend with the closural problem of paratactic structure as such because he has added to it (or surrounded it with) *another principle of thematic generation that does determine its own conclusion.* Several other factors, both formal and thematic, strengthen the closural force of the final stanza. The formal factors are of the kind that were discussed in the last chapter: for example, the terminal modification of a systematic repetition, particularly in the last two lines. Here, not only does the formulaic refrain disappear, but the rhyme-words are changed. The modification is managed with considerable subtlety. Observe, for instance, that the rhyme-sound and key word of the refrain (/ae/-*lie*) occur in the final stanza as quatrain rhymes, so that even though there is terminal modification, the continuity provided by repetition is maintained. The formal factors for closure also include the already mentioned metrical pattern of deviation to norm in the last two lines, and others that we have not yet discussed, such as occasional repetition (*stabbing-stab*) and alliteration (*stab-soul, can-kill*). Among the thematic features that strengthen closure one might note the simplicity, absoluteness, and consequent "finality" of the last line: "no stab thy soule can kill." [7]

What I have been concerned to demonstrate in this analysis are

[7] Each of these nonstructural devices is considered in greater detail in chapter 4. See pages 158–66 for "occasional repetition" and pages 182–86 for "unqualified assertion."

the ways in which a superbly skilled poet can exploit the effects of paratactic structure and solve the closural problems it presents. The devices that Ralegh uses to conclude his poem so effectively are neither the only ones available nor even the most common ones. Paratactic structure can be "wound up" in a number of ways—the point is that it does not wind itself up. In Ralegh's poem, the *additional* principle of thematic generation provided by the conceit was a crucial closural force. We may conclude this section with a brief glance at a paratactic poem in which there is no other principle, and where closure involves still other factors not discussed earlier:

The Argument of his Book

I Sing of *Brooks*, of *Blossomes*, *Birds*, and *Bowers:*
Of *April*, *May*, of *June*, and *July*-Flowers.
I sing of *May-poles*, *Hock-carts*, *Wassails*, *Wakes*,
Of *Bride-grooms*, *Brides*, and of their *Bridall-cakes*.
I write of *Youth*, of *Love*, and have Accesse
By these, to sing of cleanly-*Wantonnesse*.
I sing of *Dewes*, of *Raines*, and piece by piece
Of *Balme*, of *Oyle*, of *Spice* and *Amber-Greece*.
I sing of *Times trans-shifting;* and I write
How *Roses* first came *Red*, and *Lillies White*.
I write of *Groves*, of *Twilights*, and I sing
The Court of *Mab*, and of the *Fairie-King*.
I write of *Hell;* I sing (and ever shall)
Of *Heaven*, and hope to have it after all.[8]

Although the general contents of this catalogue are determined and limited by the obvious principle, "subjects of Herrick's verses," and the items in each line have thematic integrity, the list is fairly random in order and not fixed in length. Moreover, it is generated through a succession of closed couplets and makes systematic use

[8] *The Complete Poetry of Robert Herrick*, ed. J. Max Patrick (Garden City, N.Y., 1963), p. 11.

of verbal and syntactic repetition. All the forces for continuation implied by this description are, however, annihilated in the final two lines, which provide a completely effective conclusion. Part of the closural effect here arises from the fact that the loose syntax and flowing rhythm of the earlier lines are abruptly tightened and arrested at the beginning of line 13: "I write of *Hell;* . . . ." The effect is both to break the rhythmic continuity of the poem and to give particular emphasis and integrity to the remainder of the complet. Closure is also strengthened by the introduction of a new verb, *hope* (previously we had only *sing* and *write*), by the antithesis *Hell* . . . *Heaven* and the alliteration that reinforces it (*Hell: Heaven: hope: have*), and by a number of thematic elements. Among the latter, note particularly the phrase "ever shall," which imparts to the poem itself that quality of permanence and stability that it explicitly signifies—and, of course, the allusions to those twin ultimates of human existence, heaven and hell. Finally, the concluding phrase "to have it *after all*" (meaning not only "in spite of everything" but also "after everything else is over") is itself one of those references to finality which, as I have suggested, will tend to strengthen closure when it appears at the end of a poem.

III Sequential Structure

The coherence of development in a paratactic structure does not depend upon the sequential order of its thematic elements. In most sophisticated poems, however, it does; for the lines or verses usually "follow" from one another, either logically, temporally, or in accord with some principle of serial generation. The sequences that result may be of many kinds, and as the following list suggests, they may originate in a number of ways: spring-summer-autumn-winter, first-second-third-fourth . . . , birth-infancy-youth-manhood-old age-death, January-February-March . . . December. Of importance to us are these two facts: first, that these sequences are generated by an *extraliterary* principle of succession, and second, that they may or may not imply their own terminations.

Because the thematic structure of a poem is almost always generated by a principle already familiar to the reader from his experiences in the world of events or the world of words, he will form expectations conditioned by those experiences, expectations regarding not only the thematic development of the poem but also the probable point and nature of its conclusion. I have already emphasized the fact that our pleasure in a poem does not consist in having all our expectations gratified but, on the contrary, that the effective power of poetry lies in what it can do with those expectations. In failing to follow a certain traditional or apparently natural development, the poem may reveal a more profound principle of order; and in failing to provide the expected conventional or logical conclusion, the poem may reveal the inadequacy or triviality of convention and logic. Such revelations are effective and significant, however, only because of the reader's tendency to respond to language with certain dispositions, expectations, and assumptions. This tendency is as much the material of poetic art as is language itself. What is important for our present concern, then, is the fact that effective closure will always *involve* the reader's expectations regarding the termination of a sequence—even though it will never be simply a matter of *fulfilling* them.

The fact that a certain sequence does *not* imply a termination point will also be important for closure; but here the situation is comparable to that of paratactic structure, and the problems are solved in corresponding ways. Thus, although an indefinitely extendable series (such as first-second-third . . . , etc.) will determine the *sequence* of lines or stanzas, the *conclusion* will be determined by some other structural principle or, lacking any other principle, will be given stability and finality by special terminal features.

Two of the most common and interesting forms of sequential structure, the temporal and the logical, are also the most complex to analyze. Consequently, discussion of them will be reserved for two special sections. For the moment, I would like to expand and illustrate some of the general points already touched upon regarding sequential structure and its relation to closure. We may begin by considering a poem in which a simple arithmetic sequence is used for a generating principle:

> Finding is the first Act
> The second, loss,
> Third, Expedition for
> The "Golden Fleece"
>
> Fourth, no Discovery—
> Fifth, no Crew—
> Finally, no Golden Fleece—
> Jason—sham—too.[9]

Here the poet exploits our expectations not by surprising or fulfilling them in any obvious sense, but by taking advantage of their strength to propel us toward a conclusion "unexpected" only in its extremity. We know the legend of Jason's expedition, we know how to count upwards, and we gradually recognize a secondary sequence of progressive subtractions moving inexorably toward the zero of absolute loss. At the end, however, when we have apparently reached that zero point ("Finally, no Golden Fleece"), the principle of subtraction is given a further turn—and the possibilities of loss receive not only a chilling extension, but also (with the idea of "sham," deliberate deceit, here including self-deceit) a bitter significance.

When a principle of sequential structure does not imply its own termination point, closure must be secured either through special terminal features or through some *other* structural principle. The latter possibility is illustrated in the poem just quoted and in the other poem by Dickinson, "The heart asks pleasure first," discussed in chapter 1 (see page 6). Each of these poems is generated by two concurrent series, where one series could be

[9] *The Complete Poems of Emily Dickinson*, ed. Thomas H. Johnson (Boston, 1960), pp. 414–15.

extended indefinitely ("first . . . , second . . . , third . . . ," etc., and "first . . . , and then . . . , and then . . . ," etc.), but where the other series has an implicit terminal point (total loss in one, death in the other). What results in each poem is that the progressive loss of means, ends, and faith, or the gradual death of the heart, is given the quality of mathematical precision and neutrality—and also of mathematical certainty, which, among other things, strengthens the sense of finality at its conclusion.

We may turn now to a more detailed consideration of sequential structure in a longer and more complex poem, George Herbert's "Mortification":

How soon doth man decay!
When clothes are taken from a chest of sweets
To swaddle infants, whose young breath
Scarce knows the way;
Those clouts are little winding sheets,
Which do consigne and send them unto death.

When boyes go first to bed,
They step into their voluntarie graves,
Sleep bindes them fast; onely their breath
Makes them not dead:
Successive nights, like rolling waves,
Convey them quickly, who are bound for death.

When youth is frank and free,
And calls for musick, while his veins do swell,
All day exchanging mirth and breath
In companie;
That musick summons to the knell,
Which shall befriend him at the houre of death.

When man grows staid and wise,
Getting a house and home, where he may move
Within the circle of his breath,
Schooling his eyes;

That dumbe inclosure maketh love
Unto the coffin, that attends his death.

When age grows low and weak,
Marking his grave, thawing ev'ry yeare,
Till all do melt, and drown his breath
When he would speak;
A chair or litter shows the biere,
Which shall convey him to the house of death.

Man, ere he is aware,
Hath put together a solemnitie,
And drest his herse, while he has breath
As yet to spare:
Yet Lord, instruct us so to die,
That all these dyings may be life in death.[10]

There are three major principles of thematic structure here: two of them are sequential, one being a series, the other a logical development. The third principle, a recurrent conceit, is in effect paratactic. The conclusion of the poem derives its expressive power and stability from the complex relation of these three principles and from other nonstructural elements as well.

In certain respects the thematic structure of the poem is simple. The first five stanzas are clearly generated by the series infancy-boyhood-youth-manhood-old age. Since the series evidently corresponds to the traditionally conceived successive stages of a man's life, *death* would be a "natural" termination point. Consequently, given the existence of a sixth stanza, the reader will to some extent expect the poem to conclude with a corresponding "analysis" of that final stage, death.

This series, however, is not the only principle of thematic structure in the poem, and other thematic elements make this sort of conclusion unavailable as such. For one thing, each of the first five stanzas emphasizes the fact that death is present not only at the

[10] *The Works of George Herbert*, ed. F. E. Hutchinson (Oxford, 1959), pp. 98–99.

end of a man's life, but at every point along the way. *Death* explicitly concludes *every* stanza, both thematically and formally. Therefore, although the series implies and apparently develops toward a certain terminal item, the closural force of that item has already been more or less dissipated.

Before we consider how this situation affects the final stanza itself, we should observe that the second major principle of thematic structure is the repetition of a conceit. In each stanza except the last, an image or circumstance appropriate to that particular stage of life is seen to prefigure a funereal image or circumstance. Obviously this conceit would have little point in connection with the final stage of the series; while life may prefigure death, death itself *is* death—or is it?

In any case, the reader's expectations concerning the final stanza will reflect his awareness (at what level of consciousness need not concern us) of the fact that the internal structure of that stanza cannot merely reiterate the running conceit one last time. He will, in other words, expect some sort of turn or change in the form and nature of the assertion. What, precisely, he is most likely to expect will depend upon factors external to the poem itself: his familiarity, for example, with the traditions of Christian thought and gnomic verse, and also, perhaps, with other poems by Herbert. It will also depend upon the effects of his experience with nonliterary discourse: the extent, for example, to which he associates the development of the poem with a logical demonstration.

The combination of all these factors may very well lead the reader to look forward to a concluding stanza that draws together the implications of the first five in a resounding *memento mori.* This is not, however, the sort of conclusion he will find there. And although his expectations are thus not fulfilled, they are also not disappointed. For certain other elements throughout the poem are just as effectively preparing him for precisely the sort of conclusion that finally occurs.

As so often in *The Temple,* the grim emblems of mortality are softened by Herbert's compassion and irradiated by his faith. In each stanza a familiar circumstance of life is transformed into a funeral prop. The transformations, however, work both ways. We are always, in every act and gesture, prefiguring our own death: the infant is swathed in a version of his shroud, the old man's litter anticipates his bier. But seen the other way round, winding sheets are only swaddling bands "taken from a chest of sweets," the grave is an involuntary bed, and so forth: life is a form of dying, but "all these dyings may be life in death."

Our pragmatically derived language can hardly accommodate the nature of the typological relationship between the two sets of emblems and images, and this limitation is both reflected and overcome in the variety of verbs that indicate that relationship in each stanza. In the first, the verb suggests a relation of simple identity: "Those clouts *are* little winding sheets." Here the qualifying "little" is initially only macabre. In stanzas 3 to 5, however, the verbs "summons to," "maketh love unto," and "shows" suggest a relationship between the emblems of life and death that is more subtle and mysterious than simple identity. And while the macabre implications are not lost, another more benign quality is introduced—the quality suggested, for example, by the notion, both ironic and direct, that the funeral bell will ultimately "befriend" the convivial youth (line 18). What I have been suggesting here is that throughout the first five stanzas Herbert's expression of the relationship between the circumstances of life and the ceremonies of death is, in effect, preparing the reader for the turn in the last two lines of the poem. Although the equations have been reading "life is death," their potential reversibility is always waiting to be made explicit.

To the two major principles of thematic structure already noted (i.e., the series from infancy to old age, and the repetition of the conceit of prefiguration), we may now add the third: what Louis Martz, in *The Poetry of Meditation,* describes as meditative structure.[11] Even for the reader unfamiliar with the tradition of the

[11] New Haven, 1962. A summary description of this structure appears on p. 38 of Martz's book.

"spiritual exercise," this structural principle will be effective, for the poem's logical and dramatic coherence is perceptible in any case. The first line, what Martz would call the "composition," sets forth a general observation which the succeeding lines, from 2 to 30, clearly illustrate and develop. This central section (the "analysis" in Martz's terms) is generated with logical orderliness according to the two principles already discussed: the series and the repeated conceit. Whether or not the reader has a term for it, he will perceive that the final stanza opens with a statement that summarizes the preceding twenty-nine lines and could serve as the logical conclusion to the poem. Finally, although the reader familiar with the form of the traditional meditation would identify the last two lines as the customary "petition in colloquy with God," any reader would respond to their dramatic appropriateness. My point here is that the third principle of thematic structure is effective through its approximation to the structure of nonliterary discourse, whether or not the *specific* "meditative" form of that discourse is perceived as such by the reader.

Now let us turn directly to the dynamics of the final stanza. As it opens (with "Man . . ." now, not "When . . ."), it immediately informs the reader that the repetitive syntactic form of the preceding five stanzas is to be modified; and, for reasons we have discussed, he is likely to expect other modifications as well. Also, in referring to the general class, *man,* rather than to a particular stage or group, and in returning thus to the subject of the first line, it will suggest that a general summary is about to follow. Lines 31 to 34, which do indeed present a summary recapitulation, answer to the expectations set up by the logical structure of the poem and, more particularly, to those set up by the poem's resemblance to moral verse of a certain tradition. Although the two final lines of the poem are "surprising" with regard to *these* expectations,[12] and thus constitute what we usually refer to as a "turn," they are not at all surprising with regard to the other thematic elements discussed

[12] I am ignoring the reader's expectations regarding formal structure, which, of course, would demand that the stanza be completed.

earlier: the potentially reversible equations, the benign aspects of the funeral ceremonies, and the dramatic or conventional propriety of a concluding personal petition. In terms of the expectations created by the latter elements, the last two lines are no "turn" at all, but precisely what is needed to complete the poem.

The closural force of the final two lines is, to that degree, secure—and other nonstructural features, such as the universal *all*, the antithesis *life-death*, and the repetitions *die . . . dyings . . . death*, strengthen it. Most important, of course, is that final appearance of the conceit of transformation by which "all these dyings," now rightly understood, restore eternal life.

Temporal Sequence

> But thought's the slave of life, and life time's fool;
> And time, that takes survey of all the world,
> Must have a stop.
>
> [I *Henry IV*, Act V, scene 4, lines 81–83]

Time, however, does not stop, and the dramatic irony is evident: it is Hotspur that stops, his thoughts and his life. But time continues.

* * *

A poet may, as in narrative verse, use the passage of time as a structural principle, and temporal sequence in one form or another may be found in lyric poetry as well. The passage of time, however, is continuous; and although temporal sequence provides the poet with an excellent principle of generation, it does not provide him with a termination point. He—his story, his poem—must, at some point, stop; but the conclusion, with respect to time alone, will always be an arbitrary one.

The problem of securing closure under these circumstances—of keeping the reader from asking "What then?" or from responding to the arbitrariness of the interruption as such—is hardly unique to the poet. Works of drama and narrative fiction are almost always generated through temporal sequence, and the playwright or novelist has the same obligation to provide closure as does the poet. Although the nature of closure in these other literary modes is no less complex than that of poetry and its consideration beyond the scope of this study, a glance at some aspects of the conclusions of plays and novels will be a useful introduction to the subject of this section.

Until fairly recently, as these things go, one could safely observe that most comedies ended with the marriages, and most tragedies with the deaths, of the protagonists. And the English novel, perhaps influenced here as much by the structure of drama as by the circumstances of life, also typically concluded with marriages and deaths. We might recall here that Bulwer-Lytton prevailed upon Dickens to change the ending of *Great Expectations* so that Pip and Estella are re-united and the promise of their marriage made clear.[13] It was apparently not enough for Lytton that by the last chapter every other character in the novel, major and minor, had been brought to the altar or the grave.

What these conclusions might suggest is that dramatists and novelists typically exploited the natural or traditional stopping places of life to secure closure. And this is to some extent true. We should also observe, however, that these plays and novels inevitably had some principle of generation other than temporal sequence itself, that this additional principle could (and usually would) have its own implied termination point, and, finally, that this other thematic principle would often be of the sort for which deaths or marriages would be appropriate terminations. When, for example, the major thematic principle of a comedy is the progress of the relation between two lovers from its beginnings through a series of social or physical difficulties, the appropriately resolving conclusion would traditionally involve their marriage. (However, see n. 17 in this chapter.)

Other thematic principles imply other kinds of conclusions, and the design of a novel or play is likely to consist of a considerable

[13] Edgar Johnson, *Charles Dickens: His Tragedy and Triumph* (New York, 1952), II, 968–69.

number of them, each appropriately resolved or terminated at the conclusion of the work. In *Great Expectations* the pattern of Pip's departures from, and returns to, the values of his childhood, or the sequence of his guilt, expiation, and redemption, constituted thematic principles that implied certain terminations—and were, indeed, quite adequately terminated in the original final chapters. (The course and fate of Pip's love for Estella were apparently not important to Dickens' design in the same way they were to Lytton's response.) Similarly, in *Twelfth Night*, where the action is generated in part by such classic comic circumstances as disguises, intrigues, missing persons, and mistaken identities, the stability of the conclusion is as much the product of the final revelations of circumstantial truth as of the marriages all around.

Since there are always a number of thematic principles in any work of literature, it is notoriously difficult to define *the* theme or subject of a novel or play (or poem). For the reader or audience, however, the themes (i.e., the principles of thematic structure) are ultimately "defined" in another sense by his growing perception of how the work itself is generated. As I pointed out earlier, this perception forms a kind of running hypothesis which the reader constantly tests against the actual development of the work, and which is ultimately confirmed (or not) by its conclusion.[14] The thematic structure of James Joyce's story "The Dead," for example, is complex and elusive, but in the concluding pages the reader (as well as the protagonist, Gabriel Conroy) becomes aware of its most significant principles. Because the story concludes as it does, certain thematic elements from various earlier parts of it are brought into alignment, as it were, through what I have called "retrospective patterning": that is, connections and similarities are illuminated, and the reader perceives that seemingly gratuitous or random events, details, and juxtapositions have been selected in accord with certain principles.

It was owing to the particular nature of Joyce's story that in "The Dead" these principles remained so elusive (or the reader's

[14] The dynamics of this process were considered in chapter 1, pp. 10–13.

hypotheses so tentative) until the conclusion. In most novels and plays the themes are defined in the reader's perception with considerable certainty as the work unfolds, and his experience of the conclusion follows accordingly. If the conclusion confirms the hypothesis suggested by the work's thematic structure, closure will be to that extent secure; what presumably follows or could follow *in time* will not concern the reader—will not, to be precise, concern his experience of the work in question. In other words, the end of a play or novel will not appear as an arbitrary cut-off if it leaves us at a point where, with respect to the themes of the work, we feel that we know all there is or all there is to know. As far as the reader's experience of the work is concerned, what follows beyond the last page or scene is either of no significance (Hamlet and his problems lie dead before us), or it is completely predictable (Fortinbras will restore order to Denmark and Horatio will give a truthful account of the events), or it is, as we say, "another story," another set of themes (Horatio's further adventures, the married life of the Duke and Duchess of Illyria). If, on the other hand, closure is not secured, if we are left with the awareness that time continues and with the desire to pursue the characters or situations further into it, it is because the themes have not been adequately defined by the time the conclusion occurs or, as in Melville's *The Confidence-Man,* all the major principles of thematic structure are, like the temporal sequence itself, indefinitely extensible.[15]

The preceding discussion suggests that a reader's (or audience's) experience of temporal sequence in drama or fiction is given integrity by the relation of time to *an otherwise integrated structure.* This, of course, is exactly what divides the passage of time into integral units in our ordinary nonliterary experiences. What marks a "day" off from the succession of instants is its relation to the motion of a timepiece, to the motion of the earth (or, as we

15 The example is too striking to forego at this point, although there is reason enough to think that the open-endedness of the novel was precisely Melville's intention, especially for its corollary effect of leaving the boundary line between art and reality indistinct.

experience it, of the sun), or simply to the round of activities which defines that period in our lives. (Trapped miners, cave explorers, and others who have voluntarily engaged in experiments in human isolation invariably report that they lose track of the passage of time when no "clocks" of this sort are available.)[16] In literature, as in life, we do not respond directly to time as such; and what determines the integrity of a unit of time in either is the integrity of some attendant circumstance. Our personal histories are marked off by a multitude of such circumstances, and upon even the most random or chaotic lives night must fall and day must dawn. Not only days, years, and seasons, but jobs, homes, and roles (and excursions from them) bestow integrity upon our experience of the past, dividing it into successive and parenthetical periods. These circumstances, which determine periods of time that are not only internally coherent but also clearly distinguished from one another by beginnings and ends, are reflected in literature as principles of thematic structure. If a novel opens with the protagonist arriving in a new place, starting a new job, or assuming a new role, and concludes with him leaving the place, quitting the job, or abandoning the role, whatever thematic coherence the intervening pages do or do not have, a certain degree of structural coherence will have been suggested. And, furthermore, a certain degree of closure will be secured merely if the novel concludes with night falling, or the arrival of autumn, or if the play concludes with the protagonist slamming the door behind her. Our experience of coherence and closure in a work of literature is inevitably affected by these nonliterary experiences.[17]

[16] Although our subject touches here on the familiar philosophic problems of "subjective" and "objective" time, their more metaphysical aspects are not relevant and will be sidestepped without further comment. For a discussion of them, see Hans Meyerhoff, *Time in Literature* (Berkeley, 1955), esp. pp. 4–35.

[17] As literature begins to reflect new areas of experience, traditional thematic principles and the conclusions they imply will be abandoned for other ones. When, for example, literature began to deal with problems between the sexes that could not be resolved by marriage, weddings obviously lost their familiar closural function in plays and novels.

The relevance of the preceding discussion to the consideration of temporal sequence in poetry will become clear as this section develops, but one point must be emphasized at the outset. With reference to such obvious examples of narrative or dramatic verse as "The Eve of St. Agnes" or *Samson Agonistes,* the problems of structure and closure raised by the appearance of temporal sequence are not very different from those already touched upon. A lyric poem, however, is not so directly comparable to drama or fiction; for although a lyric may be dramatic or narrative in certain respects, what distinguishes it from a versified play or novel is the fact that it is the representation, not of an action or the chronicle of an action, but of an utterance. Lyrics cannot, for example, end in deaths, although they may (and often do) end in *references* to death. Whereas the structure of a play or novel is related to the structure of *events,* the structure of a lyric poem is related to that of personal discourse, and this relation will be reflected in the poet's use of temporal sequence as a generating principle.

There are two fundamental ways in which a poem, like any nonliterary utterance, may exhibit temporal sequence: it may develop as the report of a succession of events that either took place in the past or is taking place concurrently with the utterance itself. If the poem is cast in the form of a report of events already past, it will, of course, have some resemblance to a narration. As the following example will demonstrate, however, the poem that fits this description may be far from what we usually think of as narrative verse:

Methought I saw my late espoused Saint
  Brought to me like *Alcestis* from the grave,
  Whom *Jove*'s great Son to her glad Husband gave,
  Rescu'd from death by force though pale and faint.
Mine as whom washt from spot of child-bed taint,
  Purification in the old Law did save,
  And such, as yet once more I trust to have
  Full sight of her in Heaven without restraint,

Come vested all in white, pure as her mind:
Her face was veil'd, yet to my fancied sight,
Love, sweetness, goodness, in her person shin'd
So clear, as in no face with more delight.
But O, as to embrace me she inclin'd,
I wak'd, she fled, and day brought back my night.[18]

Although the distinction is not always so obvious, and the "narrative lyric" at some point passes into the narrative poem proper, the two may be kept separate enough for our purposes if we think of the former as essentially related to the personal anecdote, and the latter to the tale. The anecdote will be briefer, its approximation to the conventions of direct speech will be closer, its significance will lie in its relation to the speaker's own life or thought, and it will usually conclude with some comment very much in the present. Indeed, the conclusion of Milton's sonnet is exceptional in this respect: what is far more common is a poem that develops for a certain portion through the narration of past events, but concludes with a "turn" that breaks out of the strictly narrative mode, or simply continues beyond it in some other way. The following two poems are, in this respect, more representative:

Down by the Salley Gardens

Down by the salley gardens my love and I did meet;
She passed the salley gardens with little snow-white feet.
She bid me take love easy, as the leaves grow on the tree;
But I, being young and foolish, with her would not agree.

In a field by the river my love and I did stand,
And on my leaning shoulder she laid her snow-white hand.
She bid me take life easy, as the grass grows on the weirs;
But I was young and foolish, and now am full of tears.[19]

[18] John Milton, "Sonnet XXIII," *Complete Poems and Major Prose,* ed. Merritt Y. Hughes (New York, 1957), pp. 170–71.

[19] *The Collected Poems of* W. *B. Yeats* (New York, 1951), p. 21.

East London

'Twas August, and the fierce sun overhead
Smote on the squalid streets of Bethnal Green,
And the pale weaver, through his windows seen
In Spitalfields, look'd thrice dispirited.

I met a preacher there I knew, and said:
"Ill and o'erwork'd, how fare you in this scene?"—
"Bravely!" said he; "for I of late have been
Much cheer'd with thoughts of Christ, *the living bread.*"

O human soul! as long as thou canst so
Set up a mark of everlasting light,
Above the howling senses' ebb and flow,

To cheer thee, and to right thee if thou roam—
Not with lost toil thou laborest through the night!
Thou mak'st the heaven thou hop'st indeed thy home.[20]

As my description suggests, temporal sequence in such a poem presents no problem for closure because time is stopped *before* the conclusion and, as in a nonliterary anecdote, the speaker concludes by explaining its significance, adding some general or reflective comment, or otherwise "framing" the anecdote with some indication of why he told it in the first place.

When, in a wholly "narrative" lyric such as Milton's sonnet, the conclusion coincides with the last event related, closure may be secured as in drama and fiction; that is, the conclusion will be given stability with respect to the *other* structural principles by which the poem was generated. The symbolic and allegorical narrations in the poems of George Herbert and Henry Vaughan, for example, are often concluded without external comment but in a manner which is clearly terminal with respect to those poems' thematic structures. To mention only one of the most familiar

[20] *Poetical Works of Matthew Arnold* (London, 1913), pp. 180–81.

possibilities: where a poem narrates the successive stages of a search or pilgrimage, the end will coincide with the poet's discovery of his object or arrival at his destination. The conclusion of such a poem, moreover, will derive additional stability as well as emotional power from its reference to the system of traditional symbols used throughout, as in Herbert's "Redemption":

> Having been tenant long to a rich Lord,
> Not thriving, I resolved to be bold,
> And make a suit unto him, to afford
> A new small-rented lease, and cancell th'old.
> In heaven at his manour I him sought:
> They told me there, that he was lately gone
> About some land, which he had dearly bought
> Long since on earth, to take possession.
> I straight return'd, and knowing his great birth,
> Sought him accordingly in great resorts;
> In cities, theatres, gardens, parks, and courts:
> At length I heard a ragged noise and mirth
> Of theeves and murderers: there I him espied,
> Who straight, *Your suit is granted*, said, & died.[21]

Not only are the events and figures here allegorical translations of spiritual realities and experiences, but the temporal sequence itself is allegorical: the timeless relation of man and Christ, the continued re-enactment of the redemption, is transformed into a series of successive events. The conclusions of these poems are thus implied not only by their own thematic structures, but by the structure, so to speak, of that spiritual realm to which they refer and which they are intended to reaffirm. The extraordinarily moving conclusion of "Redemption" probably owes much of its power to the chilling and yet beautiful correspondence of the two. As the reader is

[21] *The Works of George Herbert*, p. 40. See also "Love (III)," pp. 188–89, "Peace," pp. 124–25, and Vaughn's "Regeneration" (*The Works of Henry Vaughan*, ed. L. C. Martin [Oxford, 1914], II, 397–99).

drawn into the allegorical world of tenants and property transactions, he follows the events as in a fictional narration—even though their religious significance is always apparent. The conclusion is experienced with a double shock of surprise and recognition.

In "narrative lyrics," then, closure may be secured through the speaker's concluding turn or framing comment, through a thematically implied termination point, and through other more or less nonstructural elements in the final lines. The latter possibility is illustrated in the sonnet by Milton quoted above:

> But O, as to embrace me she inclin'd,
> I wak'd, she fled, and day brought back my night.

The poem concludes, with expressive simplicity, as the dream which it has narrated itself concludes; the very absence of further comment becomes comment enough. The conclusion of the dream, however, is actually an interruption of it, and the significance of that incompleteness is expressed in such a way as to bring the poem itself to an appropriate completion. The last line here suggests the speaker's emotions by complementing them rhythmically: the succession of phrases corresponds, in effect, first to the swift and sharply painful transition from dream to reality, and then to the necessary resignation which ensues. The finality of the concluding words is itself, as *finality*, thematically significant ("It was over; there was no more") and draws power as well as pathos from the full implication of the last paradox, "and day brought back my night." Not only are the multiple suggestions of *night* relevant (blindness, deprivation, sorrow), but also the suggestions of the antithesis: *day*, which should be light and truth, is "my night"—darkness in every sense, and the loss of even that illuminating vision that can come in dreams. The poem concludes, then, with the interruption of the dream, but, more significantly, with the sober return to the stable ordinariness of daytime reality, and to the permanence and absoluteness of personal night.

Sequential Structure

As I mentioned above, the other form that temporal sequence may take in lyric poetry is that of "simultaneous composition," where the poem is generated in accordance with the passage of time *during which* it is presumably being composed. In Keats's "Ode to a Nightingale" the tense is present and the pretense is that the poet himself does not know, at the end of the first stanza, what will be happening by the end of the second—or if, indeed, there will be a second or third or fourth stanza. The structure of such a poem reflects and emphasizes what is true of any utterance: namely, that it takes time to say (or think or write) it, and that the physical or psychological events to which it refers may be taking place during that same period of time.

Here, the poet-speaker's presumed ignorance of how or when the poem will end would seem to imply that thematic coherence and terminal stability are likely to be more elusive. When we tell a tale or an anecdote, our sense of the whole structure, including the conclusion, inevitably determines the selection and presentation of events. In this kind of poem, however, at least the illusion of the poet-speaker's ignorance must be preserved. But the problem of coherence and closure need not be so very great, for the structure of such a poem may, like those discussed above, also be generated by some other thematic principle in addition to that of temporal sequence. Keats's ode is not merely a slice of the poet's imaginative life. The sequence of sensations, impressions, and comments is represented as originating in a particular occasion (his response to the bird's song) and maintains a constant reference to the particular experience that follows. Although the poet presumably does not know exactly what will occur from one moment to the next, the structure *and* conclusion of the poem are limited by the nature of that occasion and the integrity of that experience. (An analogy may clarify this: when a radio sportscaster reports the events of a football game, neither he nor his audience knows exactly what will happen from one play to the next, but the substance, structure, and termination of his "discourse" are limited by those of the game itself.) What the reader pursues from line to line in Keats's poem is not merely a portion of the poet's "stream-of-consciousness," but a sequence of connected psychological events: the poet's first ambiguous sensations, his desire to join the nightingale in a kind of imaginative identification, the achievement of that identification, its development, attenuation, and final loss. The conclusion of the poem thus coincides precisely with the termination of the particular experience and is stable for that reason. The final lines ("Was it a vision or a waking dream?/Fled is that music:—Do I wake or sleep?")[22] resemble the sort of "turn" we noticed above in the narrative lyric. It brings us to a present moment which, though embodied in an unanswered question, is stable with respect to the passage of time *during* the imaginative experience. That experience is already in the past ("*Was* it a vision. . . . *Fled* is that music. . . .") and there is nothing more to happen, nothing further to say.

My point here is that, as an example of "simultaneous composition," Keats's ode presents no special closural problem, even though it represents more or less interior speech and refers to more or less private experiences. With regard to the problems of temporal sequence, it is no different from any other poetic report of ongoing events—Spenser's "Epithalamion," for example, a poem which in other respects is obviously much more highly structured. For our present purposes all we need note is that in neither poem is the passage of time the only generating principle, and that in both poems the principles which give structural integrity to the events or experiences reported also give integrity and terminal stability to the report itself. Poems representing interior monologues present special closural problems when, as in Keats's "Ode on a Grecian Urn," they do not refer to a particular integral sequence of events, but develop through associative or dialectic processes; such poems will be considered in the final section of this chapter.

In concluding this section, we might consider the ways in which

[22] *The Poetical Works of John Keats*, ed. H. W. Garrod (London, 1961), p. 209.

a lyric poet may allude to the passage of time without actually making it a structural principle. Here, the effect of temporal sequence is not to raise problems of closure but to solve them, for the poet may exploit our experiences with specific units of time, borrowing *their* integrity to give additional coherence and closure to his work. The technique I have in mind may be called "temporal punctuation" and consists of introducing in the poem implicit or explicit allusions to the progress of a day, a season, a year, or some other well-defined and familiar unit of time. The technique is habitual with Milton and may be examined first in connection with "Lycidas":

> Thus sang the uncouth Swain to th'Oaks and rills,
> While the still morn went out with Sandals gray;
> He touch't the tender stops of various Quills,
> With eager thought warbling his *Doric* lay:
> And now the Sun had stretch't out all the hills,
> And now was dropt into the Western bay;
> At last he rose, and twitch't his Mantle blue:
> Tomorrow to fresh Woods, and Pastures new.[23]

This concluding passage "frames" the elegy proper, putting it into the past and creating a distinction between the poet and the elegist (now become "the uncouth Swain"). It also frames the poem by giving it an explicit temporal context: the passage of a single day from dawn to sunset. The ambivalent and changing reactions of the elegist, his vision of the procession of water deities and finally of the ascension of Lycidas, and the progress from lines 39–41 ("Thee Shepherd, thee the Woods, the desert Caves, . . . And all their echoes mourn") to line 182 ("Now *Lycidas* the Shepherds weep no more")—all presumably occurred over a period of time. Although the tenses are ambiguous, sometimes past, sometimes present, the poem—up to this concluding passage—seemed to be generated by "simultaneous composition," and transitions

[23] *Complete Poems and Major Prose*, p. 125.

such as that of line 88 ("But now my oat proceeds . . .") would emphasize the concurrent passage of time. Nevertheless, it is not until the concluding lines that this period of time is *defined* in any way; before that, it might have been a few moments or a few months. The introduction of a specific unit of time, and particularly one with well-defined limits, is what I referred to above as "temporal punctuation." If the poem had begun with an allusion to dawn and been laced throughout with references to mid-morning, noon, and dusk, this recurrent punctuation would have provided a continuing source of structural coherence. As it is, even though there had been no previous temporal reference, the concluding allusion to sunset has a strong closural effect:

> And now the Sun had stretch't out all the hills,
> And now was dropt into the Western bay.

Part of this effect, we should observe, arises from the thematic echo of line 168 ("So sinks the day-star in the Ocean bed"). Even without this, however, the reader's many experiences with sunset as a terminal limit of time would have given finality to these lines.[24]

"Lycidas" does not conclude with absolute finality, however, for the last allusion to time is not to sunset but to "Tomorrow"; and the quality that results from this and from the attendant notions of "fresh Woods, and Pastures new" is the characteristic one that I referred to sometime earlier (p. 79) as "poised repose." We find it at the conclusion of *Paradise Lost* and also in the ode "On the Morning of Christ's Nativity," the last stanza of which is as follows:

> But see! the Virgin blest,
> Hath laid her Babe to rest.
>   Time is our tedious Song should here have ending;
> Heav'n's youngest-teemed Star
> Hath fixt her polisht Car,

[24] See pp. 192–94 below, for a further consideration of closure in "Lycidas."

Her sleeping Lord with Handmaid Lamp attending:
And all about the Courtly Stable,
Bright-harness'd Angels sit in order serviceable.[25]

Throughout the poem the distinction between the present and the past is blurred: it is neither the anniversary of Christ's birth nor the nativity day itself, but both at once. Like Herbert's "Redemption," but without the allegorical superstructure, this celebration-song narrates the re-enactment of "events" that transcend chronology. In this final stanza, however, the infant, whose power had been evoked all through the poem in images of cosmic physical and historical cataclysms, rests and is put to sleep. The star which had been moving westward, guiding the "Wizards" (line 23) to this very place, itself rests "fixt." The song of praise, which is the poem we have been reading, announces itself as concluded. Nevertheless, upon this scene of stasis, order, and stability, the sun is just beginning to rise (cf. lines 229–31), the son of God is just beginning his reign, the angels sit in poised attendance, and we too are waiting: "This is the end—but more shall follow."

Logical and Syntactic Sequence

The terminology of logic includes several more or less figurative expressions which bear an obvious relation to matters already discussed in this chapter. We speak, for example, of "chains" of reasoning, of propositions which do or do not "follow," and, most important, of logical "conclusions." Each of these expressions suggests how readily the familiar forms of logical discourse can be accommodated by poetic structure and closure; and lyric poems do indeed exhibit logical structure, that is, logical sequence of one kind or another is a common thematic principle.

The structure of a lyric is not often formally syllogistic, but neither is the structure of argumentative nonliterary discourse. If we are engaged in supporting a point, making a case, or persuading

[25] *Complete Poems and Major Prose*, p. 50.

an audience to do or believe something, our argument is likely to develop informally and irregularly through analogies, examples, and inferences, and to be interrupted by digressions or elaborations. What makes a logical sequence particularly interesting for this study is that the kind of discourse it resembles is, perhaps more than any other, directed toward a *conclusion*—in both senses. It would be simple enough to say that when a poem is generated through logical sequence its end will have closural strength if it coincides with the appropriate logical conclusion. But the question of what is "appropriate" is not at all simple; for although a lyric may imitate logical discourse, that is not what it is, and the reader's experience of its conclusion (in either sense) will be determined by the fact that he ultimately responds to the poem as something other than a piece of reasoning.

We may begin by considering one of the most familiar kinds of lyrical argument, the "persuasion to love." This venerable and substantial tradition of amatory lyric inevitably offers examples of logical—or pseudo-logical—structure. No less traditional than the theme of *carpe diem* are the arguments through which it is developed: the analogies drawn between ephemerally blooming flowers and virgins, for example, or the crucial distinction made between the light of day that sets to rise again and the light of life that ends in Campion's "ever-during night." [26] The following sonnet by Samuel Daniel is a not undistinguished example of both the theme and the argument:

Look, Delia, how w'esteem the half-blown rose,
The image of thy blush and summer's honor,
Whilst yet her tender bud doth undisclose
That full of beauty time bestows upon her.

[26] "My Sweetest Lesbia," *The Works of Thomas Campion*, ed. Percival Vivian (Oxford, 1909), p. 6. Other poems in the tradition referred to include the original of this, Catullus' "Vivamus, mea Lesbia," Ausonius' "De Rosis Nascentibus," and Herrick's "To the Virgins, to make much of Time." The tradition and its conventions are extensively discussed by H. M. Richmond in *The School of Love: The Evolution of the Stuart Love Lyric* (Princeton, 1964), pp. 57–78.

No sooner spreads her glory in the air
  But straight her wide-blown pomp comes to decline;
  She then is scorned that late adorned the fair;
  So fade the roses of those cheeks of thine.
No April can revive thy withered flowers,
  Whose springing grace adorns thy glory now;
  Swift speedy time, feathered with flying hours,
  Dissolves the beauty of the fairest brow.
Then do not thou such treasure waste in vain,
But love now whilst thou mayst be loved again.[27]

The stability and appropriateness of the concluding couplet are evident enough, and numerous elements, both formal and thematic, as well as the reader's familiarity with the tradition itself, will strengthen the sense of closure here. We might observe, however, that although the conclusion is indeed appropriate, it is not, strictly speaking, logical. The same is true of one of the most famous of lyrical arguments, Marvell's "To his Coy Mistress," where it has been observed that the three divisions of the poem correspond exactly to the major and minor premises and conclusion of a formal syllogism.[28]

Had we but World enough, and Time,
This coyness, Lady, were no crime . . .

  But at my back I alwaies hear
Times winged Charriot hurrying near . . .

  Now therefore, . . .
. . . let us sport us while we may . . .[29]

[27] Sonnet "To Delia," text in *Poetry of the English Renaissance*, eds. J. William Hebel and Hoyt H. Hudson (New York, 1957), pp. 243–44.

[28] J. V. Cunningham, "Logic and Lyric," *Tradition and Poetic Structure* (Denver, 1960), pp. 41–43.

[29] *The Poems and Letters of Andrew Marvell*, ed. H. M. Margoliouth (Oxford, 1952), I, 26.

The syllogism, however, is an excellent example of a textbook fallacy known as "denying the antecedent": if P, then not Q; not P; therefore Q. "It does not follow," the lady might have replied. In each of these poems a principle of logical sequence is pursued to a conclusion which, though logically invalid, is nevertheless experienced by the reader as appropriate and stable. It might be urged that the feebleness or falseness of the logic has been obscured by rhetorical luxuriance. I think that it would be more accurate to say that logical validity has become irrelevant to the reader's experience—or not relevant in the same way that it would be to his experience of nonliterary logical discourse.

We might recall at this point the observation made in chapter 1, namely that poems imitate not only the structure but also the circumstances and motives of everyday speech. In each of these poems, very particular (though conventional) circumstances and motives are suggested: the speaker's relationship to his presumed audience, the quality of his feeling for her, and, of course, his desire to persuade her to yield to him. We may, moreover, think of the circumstances and motives of an utterance as including not merely the gross features of the attendant situation or the speaker's most apparent intentions, but *everything* that presumably gave his speech its individual form. Particular details of Marvell's poem, for example, reveal the speaker's acute and unfeigned consciousness of mutability, and a quality of playful tenderness in his feeling for the lady. These too may be regarded as motives of his speech. Taken together, all the particular circumstances and motives thus suggested will create for the reader the poem's implied context. Returning to the question of the stability of an illogical conclusion, we may now suggest that such a conclusion may nevertheless be entirely appropriate to the context of the poem, indeed *more* appropriate in this sense than a logically respectable conclusion. The argumentative lover is ostensibly concerned only with the response of his mistress, and she, perhaps, will be suspicious of the persuasive resources of rhetoric. But any other reader will respond to the argument, including its conclusions, with regard not to its ultimate persuasiveness but to its ultimate expressiveness.

I have not meant to suggest that the logical validity of a poem's conclusion is without significance in the reader's experience of closure, but rather that its significance will always be qualified by other elements in the poem, including all that distinguishes it from nonliterary discourse. The following poem illustrates how subtle the relation between logical sequence and the other elements of a lyric may be, and how powerful, also, the forces for closure that may result from that relation:

Nothing Gold Can Stay

Nature's first green is gold,
Her hardest hue to hold.
Her early leaf's a flower;
But only so an hour.
Then leaf subsides to leaf.
So Eden sank to grief,
So dawn goes down to day.
Nothing gold can stay.[30]

The sequence of lines here conforms to a logical progression which develops through a series of individual instances to a concluding generalization. The appropriateness of this conclusion is experienced without regard to the speaker's particular motives or circumstances; for, granted the metaphoric meaning of *gold,* the generalization is manifestly valid. We find, however, that it has been "supported" not so much by the instances which have apparently exemplified it as by the metaphoric significance which they have given to it. Closure here is the complex product of the interaction between logical sequence and figurative language.

The short lines and simple syntax emphasize a quality of per-

[30] *The Complete Poems of Robert Frost* (New York, 1964), p. 272.

sonal detachment, a quality that is also suggested by what appears to be, in the first six lines, the bare listing of a "naturalist's" observations.[31] At the same time, something quite other than detachment is suggested by the figurative language, which at first evokes the pathos of mutability and further on both expands the range of its significance and defines it more precisely. By the last line, the speaker has revised (and compelled us to revise with him) the relatively mild irony of his earlier understated observation (". . . gold,/Her hardest hue to hold") to the grim absoluteness of "Nothing gold can stay." The pathos of mutability—which is discovered at its most poignant not in the final stages of process (the more conventional images being of *falling* leaves, or the "going down" of *day* to *evening*) but in its very beginnings—embraces all of nature and human history. And *gold* is no longer merely the "hue" of budding leaves, but the quality of youth, innocence, untaintedness, and delicate glory that, everywhere, inevitably is betrayed or betrays itself.

The relation of logical structure to figurative language may be observed in the paradoxes of the first quatrain and in the series of "correspondences" in the second, upon both of which hinge the crucial transformation of the meaning of "gold." In the first line, *gold* is not yet figurative: the paradox is made possible by the synecdochal use of *green* to mean (the color of) growing vegetation. The concluding generalization is anticipated in the second line (and thereby given additional closural force); but here *gold* is still only a "hue." The second paradox begins the expansion of meaning by extending its implied reference from the *color* to the flowerlike *shape* of budding leaves. Consequently, by the end of the first quatrain the second line has already been retrospectively modified, and the implicit generalization is something like, "the delicate qualities of budding things are ephemeral." The fifth line

[31] Although there is thus a "catalogue" here, the thematic structure of the poem is hardly "paratactic," for, as I indicate below, the order of the items and their relation both to each other and to the conclusion are crucial to the poem's effect.

links the first quatrain to the second and initiates the series of corresponding "instances" which will culminate in the concluding generalization. The link is important because it carries with it the *implication* of "gold"; the word itself will not reappear until the last line, but then it will be with the accumulated significance established by the logical correlatives, "So Eden . . . , So dawn. . . ." The implications of this logical frame ("[As] . . . so . . . so . . .") are reinforced by the nearly synonymous verbs ("subside," "sank," "goes down"), resulting in a complex fusion of logical correspondence and metaphorical equivalence among the three "instances." They each become, in effect, mutually metaphoric; and as the fading of dawn into "the light of common day" becomes a figure for the fall of Man, the "grief" of human history is extended to the "fallings" of nature. Thus, by the end of the seventh line, the universality of the impermanence of *gold* has already been established, and in its terms, the conclusion is as valid as it is inevitable.

Frost's poem suggests how important the conventions of syntactic sequence are in the perception of logical relationships. "As . . . so . . . so . . . ," "if . . . then . . . ," "either . . . or . . ."—each of these syntactic formulae implies a logical relationship, and the occurrence of one part will cause us to expect the occurrence of the corresponding parts. Other syntactic forms, less obviously related to what we usually think of as logical sequence, affect our perceptions and expectations in the same way: "not only" implies "but also," "when" implies "then," "although" implies "yet," "once" implies "but now," and so forth. To the extent that such syntactic conventions imply a more or less definite sequence of linguistic structures, they may function as thematic principles, providing coherence throughout the poem and giving closural force to its conclusion. In the following poem, one principle of thematic structure is simply the antithetical relationship between the two stanzas implied by the frame, "When young . . . Now in my prime. . . .":

The Summing-Up

When young I scribbled, boasting, on my wall,
No Love, No Property, No Wages.
In youth's good time I somehow bought them all,
And cheap, you'd think, for maybe a hundred pages.

Now in my prime, disburdened of my gear,
My trophies ransomed, broken, lost,
I carve again on the lintel of the year
My sign: *Mobility*—and damn the cost! [32]

With the first phrase, and certainly by the end of the first stanza, all our experience with the ways of discourse will set up the expectation of a final contrast; and all our experience with the ways of youth and age will anticipate the irony of that contrast. But though the ironic contrast is indeed delivered in the final line, the poet has still artfully evaded our expectations. He has succeeded in presenting not so much a confirmation of our experience as a personal variation of it: it is not, as we might have expected, the youthful motto itself that wisdom has qualified, but rather the spirit in which it must be proclaimed and the estimation of its "cost." Closure is finally secured here not only through the *occurrence* of the anticipated contrast but also through its terms: the economic figure of the first stanza to which the conclusion returns for the language of contrast.

What I wish to emphasize once more is that while poetry imitates the structure of nonliterary discourse, it does so for its own characteristic purposes, and that successful closure is never a matter of merely gratifying the reader's conditioned expectations. At the same time, I do not mean to suggest that logical or syntactic sequence is nothing more than a convenient string on which to hang those true jewels of poetic art, metaphors. As I indicated in chapter 1, our response to any utterance is shaped by

[32] Stanley Kunitz, *Selected Poems: 1928–1958* (Boston, 1958), p. 112.

more than the bare bones of its structure and paraphrasable sense. We are always being made aware of meanings and motives as they are revealed by particular turns of expression—diction, repetitions, emphases, and so forth—that reflect and imply a particular context. My point here has been that since a lyric is the representation of an utterance, the meanings and motives suggested by a particular logical and syntactic sequence will be qualified by numerous other elements in a poem—including, of course, metaphor—and that closure will always be experienced in relation to the *total* act of speech thus represented and the *particular* context thus implied.

IV Associative and Dialectic Structure

Certain lyrics seem to represent not overt speech but the transcription, as it were, of an interior monologue. The distinction is not always clear-cut, of course, for when no particular audience is addressed or implied, the reader has no way of telling whether the speaker is externalizing his thoughts or directing an utterance to the world at large, or at least to some potentially sympathetic ear. Nevertheless, a distinction can be made between uttering what one thinks and representing the very process of thinking it; and what we may consider here are those poems in which such a representation seems to be reflected in their thematic structures.

An example of such poetry was referred to earlier as "simultaneous composition," where (as in Keats's "Ode to a Nightingale") the poem represented the record of a train of thoughts evoked by a series of ongoing events. There, however, even though the events were themselves largely interior or psychological, they formed an integral structure with respect to time; and, as we observed, the integrity of this structure gave thematic coherence to the poem itself and yielded a principle which made successful closure possible. But as we know, the life of the mind is not always so orderly; we are not always thinking about something specific, and our thoughts may develop from each other through casual associations and lead nowhere in particular. It is clear that if a lyric is to represent this kind of experience, its thematic structure will be different from any yet considered here, and closure will present a special problem. Similar problems will arise in a poem that represents not the casual connections of unfocused and undirected rumination, but the weavings and waverings of a mind pondering a specific matter of concern.

The two possibilities referred to here are obviously not merely theoretical projections, for they are reflected in some of the most characteristic poetry of the past hundred and fifty years. The extension (or withdrawal, perhaps) of lyric expression from overt to interior speech, from the utterance of thought to the representation of the process of thinking, has implications for this study which will be examined in the final chapter. Some of them, however, will be anticipated in this section in connection with the general problem that concerns us here, namely, how closure may be secured where, in the representation of interior speech, the thematic structure of a lyric becomes "associative" or "dialectic."

We realize that a poem may represent thinking in only a limited sense of either "represent" or "thinking." For one thing, true verbal activity is only part of the process of thought. Nonverbal images, sensory and kinesthetic memories, and emotional responses also float along that stream of consciousness but can be represented in poetry only insofar as words and phrases suggest them. Second, because communication is not the motive of thinking, such verbalization as does take place is freed from the demands of syntax, logic, and what would otherwise be regarded as intelligibility. Here again, a certain degree of syntactic chaos and structural incoherence can suggest the internal reality, but poetry cannot attempt to be faithful to the minutiae of interior verbalization—not if it is to be poetry. The fact that our thoughts are not intended for any audience—that they do not seek to instruct or delight anyone, or even to express anything—is reflected in the very structure of thinking.[33] But the structure of a poem, at least when it functions as art, is controlled at every point by its ultimately expressive design: its effect, that is, upon the potential reader.

The sort of poem with which we are dealing here, then, must affect its audience while pretending that it has no audience to affect. The consequences of this duplicity for the problem of closure are apparent; for the stream of consciousness, like the stream of time, does not provide any principle of termination. Not every sequence of thought is a "train," and not every train of thought reaches a destination. Some are brought to a halt by an interruption, or their elements dissipate beyond pursuit as we are "teased out of thought." But are these cessations amenable to poetic representation? And if the poem does conclude as a fragment or with the dissolution of its elements, can closure also be effected? Corresponding questions are raised by dialectic thought, for a principle of closure is readily available only when the dialectic process can be represented as internally resolved, when the poet can record his having "thought it through" to a stable conclusion. There are various answers to these questions and solutions to these problems, and not all of them can be discussed here in detail. But some of the more interesting possibilities can be suggested, and several others are implicitly covered in the preceding and following chapters. The final chapter will consider what happens when the problems are not solved or when they are no longer even regarded as problems.

It will be instructive to begin by looking at the following sonnet, where closure presents no problem to speak of because the conclusion of the poem coincides with the resolution of the dialectic process:

[33] For an excellent analysis of the relation between the forms and functions of overt and internalized speech, see *Thought and Language* by the Russian linguist and psychologist, L. S. Vygotsky, ed. and trans. Eugenia Hanfmann and Gertrude Vakar (Cambridge, Mass., 1962).

O me, what eyes hath love put in my head,
Which have no correspondence with true sight!
Or, if they have, where is my judgment fled,
That censures falsely what they see aright?
If that be fair whereon my false eyes dote,
What means the world to say it is not so?
If it be not, then love doth well denote
Love's eye is not so true as all men's 'no'—
How can it? O, how can love's eye be true,
That is so vexed with watching and with tears?
No marvel then though I mistake my view:
The sun itself sees not till heaven clears.
  O cunning love! with tears thou keep'st me blind,
  Lest eyes well-seeing thy foul faults should find.[34]

This sonnet hardly suggests a modern transcription of stream-of-consciousness, but it is not addressed to any person (a fairly unusual circumstance among the *Sonnets*) and seems to represent the poet in a quandary. By line 10, let us say, he seems to have no better idea than the reader does of how or whether those questions can be answered. The first two quatrains develop the terms of the dilemma in a somewhat formal manner, but an experiential immediacy is clearly reflected in the rhythms of line 9 (How cán it? O, how c̋an love's eye be true), which suggest the very accent of the poet's bewilderment. By the couplet, however, the questions have finally been answered, the contradictions resolved; and even though the conclusion is ironic, it is stable in terms of what had preceded it.

The structural features of this sonnet, and in particular its successful closure, are significant here primarily in that they remind us that before the development of the Romantic lyric a poet was likely to represent the dialectical complexity of thought only when he could also represent it as ultimately resolved. In other of Shakespeare's sonnets, however, as in much of the poetry of our

[34] Shakespeare, Sonnet 148.

own time, this sort of conclusion is not available because a condition of ultimately unresolvable complexity is precisely what the poem is intended to represent. In such sonnets, Shakespeare was anticipating a stylistic possibility that would not be fully realized until over two hundred years later. He also encountered the problems that this possibility entails. To put it in the terms that may be most relevant to his art, certain of the sonnets begin to sound more like soliloquies than set speeches and are generated by principles not easily accommodated by the formal structure of the English sonnet. The speaker in these poems moves from point to point as does Hamlet or Richard II in those troubled monologues in which at critical moments the character ponders his condition, or his relation to the world about him, or the possibilities of action and attitude open to him. The resemblance can be seen in Sonnet 121:

> 'Tis better to be vile than vile esteemed
> When not to be receives reproach of being,
> And the just pleasure lost, which is so deemed,
> Not by our feeling but by others' seeing.
> For why should others' false adulterate eyes
> Give salutation to my sportive blood?
> Or on my frailties why are frailer spies,
> Which in their wills count bad what I think good?
> No, I am that I am, and they that level
> At my abuses reckon up their own:
> I may be straight though they themselves be bevel;
> By their rank thoughts my deeds must not be shown—
> Unless this general evil they maintain:
> All men are bad and in their badness reign.

This sonnet is generally regarded as obscure, not only because the statements are ambiguous and allusive, but because they seem to refer to some specific circumstance or occasion, the details of which are beyond our recovery if not our surmise. The effect, in any case, is to oblige the reader to construct a circumstantial context to which the speaker's reflections would be appropriate. In other words, the poem seems to imply its own very special "Shakespearean drama." Also, the combination of gnomic observations, unanswerable questions, and unstable assertions concerning the paradoxes of morality and the speaker's own condition and self-estimation—all these are as familiar in the tragic soliloquies as they are unfamiliar in the introspective tradition of the Renaissance sonnet.

In certain respects this sonnet is comparable to the one discussed above. In neither is a particular audience addressed, and both develop largely through a series of questions and rejected answers. In 148, however, the dialectic process was ultimately resolved, whereas the conclusion of 121, though aphoristic enough, is not a resolution but a confession of desperation and perplexity. But that is the source of its power. The development of the sonnet suggests the hesitant gropings and shiftings of a mind almost overwhelmed by those elusive questions of public and private morality; and any resolution, as such, would be weak or anticlimactic, a betrayal or evasion of the speaker's own profound and compelling perceptions. Indeed, that sort of conclusion is just what we have in several other sonnets. Yvor Winters observes that "Shakespeare frequently poses his problem and then solves it by an evasion or an irrelevant cliché. . . . [He] turns aside from the issues he has raised to a kind of despairing sentimentality, and the effect is one of weakness, poetic and personal." [35] Here, however, the couplet does not provide a sentimental resolution, nor does it glide into the sort of reposeful summary or generalization common among the *Sonnets*. It offers not so much an ultimate assertion as one more turn of thought—a turn which is more extreme, but not more stable than any of those preceding it. It is introduced by a

[35] "Poetic Styles, Old and New," *Four Poets on Poetry*, ed. D. C. Allen (Baltimore, 1959), p. 48. Winters mentions Sonnets 29, 30, and particularly 66 as examples of this tendency. (See below, pp. 214–20, for an analysis of closural weakness in Sonnet 66 and a discussion of Winters' observations thereof.)

tentative (if bitter) "unless," and it proceeds to the kind of assertion that we half expect to find rejected in the next line: "But no— . . . ," etc. It is a conclusion that, in more ways than one, will not let us off the hook.

The problem, then, with this sort of structure, is to provide closure without resolution, and readers will probably vary in their sense of the poetic adequacy of the conclusion of Sonnet 121. In any case, if the reader does experience the poem as integral and well closed, it will not be because the process it represents has been resolved. It will be partly because of those nonstructural features of the final line which give it an epigrammatic form and something of the effect of epigrammatic finality; [36] but it will be primarily because the reader responds to the sonnet in the context of the other sonnets, and can thus refer it to the personal and psychological circumstances to which they apparently allude. Without this context, the poem would appear not only obscure but fragmentary. Or, to bring us back to the point from which we started, it would seem modern.

After Shakespeare's own sonnets, the soliloquies of Hamlet and Richard II find their closest lyrical counterpart in the post-Romantic tradition that eventually produces "The Love-Song of J. Alfred Prufrock." [37] Prufrock observes, with characteristic ironic self-contempt, "I am not Prince Hamlet, nor was ever meant to be." Like Hamlet's, however, his mental life is harried by "overwhelming questions," and his resolutions are similarly tentative and unstable. The resemblance is evident enough when we compare Eliot's poem to that memorable instance of dialectic and

[36] These features will be discussed in the following chapter. See sections II, III and V.

[37] T. S. Eliot, *The Complete Poems and Plays* (New York, 1952), pp. 3–7. The poem and the tradition referred to here have been examined by Robert Langbaum in *The Poetry of Experience: The Dramatic Monologue in Modern Literary Tradition* (New York, 1957), esp. pp. 197–220. Mr. Langbaum's terms, categories, and interpretations are different from but not incompatible with those offered here.

associative structure that begins, "To be, or not to be," and the resemblance extends to their conclusions. I pointed out earlier that trains of thought are frequently ended, arbitrarily enough, by some external interruption. Hamlet's troubled monologue does not on this occasion conclude with a resolution, but is broken off by the entrance of another character: "Soft you now!/The fair Ophelia . . ." (Act III, scene 1, lines 88–89). And Prufrock is recalled from "the chambers of the sea" to other rooms, as "human voices wake us, and we drown."

The conclusion of Hamlet's soliloquy is quite satisfactory with respect to the total dramatic structure of which it is itself an element. But in a lyric, an interruption of the monologue is an interruption of the poem, for the monologue is all there is. The more or less arbitrary break can, however, be adapted to lyrical closure when the dramatic context of the poem is particularly well defined. The possibility is illustrated in several of Browning's "dramatic lyrics"; the "Soliloquy in a Spanish Cloister," for example, is interrupted by the sounding of vespers, but the poem itself does not seem fragmentary. In "Prufrock" the dramatic context is only tenuously defined; the particularities of time, place, and circumstance are vague. But they are also unimportant. The reader is led to understand that the monologue reflects not so much the specific occasion as the *characteristic* inner life of the speaker: it has been this way before, it will probably always be this way. Indeed, in this respect J. Alfred is most unlike the Prince of Denmark. It is, however, this very quality of Prufrock's consciousness that is most significantly reflected in the thematic structure of the poem and in its termination: his inability to commit himself, to be resolved, to pursue the "argument of insidious intent" to its conclusion. Repeatedly on the threshold of revelation, Prufrock will be afraid to enter, and will turn instead to other rooms where distractions, however contemptible, are available. The process is endless and the dialectics unresolvable. The process is terminated on this particular occasion as it has presumably been terminated many times before—by a half-welcome interruption. When, after being interrupted in his thoughts, Hamlet later returns to the private chambers of his own mind, it is with new concerns; and the dialectics, however subtle and complex, are concluded with new resolutions: "I will speak daggers to her, but use none./My tongue and soul in this be hypocrites—/How in my words somever she be shent,/To give them seals never, my soul, consent" (III, ii, 414–17); ". . . O, from this time forth,/My thoughts be bloody, or be nothing worth" (IV, iv, 65–66). Prufrock, however, will be trapped forever in the cycle of "visions and revisions."

What I have wished to suggest here is that the "arbitrary" conclusion of "Prufrock" may provide adequate enough closure because, in its very arbitrariness, it is the only conclusion possible. As in Sonnet 121, the thematic structure of the poem and the consciousness it represents have been such that any resolution would appear to be anticlimactic. With this paradox, and with Eliot's poem in particular, we approach an aspect of this study which I shall reserve for later consideration: that is, the development in modern poetry, of deliberate anti-structure and anti-closure. Two points, however, may be anticipated here. The first is that one obvious, if radical, solution to the problem of how to conclude the representation of inconclusiveness is simply to leave it inconclusive. The second is that it is quite possible to represent a fairly unstructured or ultimately unresolved interior monologue without foregoing any of the effects of closure. As I have just suggested, the conclusion of "Prufrock," for example, owes part of its quite substantial closural force to the very fact that it affirms the intransigence of the consciousness it represents. Thus, although Prufrock himself has reached no point of stability, the poet has allowed the reader to do so. Moreover, closure is strengthened here by various formal and thematic elements, some of which are apparent in the two concluding stanzas:

> I have seen them riding seaward on the waves
> Combing the white hair of the waves blown back
> When the wind blows the water white and black.

We have lingered in the chambers of the sea
By sea-girls wreathed with seaweed red and brown
Till human voices wake us, and we drown.

As in many of Eliot's earlier poems, the free verse in "Prufrock" is actually a series of radical variations on the traditional blank verse line. In other words, the iambic pentameter line functions in the poem as the most probable pattern, always more or less expected by the reader in spite of fairly frequent deviations or, to be more precise, occasional short-range patterns of a rather different sort. And the conclusion of the poem is an example of what was referred to in chapter 2 as the terminal articulation of the metrical norm, conforming quite closely here to the conventional iambic line (exactly so in the last line), with couplet rhymes adding their share of formal coherence and stability.

Other sources of closural force exploited at the conclusion of "Prufrock"—such as the strong assonance, the frequent alliteration and word repetitions, and the obviously terminal quality of the final thematic unit ("and we drown")—will be further discussed in the chapter that follows. There we shall be considering a number of special devices that secure closural effects independent of the poem's structure, and almost any of them would answer to the purpose when the poem's thematic structure is of the sort we have been concerned with here. We may conclude this section and chapter, however, with a brief examination of another device, namely the "frame," mentioned earlier in connection with the closural problems presented by the inherent interminability of paratactic structures—problems obviously comparable to those of associative and dialectic structures.

It is clear from many of the sonnets in Sidney's *Astrophel and Stella* that the poet was well aware of the dramatic possibilities of the Petrarchan mode; and although his sonnets never achieved the psychological complexity of Shakespeare's, they often surpassed them in dramatic vividness and immediacy. In the following poem, extraordinary for its time, Sidney *represents* that state of psychological disorder which other Petrarchan poets had, for centuries, merely described:

> Come, let me write. 'And to what end?' To ease
> A burdened heart. 'How can words ease, which are
> The glasses of thy daily vexing care?'
> Oft cruel fights well pictured forth do please. 4
> 'Art not ashamed to publish thy disease?'
> Nay, that may breed my fame, it is so rare.
> 'But will not wise men think thy words fond ware?'
> Then be they close, and so none shall displease. 8
> 'What idler thing than speak and not be heard?'
> What harder thing than smart and not to speak?
> 'Peace, foolish wit; with wit my wit is marred.'
> Thus write I while I doubt to write, and wreak 12
> My harms on ink's poor loss: perhaps some find
> *Stella*'s great powers, that so confuse my mind.[38]

Although the thematic structure here is considerably more formal and stylized than that of the other poems discussed in this section, it is obvious that Sidney is attempting to suggest the quality of interior speech, and more particularly the interior speech that would accompany the composition of a poem. The first eleven lines imitate directly the sort of sequence of bitter questions, tentative answers, and provoking reflections that might be expected to occur in the mind of a distraught poet-lover. In the last three lines, however, he generalizes *about* the internal dialogue just represented; the transcription of the dialogue has become the poem he is trying to write, but it is framed, as it were, by another poem. In the last three lines, our attention is explicitly directed toward the very qualities of the process which would otherwise have made closure a problem: that is, its disorder and inconclu-

[38] Sonnet 34, *The Poems of Sir Philip Sidney*, ed. William A. Ringler, Jr. (Oxford, 1962), pp. 181–82. I have modernized the spelling and punctuation here to clarify the dialogue between the two "voices."

siveness. The problem has been solved, however, by the creation of two fairly distinct orders or levels of representation: first, the representation of interior speech, and second, framing it, the more traditional order of lyrical mimesis, the representation of direct nonliterary speech. Most significant is the fact that, by making a rational and stable comment from "outside," the framing lines allow Astrophel's problems to retain the psychological realism of irresolution while leaving the reader with a sense of closure.

The type of reflexive reference illustrated by this sonnet ("Thus write I . . .") or by such phrases in other Renaissance poems as "these poor rude lines," "this powerful rhyme," or "our song" is possible only in a poetic tradition in which the concept of the poem as a literary artifact is acceptable. As we would expect, it is rare in the Romantic lyric or wherever the illusion of the poem as a direct unartful utterance must not be jeopardized. There are other ways, however, in which the closural effect of the frame may be secured without losing the dramatic vividness of the poem as an overt speech or the psychological realism of the poem as overheard internal monologue. Turning again to Eliot, we may observe that in "Gerontion" the old man's fruitless ruminations conclude with this more subtle reflexive reference:

> Tenants of the house.
> Thoughts of a dry brain in a dry season.[39]

The tenants of his brain will continue, presumably, to move aimlessly from room to room, unable to rest. The poem and reader do rest, however, for in affirming the fact of irresolution, the last line separates itself from the structure of irresolution, and in acknowledging that affirmation, the reader has drawn an appropriate "conclusion."

[39] *Complete Poems and Plays*, p. 23.

4 Special Terminal Features

I Introduction: Closure and the Sense of Truth

In the preceding two chapters we have considered the relation of closure to a variety of structural principles, and at least one fairly simple generalization emerges, namely that the formal and thematic principles by which a poem is generated sometimes do and sometimes do not imply a specific termination point or kind of conclusion. And, as we have repeatedly observed, when a conclusion is not structurally predetermined, closure must be secured—if at all—through some other means. Moreover, we have seen that even when a particular conclusion seems to be implied by the poem's generating principles, the poet might for the sake of certain expressive effects evade that conclusion. Finally, as several of the examples illustrated, even when the conclusion of a poem more or less conforms to the expectations established by its structure, the poet may in various ways reinforce the reader's sense of its stability or finality.

In each of these instances, a sense of finality and stability is secured or strengthened by certain terminal features or special devices that tend to have closural force more or less independent of the poem's particular formal or thematic structure. I refer to these devices as "nonstructural," not to suggest that they are external to the poem's structure—like tacked-on signs reading FINIS—but because they do not necessarily "follow" from the poem's structural principles or affect the reader in relation to such over-all expectation-sets as may arise from those principles. Many of the features that I discuss in this chapter (e.g., alliteration, formal antithesis, and allusions to death) may, moreover, occur at any point in a poem, not only in its concluding lines. However, for reasons I shall elaborate or speculate upon later, such features apparently tend to have substantial closural force when they *do* occur at the end of a poem, and we may thus speak of them as closural devices.

Before turning to an examination of these devices individually, I should like to introduce a more general point, namely the relation between the sense of closure in poetry and something we might call "the sense of truth." The devices of closure often achieve their characteristic effect by imparting to a poem's conclusion a certain quality that is experienced by the reader as striking *validity*, a quality that leaves him with the feeling that what has just been said has the "conclusiveness," the settled finality, of apparently self-evident truth.

As these remarks imply, the sense of truth that concerns us here is a psychological epiphenomenon and in certain respects illusory. I would suggest, however, that it is not, for that reason, unrespectable—not even when we acknowledge that the devices which produce it are the common property of not only poets but political and commercial propagandists as well: all those rhetoricians, in other words, who for the sake of their particular ends exploit our responses to the marginal properties of language.

It has always been difficult to define the relation between truth and poetry, partly because our claims have a way of turning into concessions. Accused of lying, the poet (or his advocate) may reply that he tells a better truth than history, philosophy, or science: he tells what may be or ought to be rather than what is; he reveals the ideal truth (if not the real truth), the truth of the heart (if not of the intellect). Thus, through the diplomatic introduction of the notion of two kinds of truth, the poet makes his peace with those who dispute his claim to any truth at all.[1] The truce is threatened, however, by the current crisis in epistemology. The growing ascendancy of various forms of philosophical realism (e.g., positivism and pragmatism) and the associated activity of linguistic analysis in both philosophy and science have undercut whatever traditional notions of truth remained to us; and as we see even the rock of verifiable scientific truth pulverized into "statements of probability" and "operational definitions," any simple division of the territory appears increasingly irrelevant or inadequate.[2] Although this situation obviously complicates the relation of poetry to truth, it is also something of a boon to the literary partisan or theorist. It is evident, for example, that poetry need no longer be so much on the defensive with respect to its claims to truth, for no one else is claiming to have cornered the real thing. More important for our present purposes is the fact that we can now use such a notion as "the sense of truth" without feeling that we have betrayed poetry to its arrogant rivals. Or, to put it another way, we may speak of that sense of truth produced by a poem not as a qualified, inferior or illusory truth, but as a significant response to an experience.

The concept of the poem as "a possible utterance" suggests one of the ways in which poetic language can be true while being fictional. Poems are obviously *impossible* utterances in several respects (no one really talks in couplets), but the contexts and motives they imply are recognizable human situations, emotions, and desires. Perhaps there was no *real* "fair youth" in Shake-

[1] In recent years, for example, especially in America, the distinction between "denotations" and "connotations" has done wonders to produce genial relations, the distribution of land, and the adjustment of boundaries between literature and science. Denotations are granted to the scientist and connotations claimed for the poet. Meanwhile, each secretly believes he has the best of the bargain in that his portion of language is the ultimate source or revelation of the best kind of truth.

[2] A good summary and examination of the numerous aspects and implications of this development appear in Brand Blanchard's *Reason and Analysis* (La Salle, Ill., 1962), esp. chaps. 1, 3, 5, 7, and 8.

speare's life, or perhaps, if there was, the poet did not care whether or not he got married or had children; and perhaps no poem ever bestowed immortality upon its subject in any sense of immortality that really matters. But fair youths do exist, and we do delight in their beauty and lament its transience, and we do sometimes wish desperately for some way to evade mortality. The point is not that a poem allows us the momentary entertainment of illusions, but that it allows us to know what we know, including our illusions and desires, by giving us the language in which to acknowledge it.

The corollary concept of the poem as "a fictional utterance" suggests another way in which poetry may be true while being false, as we discussed earlier in connection with the "appropriateness" of illogical conclusions. That is, we may speak of the validity of a poetic statement as referring not to our own sense of what is right and real, but to the implied circumstances and motives of the speaker.

The "sense of truth" with which I shall be most concerned, however, is something a little different from either of these, although they are all related. Since closure is our primary interest here, we will be focusing on that particular experience of validity which, when it occurs at the conclusion of a poem, strengthens or secures the reader's sense of finality and stability. In general, it appears that the conditions which contribute to the sense of truth are also those which create closure. We have already seen that when a certain syntactic form (e.g., "not only . . .") implies a particular counterpart ("but also"), the occurrence of the completing part will obviously have closural force; or, more broadly, that any terminal element that has been in some way predetermined will strengthen closure by fulfilling the reader's expectation of it. One may observe, however, that the occurrence of predetermined elements also increases the reader's experience of validity: that is, by conforming to his expectations, such an element becomes both stable and self-validating and extends these effects to the whole utterance of which it is a part. It would seem, then, that any device that predetermines the occurrence or form of terminal elements will tend to strengthen both closure and the sense of validity.

We shall find, therefore, that what we examined earlier as *structural principles* can, when concentrated in the conclusion of a poem, function as nonstructural devices of closure. In other words, the principles that organize (or generate) an entire poem and determine the general form of its conclusion may also, in miniature as it were, organize a single concluding line and strengthen whatever other closural forces may be present. Antithesis, for example, as we saw in the discussion of syntactic sequence, may operate as a structural principle from one stanza to the next. Compressed in one concluding line, however, an antithesis operates as a *nonstructural* device for strengthening closure. (Repetition of formal elements may also work both ways: as a generating principle throughout a poem—as in meter, end-rhyme, and so forth—and as a nonstructural device in its concluding lines. As we shall see later, however, nonstructural repetition has its own very special dynamics.)

If, as I have been suggesting, we entertain the notion that whatever conditions contribute to our sense of the validity of an utterance also strengthen our sense of its closure, we may then find it profitable to ask what these conditions usually are. The condition that I have just been speaking of can be referred to for convenience as *predetermination:* that is, when the form or occurrence of a certain terminal element has been previously implied and is consequently expected by the reader. An utterance tends to seem valid, however, not only when it conforms to our expectations, but also when it confirms our experience. If someone says, "It is raining outside," we need not have *expected* him to say it in order to feel that it is true—not if we have just observed that it is, indeed, raining outside. I have already mentioned the broader sense in which poems confirm our own experience, but in that sense it is not particularly relevant to closure. It becomes most significant, however, when we add that the "experience" confirmed by an utterance may be, in itself, a *verbal* experience. When someone says, "MacBride wants to repeal the Federal Income Tax," we may reply, "Yes, I know, I just read it in the paper." Here, what we are told seems valid because it confirms not a direct experience but something that we "know" only in the sense that we had been told it before. (Part of what makes the newspaper account itself seem valid will be considered in a moment.) The fact remains, however, that when an utterance is repeated, its second occurrence, by confirming our experience of the first, will to that extent tend to appear valid.

It would seem, moreover, that this psychological tendency is so subtle, strong, and pervasive that it will affect our experience of even the most minute elements of an utterance. In other words, when a line, phrase, or even a sound is repeated, the second occurrence will confirm (by conforming to) our experience of the first and, to that extent, acquire a measure of validity. Lewis Carroll whimsically depicted this psychological susceptibility in "The Hunting of the Snark":

> "'Tis the voice of the Jubjub!" he suddenly cried.
>   (This man, that they used to call "Dunce.")
> "As the Bellman would tell you," he added with pride,
>   "I have uttered that sentiment once.
>
> "'Tis the note of the Jubjub! Keep count, I entreat,
>   You will find I have told it you twice.
> 'Tis the voice of the Jubjub! The proof is complete.
>   If only I've stated it thrice."
>
> The Beaver had counted with scrupulous care,
>   Attending to every word:
> But it fairly lost heart, and outgrabe in despair,
>   When the third repetition occurred.[3]

We are also familiar with it as it is exploited by the techniques of the "hard sell," and it is likely that rumor works the same way: the

[3] "Fit the Fifth," lines 29–40. *Logical Nonsense: The Works of Lewis Carroll,* eds. Philip C. Blackburn and Lionel White (New York, 1934), p. 279.

second or third time around, the otherwise questionable proposition has been confirmed, as it were, by having been previously affirmed. "Yes," one says, "I heard that before."

We should not be surprised, then, that certain forms of verbal repetition are especially effective closural devices. A very important distinction must be made, however, between systematic repetition and nonstructural (or, as I have called it before, "occasional") repetition. In the former, a pattern of recurrence sets up an expectation which, though it is repeatedly fulfilled, is also strengthened with each successive recurrence. And, as I pointed out in chapter 2, the systematic repetition of formal elements (as in rhyme, meter, couplet series, etc.) is consequently more a force for continuation than for closure. *Occasional* repetition, however (as in irregular internal rhyme or alliteration), by imparting validity to the terminal recurrence of a formal element, does operate as an effective closural device.

Our allusion just above to newspaper accounts brings up a third condition for the sense of truth which also has significance for poetic closure. Certain utterances which neither conform to our expectations nor confirm our experiences (verbal or otherwise) may nevertheless have the ring of truth because of a quality that we might call the *tone of authority*. The impersonality of press releases, for example, and the brevity of newspaper headlines certainly do not detract from this tone. Indeed, it would seem that the very fact that the assertions they offer are so unqualified enhances their immediate effect.

The authority of unqualified assertion is familiar to us from other more literary quarters. Dr. Johnson, most notably, made a personal style out of absolute declarations: "No, Sir, riches do not gain hearty respect; they only procure external attention. . . . Sir, there is no harm. What philosophy suggests to us on this topic is probable: what scripture tells us is certain. . . . No, Sir; a man always makes himself greater as he increases his knowledge." In spite of all the qualifications of his critical pronouncements that later literary sophistication has imposed, one still tends to be humbled by the great man's tone. We may make the transition to our special concerns here by observing that Johnson always seemed to have the last word in any conversation. Even when Boswell does record a rejoinder, no matter how reasonable and considered it was, it usually sounds feeble after that firm and stable Johnsonian thump.

Johnson's prose style has obvious affinities (formal as well as historical) with the neoclassical epigrammatic couplet, and, as we shall see later, the characteristics that define the epigram almost all either produce or arise from exceptionally strong closural effects. What I wish to point out here is that particular quality of Johnson's style which I have called "the tone of authority" and the features that can be found associated with it: the relative frequency of universals, superlatives, and absolutes (*all* Scotchmen, *no* woman, the *only* man in England, the *best* way, etc.), and the relative infrequency of self-qualifying expressions (perhaps, maybe, usually, more or less, I sometimes think, etc.). As we might expect, these are features which, when they appear in the concluding lines of a poem, will give it the ring of truth and strengthen the sense of closure.

The relation suggested in this section between the conditions of validity and those that secure closure does not prepare us for the effectiveness of all the devices I shall take up in the following pages. Rather than extend these general remarks, however, I shall now turn directly to the examination and illustration of the most common or otherwise interesting of them, reserving further introductory comments and speculations for the sections where they will be most appropriate.

II Formal Devices and Nonsystematic Repetition

Anyone who has worked with translations of poetry knows how difficult it is to reproduce in another language the crispness of the original poem. Translations tend to seem flat or two-dimensional not only because they lack or distort the connotations of the original words, but also because they lack or distort their mutually resonating sounds. Even if the translator has duplicated the meter and rhyme-scheme of a poem, the more subtle and less systematic organizations of sound—in alliteration or assonance, for example—will usually elude his efforts. The flatness of a translation is often most conspicuous at its conclusion, and where the power of a poem is closely related to its closural effects, as in an epigram, successful translation may be altogether impossible.

Consider, for example, Shakespeare's eighteenth sonnet:

> Shall I compare thee to a summer's day?
> Thou art more lovely and more temperate:
> Rough winds do shake the darling buds of May
> And summer's lease hath all too short a date;
> Sometime too hot the eye of heaven shines
> And often is his gold complexion dimmed,
> And every fair from fair sometime declines,
> By chance or nature's changing course untrimmed;
> But thy eternal summer shall not fade
> Nor lose possession of that fair thou ow'st,
> Nor shall Death brag thou wand'rest in his shade
> When in eternal lines to time thou grow'st:
> So long as men can breathe or eyes can see,
> So long lives this, and this gives life to thee.

With respect to the poem's thematic structure, even a bluntly prosaic paraphrase of the concluding couplet would be adequately "conclusive." The particular power of these last lines, however, their striking sense of conviction and aphoristic rightness, is partly a product of elements that do not yield to facile translation. For one thing, the complete regularity of the meter, reinforced by the entirely monosyllabic diction, produces a strong, slow, and steady beat that hammers out each word distinctly and emphatically. Secondly, formal repetition and syntactic parallelism create a series of mutually reinforcing echoes: "So long . . . so long," "this . . . this," "lives . . . life," "man can breathe . . . eyes can see." To the extent that these repetitions involve whole words and phrases, they could be duplicated in another language. But there is also a complex pattern of alliteration, assonance, and internal rhyme, for which the translator might devise counterparts, but which he could not duplicate: "br*ea*the . . . *see*," "*l*ong . . . *l*ive . . . *l*ife," "l*iv*es . . . *giv*es," "*eye*s can *see* . . . l*i*fe to th*ee*." Although none of the formal features noted in this couplet could secure closure independently, their cumulative effect at the end of a poem is obviously strong. Conversely, any of the formal devices noted here will contribute some closural force when it appears as a terminal feature.

Metrical regularity at the end of a poem, especially when accompanied by monosyllabic diction, has closural effects for several reasons. First it is a re-establishment of the norm, the most probable and therefore the most stable arrangement of stresses. (Its closural effect will be strongest, of course, when the preceding lines or the poem as a whole have exhibited the widest metrical variations.) Also, as Sonnet 18 illustrates, metrical regularity may have an expressive effect that enhances closure; it suggests control, authority, and, in both senses, dependability. Finally, when metrical regularity is combined with monosyllabic diction, it will also suggest a slowing down of pace, which, because of the reader's innumerable extraliterary experiences, will be associated with an approaching halt. Some of these effects are illustrated in the final line of this poem by Walter Savage Landor:

> Stand close around, ye Stygian set,
>   With Dirce in one boat conveyed!
> Or Charon, seeing, may forget
>   That he is old and she a shade.[4]

[4] *Poems,* selected and introduced by Geoffrey Grigson (Carbondale, Ill., 1965), p. 62.

The closural force of this line arises not only from the regular meter and monosyllabic diction, but also from the alliteration, assonance, internal rhyme, and the rhythmic parallelism of the balanced antithesis. As I pointed out earlier, it is important to recognize the difference between such irregular or "occasional" sound-recurrence and the systematic or structural repetition of sounds, as in end-rhyme or true alliterative verse. When sound-recurrence is a structural principle it is not a closural force but, on the whole, a force for continuation. The principle is experienced by the reader as an expectation of recurrence, and while each occurrence confirms the expectation, it also extends it. Nonsystematic recurrence, on the other hand, does not operate upon the reader's expectations because by definition it is not systematic enough to create any. In the body of a poem, these occasional repetitions of formal elements have various effects ranging from euphony to emphasis. When they occur at the conclusion of a poem they also have closural effects of the general kind suggested in the previous section. That is, formal repetitions appear to give additional validity and thus stability to the terminal lines of a poem by introducing a verbal experience which is immediately "confirmed" by its recurrence.

As closural devices, alliteration, assonance, internal rhyme, and balanced antithesis (as well as the recurrence of whole words and phrases) are not only extremely common but also very conspicuous in styles which admit flagrant rhetorical figures, as may be readily seen in these concluding lines from some Tudor and Stuart lyrics:

> Thou farest as fruit that with the frost is taken:
> Today ready ripe, tomorrow all to shaken.[5]

> That happy, heavenly night, that night so dark and shady,
> Wherein my love had eyes that lighted my delight.[6]

[5] Henry Howard, Earl of Surrey, "Brittle Beauty"; text from *Silver Poets of the Sixteenth Century*, ed. Gerald Bullett (London, 1960), p. 119.

[6] "O night, O jealous night," from R. S.'s *Phoenix Nest* (1593); text from *Poetry of the English Renaissance*, eds. J. William Hebel and Hoyt H. Hudson (New York, 1957), p. 198.

For till to-morrow we'll prorogue this storm,
Which shall confound with its loud whistling noise
Her pleasing shrieks, and fan thy panting joys.[7]

Even when the repetition of formal elements is considerably less conspicuous than this, it may have comparable effects. Alliteration, for example, may be effective even when it does not involve initial sounds or stressed syllables. Consider this final couplet from Shakespeare's Sonnet 29:

For thy *s*weet *l*ove rememb'red *s*uch *w*ea*l*th brings
That then I *s*corn to change my *s*tate with *k*ings.

The sequence /swl/ in "sweet love" recurs in "such wealth," and the /sk/ of "scorn" is repeated in "state . . . kings." Although the second of these repetitions is subtle, it is perhaps even more effective for closure than the first, for after being broken by an intervening syllable, the "alliteration" is completed on the last word of the poem. A striking example of the closural effect of this sort of repetition appears in the final couplet of Spenser's *Amoretti* XV, in which the poet has catalogued his lady's physical charms:

But that which fairest is, but few behold,
Her mind adornd with vertues manifold.[8]

The final word *manifold* is not only end-rhymed, but it repeats the /mnd/ sequence of *mind* and echoes the prominent /f/ (*fairest, few*) of the previous line, thus constituting through sound alone a summary and reiteration of the entire couplet—decidedly "manifold."

The kind of formal recurrence illustrated by these lines has been

[7] Thomas Carew, "On the Marriage of T[homas] K[illegrew] and C[ecilia] C[rofts] . . ."; text from *Minor Poets of the Seventeenth Century*, ed. R. G. Howarth (London, 1959), pp. 129–30.

[8] *The Poetical Works of Edmund Spenser*, ed. J. C. Smith and E. de Selincourt (London, 1957), p. 565.

discussed by Kenneth Burke,[9] who mentions some other possibilities that are also of interest to us. He points out, for example, that phonetic "cognates" such as /m-b-p/, /f-v/, /n-d-t/, /j-ch/ or /z-s-sh/ may figure in what he calls "concealed alliteration"; and in the following couplet he would no doubt regard the repetitions of /m/, /p/, and /b/ as mutually alliterative:

> If *my* slight *M*use do *p*lease these curious days,
> The *p*ain *b*e *m*ine, *b*ut thine shall *b*e the *p*raise.[10]

Burke also mentions the possibility of "acrostic alliteration," where a sequence of consonants recurs in scrambled order, as in his example "tyrannous and strong" where "the consonant structure of the third word is but the rearrangement of the consonant structure of the first: t-r-n-s is reordered as s-t-r-ng." [11]

Burke's main concern with these more subtle forms of verbal recurrence involves, as the title of his essay indicates, their contribution to the total euphony of a poem. His major point, however, is that when one investigates the "musicality of verse," one cannot go about it by simply noting the recurrence of initial consonants in stressed syllables. To the extent that these formal features also contribute to closure, his observation serves us here as well.

Up to this point, we have considered those forms of verbal repetition which, conspicuously or subtly, tend to strengthen closure when they appear as terminal features. Closural effects may also be secured, however, when certain formal elements that appear *throughout* the poem (but not systematically) recur in its concluding lines. In a rigorously statistical study of a group of English sonnets, the linguist Dell H. Hymes observed that in a number of his sample poems a single word in the concluding line

[9] "On Musicality in Verse," in *The Philosophy of Literary Form* (New York, 1957), pp. 369–78.

[10] Shakespeare, Sonnet 38.

[11] *The Philosophy of Literary Form*, p. 371.

had what he called a "summative" relation to the poem as a whole.[12] Such a word not only "express[es] the theme of the poem (or octave or sestet)," but also contains the sounds that are dominant throughout it.[13] That is, certain vowels and consonant groups that occurred with particularly high frequency in the body of a poem would recur at the conclusion in a word that was also thematically significant.

Hymes was more interested in testing a particular approach than in reaching any general conclusions, but his investigations are certainly suggestive. One of the poems he considers is Keats's sonnet "To Sleep":

> O soft embalmer of the still midnight,
>   Shutting with careful fingers and benign,
> Our gloom-pleas'd eyes, embowr'd from the light,
>   Enshaded in forgetfulness divine:
> O soothest Sleep! if so it please thee, close
>   In midst of this thine hymn my willing eyes,
> Or wait the amen, ere thy poppy throws
>   Around my bed its lulling charities.
> Then save me, or the passèd day will shine
> Upon my pillow, breeding many woes,—
>   Save me from curious Conscience, that still lords
> Its strength for darkness, burrowing like a mole;
>   Turn the key deftly in the oiled wards,
> And seal the hushed Casket of my Soul.[14]

Hymes calculates that the dominant consonants are /sl/ (note *still, sleep, close, seal,* and the frequency of /s/ and /l/ individually) and that the dominant vowel sound in the sestet is /ow/

[12] "Phonological Aspects of Style: Some English Sonnets," in *Style and Language,* ed. Thomas A. Sebeok (New York, 1960), pp. 109–31.

[13] *Ibid.*, p. 118.

[14] *The Poetical Works of John Keats,* ed. H. W. Garrod (London, 1956), p. 368.

(*pillow, woes, burrowing, mole,* which are themselves echoes of the octaves' rhymes, *close* and *throws*). Both sound-groups, /sl/ and /ow/, recur in the "summative" word *Soul,* which is the final word of the poem. We may also surmise that the closural effect (with which Hymes was not concerned as such) is strengthened by terminal alliteration of *seal* and *Soul.*

Hymes also establishes a set of criteria (frequency and thematic significance) for what he calls "key words," and his procedure suggests that when such words recur at the conclusion of a poem they will also be "summative"—and, we might add, closural. In a less elaborately statistical reading of Frost's "After Apple-Picking," Reuben Brower observes that "since the [final] word 'sleep' has already occurred five times, it completes the rhyme and the poem with a special finality of sound and meaning." [15] And numerous other studies of the sound-patterns in particular poems have emphasized the quality of "rightness" that results from such terminal recurrences of key words or dominant sounds, or their tendency to make "the words come to us with all the force of inevitable verities. . . ." [16]

Hymes observes in passing that the notion of *summative* words does not take account of the effects of contrast, and that in certain poems the force of the final words may owe something to " 'surprise' value." [17] The "contrast" that he refers to is probably related to what we have called "terminal modification" (see chapter 2), which we might here describe as a failure of expected repetition at the conclusion of a poem. Certainly our consideration of the closural force of repetition is complicated by terminal modification, for the same effect would seem to arise from two

[15] *The Poetry of Robert Frost* (New York, 1963), p. 25.

[16] T. Walter Herbert, "Sound and Sense in Two Shakespeare Sonnets," *Tennessee Studies in English* (1958), p. 52. See also David I. Masson, "Free Phonetic Patterns in Shakespeare's Sonnets," *Neophilologus,* 38 (1954): 277–89.

[17] "Phonological Aspects of Style," pp. 121 and 130.

more or less opposite conditions: repetition and the failure of repetition. There is no inconsistency, however, for the dynamics of closure are different for each condition, and they are not, in any case, really opposite. In nonsystematic repetition, the terminal recurrence of sounds used earlier strengthens closure by confirming the reader's experiences, thus reinforcing his sense of the "rightness" of the lines in question. In terminal modification, on the other hand, a final failure of systematic repetition strengthens closure by qualifying the reader's expectation of continuation; it suggests to him that something different is happening and that his earlier expectations are no longer appropriate. There is no reason why both devices cannot be present in the same lines; for since the dynamics of each are independent, one device compounds rather than cancels out the effect of the other.

III Puns, Parallelism, and Antithesis

Certain devices are not easily distinguished as either formal or thematic precisely because their effects arise from a relation between both formal and thematic elements. Puns, for example, depend upon homonyms, words that are formally identical (or similar) and thematically different. A pun might be described as a linguistic structure that creates expectations in terms of which the different meanings of a homonym have equal appropriateness. Their witty effect arises from the consequent havoc they play with the reader's expectations, simultaneously fulfilling and surprising them. The effectiveness of a pun obviously depends upon its context; a list of homonyms is not witty.

Puns are not in themselves closural devices, but their interesting relation to closural effects makes it worth our while to give them some attention here. The last line of the following epigram makes use of what is probably the most poetically fruitful homonym in English, "lie":

Of a Cozener

And was not death a lusty struggler
In overthrowing James the Juggler?
His life so little truth did use
That here he lies—it is no news.[18]

The effect of the pun here depends to a large extent upon its position in the line, and particularly upon its relation to the rhyme. As it stands, the pun is, in itself, anti-closural, for it occurs at that point in the line where the *demand* for completion seems to be greatest. Since the epigram is evidently of the post-mortem variety, the phrase "here he lies" will clearly have its sepulchral meaning. At the same time, the title and the sequence "so little truth . . . that . . ." will make the meaning of "prevaricates" equally appropriate. The result is a full ambiguity, with two possible meanings of equal strength—a psychological circumstance of maximum instability for the reader. The last phrase, "it is no news," does not resolve the ambiguity, but affirms it. Nevertheless, the phrase has closural force, for the affirmation (its authority reinforced by rhyme) transforms an unstable ambiguity into a stable one. Both expectations are allowed to be fulfilled and closure is secured.

If we rewrite the last two lines slightly, the pun can have a completely different effect with respect to closure:

Since never truth did he advise,
It is no news that here he lies.

Here the pun is far from being anti-closural or creating instability. On the contrary, its position at the very end of the poem, suggesting that no further explanation or resolution will be offered, functions as an affirmation of its own double meaning. The affirmation

[18] John Hoskins; text from Hebel and Hudson, *Poetry of the English Renaissance*, p. 527.

is given further authority by the explicit "it is no news" that introduces it, by the rhyme, and by all the other structural forces such as meter and syntax which determine that the line end at that point—with a monosyllabic verb. The *wit* of the pun remains, however, for its ambiguity continues to juggle our responses back and forth; and we are delighted, as it were, to see ourselves catch the ball each time.

Puns, then, are neither closural nor anti-closural in themselves, but they are common terminal features, because either they enhance the effect of other closural devices (setting them up through maximized instability), or their characteristic effect, wit, is maximal when combined with strong closure.

The devices of parallelism and antithesis arise, like puns, from a relation between formal and thematic elements, the relation here being that of *coincidence.* W. K. Wimsatt, Jr. has pointed out that while there are numerous instances of parallelism and antithesis implicit in the most casual utterance, we tend to regard and record them as such only when they are emphasized by the positions of, or formal similarities among, the members.[19] The same factors are involved when parallelism and antithesis have closural force. That is, when a thematic connection or opposition is to some degree reinforced by syntactic correspondence and formal repetition, the linguistic structure so formed appears particularly stable and authoritative.

The effect is familiar in maxims, *sententiae,* and traditional proverbs. What distinguishes the snappy force of "Look before you leap" from the flatness of "Look before you jump" is simply the alliteration of the antithetical verbs. Similarly, it is partly the formal reinforcement of alliteration, assonance, and syntactic parallelism that gives the following maxims their intimidatingly oracular quality, that makes them seem so incontrovertibly *so:* "An ounce of discretion is worth a pound of wit"; "Dead men don't

[19] *The Prose Style of Samuel Johnson* (New Haven, 1941), pp. 15–20, 38–43.

bite" (doubly alliterated if we regard /m/ and /b/ as phonetic cognates); "If you sing before breakfast you'll cry before night"; "Love comes in at the window and goes out at the door"; "Out of debt, out of danger." [20]

The closural force of formal parallelism and antithesis would seem to be the result of the psychological principles mentioned at the beginning of this chapter. These devices involve sound-repetitions that "confirm" a linguistic experience by duplicating its elements, and the measure of control suggested by emphatically patterned speech will reinforce the reader's or hearer's sense of its authority.

Parallelism and antithesis are common features of the concluding couplets of the English sonnet, where the rhyme pattern and formal structure of the poem encourage and enhance epigrammatic closure. Spenser's *Amoretti* XLVII concludes as follows:

> O mighty charm which makes men loue theyr bane,
> and thinck they dy with pleasure, liue with payne.[21]

The parallelism of the last line involves the repetition not only of certain parts of speech in a certain order but of whole words as well: [verb] *with* [noun], [verb] *with* [noun]. The double antithesis ("dy"–"pleasure"; "liue"–"payne" and its permutation "dy"–"liue"; "pleasure"–"payne") sets up something like a mathematical ratio, where the reader can easily "solve for x," in this case the final word, "payne." The alliteration seems to confirm the solution, and its stability is further reinforced not only by the rhyme but by the repetition of other formal elements from the last phrase in the line above: "loue theyr bane"—"liue with payne."

The effect of such devices may be readily appreciated in the

[20] *The Oxford Dictionary of English Proverbs*, compiled by William George Smith (Oxford, 1935), pp. 43, 83, 215, 279, and 350. An equally important source of the oracular quality of maxims is discussed below in section V as "unqualified assertion."

[21] *Poetical Works*, p. 570.

concluding couplet of Shakespeare's Sonnet 124, since its meaning has eluded most readers [22] although its closural force is apparent:

> If my dear love were but the child of state,
> It might for Fortune's bastard be unfathered,
> As subject to Time's love or to Time's hate,
> Weeds among weeds, or flowers with flowers gathered.
> No, it was builded far from accident:
> It suffers not in smiling pomp, nor falls
> Under the blow of thrallèd discontent,
> Whereto th'inviting time our fashion calls;
> It fears not policy, that heretic
> Which works on leases of short-numb'red hours,
> But all alone stands hugely politic,
> That it nor grows with heat nor drowns with showers.
> To this I witness call the fools of Time,
> Which die for goodness, who have lived for crime.

The syntactic parallelism of the last line gives to the double antithesis ("die"–"lived"; "goodness"–"crime") a stability and authority which very little in its apparent significance will countenance. The "fools of Time" are not as effective as witnesses to the validity of the poem's statement as are the devices through which they are characterized.

The closural effects of parallelism and antithesis may also be reinforced by the more subtle kinds of alliteration mentioned in the preceding section, as this concluding passage from Sir John Suckling's "Against Absence" shows:

> Return then back, and feed thine eye,
> Feed all thy senses, and feast high:

[22] For a review of the problem and two noble (but conflicting) attempts at a solution, see Arthur Mizener's "The Structure of Figurative Language in Shakespeare's Sonnets," *The Southern Review*, 5 (1940): 730–47, and more recently, John Dover Wilson, *An Introduction to the Sonnets of Shakespeare . . .* (New York, 1964), pp. 69–70.

Spare diet is the cause love lasts,
For surfeits sooner kill than fasts.[23]

The last line here illustrates Burke's "acrostic alliteration" and Hymes's "summative words." The dominant consonant group in the quatrain is /f-s/ (*feed, senses, feast, spare, for, surfeits, sooner*), appropriately "summed" in the final word, *fasts*. This word also alliterates acrostically with its antithesis *surfeits* and doubly with *feast*, which might be regarded as its more remote antithesis. All these repetitions combine with the most obvious one, rhyme, to give closural force to the final word.

We may conclude this section with a glance at the last lines of another of Suckling's poems, "Love and Debt Alike Troublesome":

And he that is content with lasses clothed in plain woolen,
May cool his heat in every place: he need not to be sullen,
Nor sigh for love of lady fair; for this each wise man knows—
As good stuff under flannel lies, as under silken clothes.[24]

The aphoristic quality that Suckling intended for the last line (what "each wise man knows") requires strong closure, and it is secured through an antithesis reinforced by the pun on *stuff* as well as syntactic parallelism and multiple alliteration. *Stuff . . . flannel lies* alliterates with *silken clothes* (/s-l-n-l-s/), and the antithesis of "flannel" and "silken" also involves repetition of sounds that had been dominant in the quatrain up to that point: /f/, /l/ and /s/. A high incidence of formal parallelism and antithesis obviously tends to produce what we call "epigrammatic" effects; and when such devices occur at the conclusion of a poem they also have striking closural force. The relation between epigram and closure has, of course, been widely recognized. It is significant and revealing enough, however, to deserve special consideration in this study, which it will receive in chapter 5.

[23] Text in Howarth, *Minor Poets of the Seventeenth Century*, p. 201.
[24] *Ibid.*, p. 219.

IV Thematic Devices: Closural Allusions

One of the most obvious ways in which a poem can indicate its own conclusion thematically is simply to say so. In the final stanza of Milton's ode "On the Morning of Christ's Nativity," for example, there occurs the line, "Time is our tedious Song should have its ending." [25] It is also obvious that this sort of explicit announcement can only rarely be accommodated by a poem's thematic structure, and that its closural force is gained at the expense of the illusion of dramatic immediacy. Explicit self-closural references are, in fact, only rarely encountered, but something a little different, closural *allusions*, are extremely common. The most casual survey of the concluding lines of any group of poems will reveal that in a considerable number of them there are words and phrases such as "last," "finished," "end," "rest," "peace," or "no more," which, while they do not refer to the conclusion of the poem itself, nevertheless signify termination or stability. The following examples (italics mine) will suggest how, in a variety of styles, this possibility can be realized, and with what effect.

> His servants he with new acquist
> Of true experience from this great event
> *With peace* and consolation hath *dismist,*
> And *calm* of mind, *all passion spent.*
>
> [John Milton, *Samson Agonistes*] [26]

> Thou at stupendous truth believ'd;—
> And now the matchless *deed's atchiev'd,*
> DETERMINED, DARED, and DONE.
>
> [Christopher Smart, "A Song to David"] [27]

[25] *Complete Poems and Major Prose,* ed. Merritt Y. Hughes (New York, 1957), p. 50.

[26] *Ibid.,* p. 593.

[27] *The Collected Poems of Christopher Smart,* ed. Norman Callan (Cambridge, Mass., 1949), I, 367.

Thus Nature spake—*The work was done—*
How soon my Lucy's race was run!
She died, and left to me
This heath, this *calm,* and quiet scene;
The memory of what has been,
And *never more will be.*
[William Wordsworth, "Three years she grew"] [28]

Oh, *cease!* must hate and death return?
Cease! must men kill and die?
Cease! drain not to its dregs the urn
Of bitter prophecy.
The world is weary of the past,
Oh, might it die or *rest at last.*
[Percy Bysshe Shelley, *Hellas*] [29]

I've known her—from an ample nation—
Choose One—
Then—*close* the Valves of her attention—
Like Stone—
[Emily Dickinson, "The Soul Selects her Own Society"] [30]

I look and see it there, shrinking, shrinking,
I look back at it amid the rain
For the *very last time;* for my sand is sinking,
And I shall traverse old love's domain
Never again.
[Thomas Hardy, "At Castle Boterel"] [31]

[28] *The Poetical Works of Wordsworth,* ed. Thomas Hutchinson, rev. ed. E. de Selincourt (London, 1961), p. 148.

[29] *The Complete Poetical Works of Shelley,* ed. Thomas Hutchinson (London, 1960), p. 478.

[30] *The Complete Poems of Emily Dickinson,* ed. Thomas H. Johnson (Boston, 1960), p. 143.

[31] *Collected Poems* (New York, 1931), p. 331.

You are nomad yet; the lighthouse beam you own
Flashes like Lucifer, through the firmament.
Earth's axis varies; your dark central core
Wavers a candle's shadow, *at the end.*

[William Empson, "Legal Fiction"] [32]

The still figure
Beyond the flow
Listens, listened
Aeons ago.
Ever a-flutter
Must all words be.

Here is an end.

[I. A. Richards, "By the Pool"] [33]

Among these passages, only the concluding lines of *Samson Agonistes*—which reflect Milton's effort to suggest or create the classical cathartic effect of tragedy—would seem intended as specifically closural. In all of the others, the words and phrases to which I have drawn attention obviously have functions and effects not directly related to closure. In Emily Dickinson's lines, for example, the soul's "closure" is, of course, the point of the poem, and we might hesitate to think of it as a "device" to secure poetic closure. It might, in fact, seem improper to speak of any of these allusions as nonstructural devices, for they are hardly gratuitous and clearly of importance in, if not actually determined by, the

[32] *Collected Poems* (New York, 1949), p. 26. This example and the one below happen to be from the two particular poems discussed by I. A. Richards in the essay mentioned earlier, "How Does a Poem Know When It is Finished?" (see pp. 96–98 above). They are certainly handy illustrations of our point here; but although Richards scrutinized these poems quite closely from his own point of view, he did not comment upon, and apparently did not notice, the rather striking similarity of their conclusions. His concept of self-determination would not, of course, account for the occurrence or effect of the closural allusions.

[33] I. A. Richards, *Screens and Other Poems* (New York, 1959), p. 87.

poem's thematic structure. I think it may be maintained, however, that even when the appearance of such an allusion in the concluding lines of a poem can be completely accounted for in terms of the poem's thematic structure, the allusion will nevertheless have closural force. It is also likely that in certain instances the allusion may be regarded as an option, selected from other possibilities precisely for its closural effect. And, taking this one step further, it is possible to regard the thematic structure that seems to call for this sort of allusion as itself an option, selected just because it will, at the end of its development, yield a closural allusion.

In other words, the frequency of these allusions may testify not to their necessary relation to certain common thematic principles but to their extraordinary effectiveness in securing closure; and certain thematic principles may be common in poetry precisely because they set up the possibility for such references at their conclusions. This point is slippery because in speaking of art the distinction between causes and effects is often meaningless. A poem is, in a sense, caused by its own effects. That is, the poet is constantly making choices that are determined by his sense of their ultimate effectiveness. Given an infinity of experiences, attitudes, emotions, and recognitions, what the poet perceives as the occasion (broadly speaking) for writing a poem will depend not only upon his temperament, style, and motives, but upon his notions of the nature of poetry. Since these notions have usually involved the concept of the poem as an integral and well-closed work, we may surmise that certain experiences or themes (again broadly speaking) have offered themselves repeatedly as appropriate for poetic expression because they *could* be developed so as to yield adequate closure. It must often happen, in fact, that the *donnée* of a poem is its conclusion, that the poet began with the end, and that what the reader perceives as an ending determined by the poem's thematic structure may, from the poet's point of view, have been what determined that structure in the first place.

Some of these points are given further substance, and others are raised, by another form of closural allusion: references not to termination, finality, repose, or stability as such, but to events which, in our nonliterary experiences, are associated with these qualities—events such as sleep, death, dusk, night, autumn, winter, descents, falls, leave-takings and home-comings. The examples that follow have been selected to illustrate such allusions and, hopefully, to remind the reader of how often he has encountered them in poems of various periods and styles (italics again mine):

Western wind, when will thou blow?
The small rain down can rain—
Christ, if my love were in my arms
And *I in my bed* again!
[Anonymous, 15th century?] [34]

Ye warbling nightingales repair
From every wood to charm this air,
And with the wonders of your breast,
Each striving to excel the rest.
When it is time to wake him, *close your parts,*
And *drop down* from the trees with broken hearts.
[James Shirley, *Triumph of Beauty,* 1646] [35]

. . .—then on the shore
Of the wide world I stand alone, and think
Till love and fame *to nothingness do sink.*
[John Keats, "When I have fears"] [36]

The pallor of girls' brows shall be their pall;
Their flowers the tenderness of patient minds,
And each slow *dusk* a *drawing-down* of blinds.
[Wilfred Owen, "Anthem for Doomed Youth"] [37]

[34] Text from Hebel and Hudson, *Poetry of the English Renaissance,* p. 42.
[35] *Ibid.,* p. 406.
[36] *Poetical Works,* p. 366.
[37] *Collected Poems,* ed. C. Day Lewis (Norfolk, Conn., 1964), p. 44.

Only at unconjectured intervals,
By will of him on whom no man may gaze,
By word of him whose law no man has read,
A questing light may rift the sullen walls,
To cling where mostly its infrequent rays
Fall golden on the patience of *the dead.*
[Edward Arlington Robinson, "Many are Called"] [38]

The eminence *is gone* that met your eye;
The winding savage, too, has *sunk away.*
Now, like a summer myth, the meadows lie,
Deep in the calm of silvan slow decay.
[Yvor Winters, "John Day, Frontiersman"] [39]

And, in the isolation of the sky,
At *evening,* casual flocks of pigeons make
Ambiguous undulations as they *sink*
Downward to darkness, on extended wings.
[Wallace Stevens, "Sunday Morning"] [40]

In none of these passages is the noted allusion gratuitous with respect to the poem's thematic structure; even without these structures before us, however, I think the independent effectiveness of the allusions in strengthening our sense of stability, finality, and repose is quite evident. We could attribute the closural effects here to that psychological catchall, "association," noting that death, night, autumn, and farewells are terminal events, that references to them would presumably signify or suggest that something was ending, and that by some process of psychological conduction this significance might be conveyed to the reader's experience of the poem itself. It is possible, however, that the closural effect of these allusions sometimes arises from a phenomenon more specific than

[38] *Collected Poems* (New York, 1937), pp. 581–2.
[39] *Collected Poems* (Denver, 1960), p. 106.
[40] *The Collected Poems* (New York, 1961), p. 70.

"association." For we may observe that, in those lines which involve references to terminal *motion* (such as falling or sinking), there is a kinesthetic aspect to our responses, as if we were subliminally, but nevertheless physically, participating in the motion so described. We recognize that the phrase "large red apple" can evoke a visual image, and that the phrase "mournful winter wind" can evoke an auditory image. Similarly, the phrases "stretched painfully" or "stood on tiptoe" or "crumpled into a heap" can evoke what might be called a "kinesthetic image": not a picture of the event from the outside, as it were, but a sense of what it feels like to be engaged in it. If the possibility of this phenomenon is granted (recognizing that it would probably vary greatly among readers), then we can refer to it the closural effect of certain kinds of terminal allusions. In other words, references to terminal motion may strengthen the reader's experience of closure by inviting him to re-enact a physical event which itself terminates in repose or stability.[41]

A final observation of general relevance to this chapter perhaps needs emphasis. In none of the passages quoted above does closure depend exclusively upon the particular device it was selected to illustrate. We may, in fact, observe in most of them the other closural devices discussed earlier in this chapter. Nonsystematic alliteration, for example, appears in the lines from Stevens and Winters, syntactic parallelism in "Western wind," and metrical regularity and monosyllabic diction in Owen's poem. The point is not that any of these devices can secure closure in itself, but that it will, occurring as a terminal feature, strengthen the reader's sense of stability, climax, finality, or ultimateness. Like almost all the other devices described here, allusions to closure may appear at points in a poem where closure itself is undesirable, even in the same poem in which they ultimately occur as terminal features. It

[41] More or less subliminal kinesthetic identification is not, of course, confined to the experience of poetry or even of language or art. A spectator at a ballet performance or a football game may be physically exhausted at the end of it though he never left his seat.

could hardly be claimed, for example, that alliteration, parallelism, or references to night and death appear only in the last lines of poems. They will, however, have closural effects when they *do* occur at the conclusion of a poem, for there they can combine either with structural forces for closure or with other nonstructural devices.

Thomas Carew's "Song" provides an interesting illustration of this last point, for references to closure appear in each of its stanzas, but with appropriate closural *effect* only in the concluding one:

> Ask me no more where Jove bestows,
> When June is past, the fading rose;
> For in your beauty's orient deep
> These flowers, as in their causes, sleep.
>
> Ask me no more whither doth stray
> The golden atoms of the day;
> For in pure love heaven did prepare
> Those powders to enrich your hair.
>
> Ask me no more whither dost haste
> The nightingale, when May is past;
> For in your sweet dividing throat
> She winters, and keeps warm her note.
>
> Ask me no more where those stars light,
> That downwards fall in dead of night;
> For in your eyes they sit, and there
> Fixed become as in their sphere.
>
> Ask me no more if east or west
> The phoenix builds her spicy nest;
> For unto you at last she flies,
> And in your fragrant bosom dies.[42]

[42] Text from Howarth, *Minor Poets of the Seventeenth Century*, pp. 148–49.

The thematic structure of this poem is what was described in chapter 3 as "paratactic"; that is, it "develops" not through any sequence but through thematic repetition, here a conceit that is repeated with variations in each stanza. This structural principle of "variations on a theme" is, moreover, emphasized by extensive verbal repetitions sustained through the final stanza. There is, in other words, no apparent terminal modification; and since a paratactic structure does not determine its own conclusion, and systematic repetitions are themselves forces for continuation, the *structural* sources of closure in this poem are minimal. Most readers would agree, however, that Carew's lyric concludes with a strong sense of climax, stability, and repose. The sources of closure here, then, must be primarily nonstructural, the product of certain features of the final stanza that distinguish it from the others.

Now it is obvious that this stanza offers closural allusions ("at last" and "dies"), but so does each of the other stanzas (except, to be precise, the second); the fourth stanza in particular contains several strong references of this kind ("*light* [i.e. settle]," "*downwards fall* in *dead* of *night*," "they *sit* . . . *fixed*"). These repeated allusions to termination and stability in the earlier stanzas might be expected to weaken the closural effect of any *terminal* reference of this kind, for when one has said "finally" too often, the finality of its really last occurrence will not be very strong. It is like the boy crying "Wolf!" And yet the final stanza is not at all anticlimatic, nor would any of the other stanzas, including the fourth, have been so effective a conclusion. What, then, makes the difference?

We might observe, to begin with, that although the conceit repeated in each stanza involves a closural concept (fading, falling, disappearing, or dying), it also involves the idea of rebirth. The phoenix dies, but will, of course, be reborn. The poet's mistress is not its grave, nor was she the grave of the roses, which sleep in her beauty "as in their causes"; that is, the flowers return in her to their condition of unrealized essence. The death of the phoenix is, then, the counterpart to the disappearance of the roses, "golden atoms," nightingale, and stars of the earlier stanzas, with the lady conceived of as something like a link between one appearance (or incarnation) and the next in the natural cycle of each. But it is only in this final stanza that the idea of rebirth, though still implicit, is effectively subordinated to the idea of transcendent permanence and finality. This particular hyperbolic conceit, involving the death of the phoenix, the terminal point of a lengthy and eternally repeated cycle of process, offers a symbol of ultimateness that could hardly be surpassed.

Secondly, there is, after all, a very subtle terminal modification in the third line of this stanza, the effect of which can be best appreciated when it is compared to the earlier corresponding lines:

> For in your beauty's orient deep . . .
> For in pure love heaven did prepare . . .
> For in your sweet dividing throat . . .
> For in your eyes they sit, and there . . .
> For unto you at last she flies, . . .

The difference is not only in the substitution of the climactic "unto you" for "in . . . ," but in the fact that only here is the line end-stopped, obliging a slight pause before the concluding line of the stanza. This rhythmic change is effective not only in *being* a change, but in giving special integrity and emphasis to the final line of the poem. It suggests, and also functions very much like, the rhetorical pause that a speaker may make to set the stage for his last clinching statement.

Finally, the closural references in this stanza may not be more numerous or, in a sense, stronger than those in the fourth, but they are especially effective. The phrase "at last," reinforced by its own assonance and duration, announces a conclusion, and that conclusion is sealed by the final word, "dies." Because of the obvious effect of end-rhyme, and here also because of the syntactic suspension resolved only with the verb, *that* word in that position will draw to itself all the forces of termination and repose discussed above—and all those created by the reader's response to what is, more than sleep, winter, or the permanence of the fixed stars, the most personal and ultimate of ultimates.

V Thematic Devices: Unqualified Assertion

An utterance apparently tends to sound particularly valid when it is delivered in the form of an unqualified assertion. Consider, for example, the following group of remarks:

> He probably tells the truth.
> No doubt he tells the truth.
> I do believe he tells the truth.
> I assure you he tells the truth.
> He tells the truth.

The last is clearly the most convincing, for even where the qualifying phrases have ostensibly been added to strengthen credibility, they actually have the effect of weakening it. They suggest that the speaker has some reason to emphasize the validity of his assertion, and our experiences with our own speech and that of others will make us sense that among those reasons is his own doubt of its validity or his recognition of the grounds for his listener's doubt. The *unqualified* assertion, on the other hand, conveys a sense of the speaker's security, conviction, and authority. Since he did not guard or cover himself with implicit or explicit reservations, we assume that he did not need to.

The closural force of unqualified assertion is also suggested by this series; for in the order in which they are listed they evoke a simple but structured dramatic situation, and we can readily imagine the final remark as the conversation stopper. The last speaker is appropriately so because, in its unqualified absolutness, his assertion is effectively "the last word." It has a quality of ultimateness and stability, as if nothing further need be or could be said.

Since nonqualification is essentially a negative characteristic, its closural force is difficult to illustrate in particular poems; one could only indicate the *absence* of certain words and phrases in their concluding lines. There is, however, another aspect to nonqualification which does involve positive characteristics, the effects of which can be observed in individual poems and discussed more generally. We may recognize, that is, that there are words and phrases which, although they are qualifiers grammatically, are nevertheless nonqualifying in expressive function or effect. There is, for example, more than a numerical difference between "99 per cent" and "all," and a world of difference between "for twenty years" and "forever," or between "rarely" and "never." The point is that when universals and absolutes (words such as "all," "none," "only," and "always") occur in assertions, they are themselves the expressions of the speaker's inability or refusal to qualify. And we may add superlatives to this category, for they have the same expressive effect. To speak of what is "highest," "last," "best," or closural effects when they occur as terminal features in an utter- "most" is, of course, also to assert extremities, absolutes, and ultimates. All such nonqualifying words and phrases tend to have ance or a poem, for they not only reinforce our sense of the speaker's conviction but are themselves expressions of comprehensiveness, climax, or finality. They imply that a point has been reached beyond which nothing further can or will be said because all that could be said has been. Some of these effects can be observed in the following examples, all of them the concluding lines of fairly familiar poems (italics mine):

> For vertue hath this better lesson taught,
> Within my selfe to seeke my *onelie* hire:
> Desiring *nought* but how to kill desire.
> [Sir Philip Sidney, "Thou Blind Man's Mark"] [43]

[43] *The Poems of Sir Philip Sidney*, ed. William A. Ringler, Jr. (Oxford, 1962), p. 161.

Lo! thy dread Empire, CHAOS! is restored;
Light dies before thy uncreating word:
Thy hand, great Anarch! lets the curtain fall;
And *Universal* Darkness buries *All.*
[Alexander Pope, *The Dunciad*] [44]

Oh heart! oh blood that freezes, blood that burns!
Earth's returns
For whole centuries of follies, noise and sin!
Shut them in,
With their triumphs and their glories and the rest!
Love is best.
[Robert Browning, "Love Among the Ruins"] [45]

And thou, who didst the stars and sunbeams know,
Self-school'd, self-scann'd, self-honour'd, self-secure,
Didst walk on Earth unguess'd at. Better so!
All pains the immortal spirit must endure,
All weakness that impairs, *all* griefs that bow,
Find their *sole* voice in that victorious brow.
[Matthew Arnold, "Shakespeare"] [46]

Deep with the first dead lies London's daughter,
Robed in the long friends,
The grains beyond age, the dark veins of her mother,
Secret by the unmourning water
Of the riding Thames.
After the first death, *there is no other.*
[Dylan Thomas, "A Refusal to Mourn the Death,
by Fire, of a Child in London"] [47]

[44] *The Poems of Alexander Pope,* ed. John Butt (New Haven, 1963), p. 800.

[45] *The Poetical Works of Robert Browning* (London, 1957), p. 218.

[46] *Poetical Works of Matthew Arnold* (London, 1913), p. 3.

[47] *Collected Poems* (New York, 1953), p. 112.

As these passages might suggest, the effect of unqualified assertion, of universals, absolutes, and superlatives, is not necessarily to reinforce our sense of the speaker's authority or of the actual validity of his assertions. Almost all of the examples, in fact, involve obvious hyperbole or overstatement. Hyperboles, however, can have the same sort of dramatic or contextual validity that we observed earlier in connection with the "illogical" conclusions of pseudo-logical poems, and may have closural force for similar reasons. They are experienced with reference to the speaker's motives, feelings, and circumstances; and, as we know from nonliterary situations, a speaker's desire or willingness to make hyperbolic assertions—"I shall love you forever," "All my thoughts are with you," "I wish only to make you happy"—reveals something of interest and value to us even though we recognize that the statement is improbable or the promise, like all promises, subject to time and fortune. Like italics or shouts, they reveal the pressure of intentions and circumstances so compelling or unusual that the ordinary resources of language are strained. The occurrence of hyperbole at the conclusion of a poem, then, is often a reflection and signal of emotional climax or extremity, a point at which the speaker is apparently striving for the ultimate, consummate, and most comprehensive expression of the motives and emotions that are the occasion of the poem. What is most significant here, of course, is the implication that, having reached that point, he cannot and need not go further.

These last observations are interestingly illustrated in Shakespeare's thirty-first sonnet, which develops through the logic and mathematics of hyperbole to a conclusion of comprehensive absoluteness:

> Thy bosom is endearèd with all hearts
> Which I by lacking have supposèd dead;
> And there reigns Love and all Love's loving parts,
> And all those friends which I thought burièd.
> How many a holy and obsequious tear

Hath dear religious Love stol'n from mine eye
As interest of the dead, which now appear
But things removed that hidden in there lie.
Thou art the grave where buried Love doth live
Hung with the trophies of my lovers gone,
Who all their parts of me to thee did give,
That, due of many, now is thine alone.
  Their images I loved I view in thee,
  And thou, all they, hast all the all of me.

In terms of the sonnet's central conceit, this last line is both logical conclusion and mathematical sum. Also, in the purity and extremity of its absoluteness, it brings the poem to a point where any further development would be superfluous and anticlimactic.

As we have seen, both the expressive and closural effects of unqualified assertion are complex and various. In the sort of bare, spare, or economical statements that we refer to as "epigrammatic," nonqualification suggests reserve, a sense of control, security, and authority. But there is a considerable difference in tone and effect between Thomas' "After the first death, there is no other," and Browning's "Love is best!" The refusal or inability to qualify may produce understatement or overstatement, both having closural force but each in a somewhat different way. The difference is obviously significant for poetic style and, as we shall see in the next chapter, it is reflected in what choice among these two possibilities is most congenial to the temper of modern poetry.

VI The Poetic Coda

In informal verbal situations such as chance encounters, letters to friends, or telephone conversations, the eventual obligation to conclude confronts the fact that unstructured discourse offers no handy termination point. Since abrupt cutoffs are psychologically unpleasant as well as impolite, we usually make use of some formula of conclusion to signal the approaching termination: "Well, it's been good to talk to you—give my regards to your wife . . . ," "So, that's about it for now . . . ," "Okay, I'll be seeing you soon—Good-bye." This last expression, "good-bye," has become almost obligatory in telephone conversations, probably because the speaker's gestures and facial expressions cannot be seen and the only signals are vocal ones. It is a particularly interesting expression, because it has retained hardly a vestige of its original meaning and form ("God be with ye"), and the corruption suggests that its "meaning" was always less significant that its function. It is likely that it always served the purpose of providing a genial signal of conclusion.

There is probably no language that does not have some conventional signal of this kind, and a poetic form of it is found in the Japanese *haiku*. Many of these poems conclude with a "word" (such as *kana* or *yo*) which, we are told, has no independent meaning and functions somewhat as a punctuation mark, thus frequently translated as "Ah," "Oh," or simply "!".[48] These terminal forms are called "cutting-words" (*keriji*), and if they mean anything at all, it is simply "this poem ends here." The effect and even the possibility of such a poetic convention is probably related to the long tradition and rigid specifications of the *haiku*. Nothing like it is found in modern European poetry, where no linguistic element appears that does not also appear in the language of ordinary discourse.[49] Perhaps the nearest comparable convention is the envoy of the medieval ballad, which, although it is not a word but a whole stanza and contains meaningful thematic material, nevertheless serves, like the *keriji*, as a terminal signal, a poetic farewell to the reader. The envoy is best considered, however, as a particularly obvious instance of a more general kind of closural

[48] Harold G. Henderson, *An Introduction to Haiku* (New York, 1958), pp. 175–8.

[49] The word *"amen,"* while not strictly speaking "European," may be regarded as an exception to this rule and is an interesting counterpart to the *keriji*. Cf. also, *"selah."*

device which in form and function is the counterpart of the musical coda.

In music, the coda is a terminal section of a piece or movement, added for the specific purpose of securing closure and clearly distinguished from the preceding portion by its structure. A counterpart is found in poetry wherever the conclusion of a poem forms a more or less discrete section, involving new formal or thematic principles, or (as in the envoy) both. As a closural force, the essential characteristics of the poetic coda have already been examined: first, in the discussions of terminal modification and, later, of "frames." As we observed, the terminal modification of formal principles arrests the reader's expectations of further development and thus prepares him for cessation. The frame could be thought of as a terminal modification of thematic principles. In any case, it achieves its closural effect by separating itself from the thematic structure of the rest of the poem and making a generalized or in some way stable comment upon it from "outside." (Both terminal modification and framing are characteristics of the envoy, which is commonly a truncated stanza and separates itself in various ways from the thematic structure of the poem proper.)

The following description of the function of the musical coda is suggestive:

> When a number of parts or voices were made to imitate or follow one another according to rigorous rules, it would often occur that as long as the rules were observed a musical conclusion could not be arrived at. Indeed sometimes such things were constructed in a manner which enabled the piece to go on forever if the singers were so minded. . . . In order to come to a conclusion a few chords would be constructed apart from the rigorous rules, and so the coda was arrived at. . . . In a series of variations, each several variation would only offer the same kind of conclusion as that in the first theme, though in a different form; and in . . . the very nature of things it would not be aesthetically advisable for such a conclusion to be very

> strongly marked, because in that case each several variation would have too much the character of a complete set piece to admit of their together forming a satisfactory continuous piece of music. Therefore it is reasonable when all the variations are over to add a passage of sufficient importance to represent the conclusion of the whole set instead of one of the separate component parts.[50]

As in music, so also in poetry, the coda is most often found as a special closural device when the structure of the work does not itself adequately determine a conclusion. As we might expect, then, a poetic coda of some sort is likely to appear when the thematic structure of a poem is paratactic, associative, or dialectic. Its effect may be illustrated first in the following poem, which is generally associative-paratactic in structure and concludes with an envoy-like stanza:

The Aged Lover Renounceth Love

  I loathe that I did love;
In youth that I thought sweet,
As time requires for my behove,
Me thinks they are not meet.
  My lusts they do me leave,
My fancies all be fled,
And tract of time begins to weave
Gray hairs upon my head.
  For age, with stealing steps,
Hath clawed me with his crutch;
And lusty life away she leaps
As there had been none such.
  My muse doth not delight
Me as she did before,

[50] "Coda," art. by C. Hubert H. Parry, *Grove's Dictionary of Music and Musicians*, ed. Eric Blom (London, 1954), II, 362.

My hand and pen are not in plight
As they have been of yore.
  For reason me denies
This youthly idle rhyme,
And day by day to me she cries,
Leave off these toys in time!
  The wrinkles in my brow,
The furrows in my face,
Say limping age will hedge him now
Where youth must give him place.
  The harbinger of death,
To me I see him ride;
The cough, the cold, the gasping breath,
Doth bid me to provide
  A pickaxe and a spade,
And eke a shrouding sheet;
A house of clay for to be made
For such a guest most meet.
  Me thinks I hear the clerk
That knolls the careful knell,
And bids me leave my woeful work
Ere nature me compel.
  My keepers knit the knot
That youth did laugh to scorn;
Of me that clean shall be forgot
As I had not been born.
  Thus must I youth give up,
Whose badge I long did wear;
To them I yield the wanton cup
That better may it bear.
  Lo, here the barëd skull
By whose bald sign I know
That stooping age away shall pull
Which youthful years did sow.
  For beauty, with her band,

These crooked cares hath wrought,
And shippëd me into the land
From when I first was brought.
  And ye that bide behind,
Have ye none other trust;
As ye of clay were cast by kind,
So shall ye waste to dust.[51]

The sequence of quatrains here is certainly not arbitrary; several of them are syntactically or in other ways thematically continuous, and the connectives "for" and "thus" in lines 9, 17, 41, and 49 suggest logical development. The structure is not logical, however, but associative and iterative. The poet is confronted by his own mortality, which he almost dispassionately acknowledges as it reveals itself in the signs, symptoms, and visions of his own decay and death. His reflections reach a climax of sorts in lines 25–40, but the "thus" of line 41 introduces a section that does not so much clinch as dissipate it; and since lines 41–48 are very similar to lines 21–24, they will seem either anticlimactic or repetitive. Indeed, at this point the poem threatens to become intolerably monotonous or obsessive, for the reader has been assailed by a relentless succession of "last things," and the question "Where do we go from here?" is beginning to press itself. The repetitive and associative structure of the poem has not yielded any principle that could determine a concluding point, and since almost every quatrain has rung with the finality of death, the closural force of any such allusion has been exhausted well before the last lines. In the conclusion of the poem, however, the poet unexpectedly turns from the incantatory evocation of his own death to a chilling envoy that sweeps the reader into the dismal fellowship of mortality. Though blunted by iteration, in this coda death's sting is sharpened once again, for here the poet has made it our own.

[51] Vaux, Thomas, Lord; text from Hebel and Hudson, *Poetry of the English Renaissance*, pp. 38–39.

We have already referred to the framing conclusion of "Lycidas" (see pp. 129–30, above) and observed how, in the final lines of the poem, Milton separates the identity of the poet-speaker from that of the elegist, "the uncouth Swain," and establishes a temporal context for the elegy proper. We might also notice that this passage is a self-contained formal unit, more regular (and conventional) in its rhyme pattern than the poem as a whole. In formal as well as thematic structure, then, it clearly isolates itself from the body of the poem. If, as has been suggested, the formal structure of "Lycidas" owes something to the *canzone*, this last section may very well reflect Milton's intention to provide the envoy (or *commiato*) common to that form.[52]

As a coda, the concluding lines of "Lycidas" are more like the fairly elaborate and gratuitously added section of a Beethoven symphony than the necessary closural section of a madrigal, rondel, or set of variations. In the latter musical forms, as in the envoy of a medieval lyric, a special conclusion is *required* because the generating principles of the work do not determine any concluding point or, of themselves, allow completion. In "Lycidas," however, as in some of Beethoven's works,[53] a coda appears after an otherwise adequate conclusion and serves not only as a locus of additional closural forces but also as a small "movement" in its own right, with significant new thematic material. It would certainly seem that the dialectic development of the themes in the elegy proper had reached a stable resolution in lines 165–85 (i.e., before the coda):

> Weep no more, woeful Shepherds weep no more,
> For *Lycidas* your sorrow is not dead,
> Sunk though he be beneath the wat'ry floor,
> So sinks the day-star in the Ocean bed,

[52] F. T. Prince, *The Italian Element in Milton's Verse* (Oxford, 1954), pp. 72–73.

[53] Cf. the sonatas Opp. 81 and 100, for example, and the "Eroica" Symphony. The construction of the coda in the latter work is discussed by Hugo Leichentritt in *Musical Form* (Cambridge, Mass., 1951), pp. 156–57.

And yet anon repairs his drooping head,
And tricks his beams, and with new-spangled Ore,
Flames in the forehead of the morning sky:
So *Lycidas*, sunk low, but mounted high,
Through the dear might of him that walk'd the waves,
Where other groves, and other streams along,
With *Nectar* pure his oozy Locks he laves,
And hears the unexpressive nuptial Song,
In the blest Kingdoms meek of joy and love.
There entertain him all the Saints above,
In solemn troops, and sweet Societies
That sing, and singing in their glory move,
And wipe the tears for ever from his eyes.
Now *Lycidas*, the Shepherds weep no more;
Henceforth thou art the Genius of the shore,
In thy large recompense, and shalt be good
To all that wander in that perilous flood.[54]

The elegist whose earlier reflections and reactions to his friend's death had moved irregularly through bitterness, despair, and nihilism has here reached the point where the death of promising and virtuous young men is seen as justified in a larger supernatural scheme of rewards and punishments, and where, finally, he has a more than consoling vision of Lycidas exalted to permanent blessedness. This penultimate passage, moreover, contains many of the "terminal" features that we have discussed before in this chapter, the repeated "weep no more," the ultimates and absolutes of "*all* the Saints" (178) who "wipe the tears *for ever* from his eyes" (181), and Lycidas himself "henceforth . . . the Genius of the shore, . . . good to *all* that wander in that perilous flood."

For those readers, however, to whom the questions raised in "Lycidas" remain more compelling than the answers, the coda itself is the more effective and perhaps the only possible "resolution." For, in focusing on the character of the speaker himself, it

[54] *Complete Poems and Major Prose*, pp. 124–25.

emphasizes that quality of the poem that associates it more closely with dramatic monologue than formal elegy, and it allows the reader to relate the earlier resolution to particular personal motives and circumstances.[55] Thus, whatever stability is lacking in the consolations themselves (and when a poem has offered and developed such profoundly disturbing reflections as are found here, the ultimate stability of any consolation would naturally remain retrospectively qualified) is provided by their referral to an implicit context. As I pointed out in the earlier discussion of these lines, the final quality of the conclusion is something more complex than closural repose, for it looks ahead to an undefined future:

> Thus sang the uncouth Swain to th'Oaks and rills,
> While the still morn went out with Sandals gray;
> He touch't the tender stops of various Quills,
> With eager thought warbling his *Doric* lay:
> And now the Sun had stretch'd out all the hills,
> And now was dropt into the Western bay;
> At last he rose, and twitch't his Mantle blue:
> Tomorrow to fresh Woods, and Pastures new.

Nevertheless, its stability is evident, and a number of clearly closural features mark it: simple and chiasmic parallelism (lines 190–91, and "fresh Woods, and Pastures new"), closural allusions (lines 187, 190–91, and "At last"), and, of course, the terminal rhyming couplet after a series of alternating rhymes.

A musical coda is often more than a few chords and may have an independent structure with the same characteristics, only more concentrated, as any integral piece or movement. When this structure is itself particularly well completed, the closural effect will be

[55] By "personal" I do not mean "autobiographical." The relation of the elegist to John Milton is another matter altogether. As always, I am speaking here of the fictional person whose utterance the poem represents. And Milton himself, by introducing a framing conclusion evidently written by someone other than "the uncouth Swain," certainly emphasizes this fiction.

carried over the entire piece of which it is the terminal portion. Consequently, one may secure closure for even the most unstructured work simply by appending to it an independently well-closed section. A corresponding poetic possibility is illustrated by numerous Romantic and post-Romantic poems, where an associative structure is concluded with this sort of terminal section. The last stanza, particularly the last five lines, of Keats's "Ode on a Grecian Urn" offers an independent structure that concludes with resounding finality:

When old age shall this generation waste,
Thou shalt remain, in midst of other woe
Than ours, a friend to man, to whom thou say'st,
'Beauty is truth, truth beauty,'—that is all
Ye know on earth, and all ye need to know.[56]

Every device that has been discussed in this chapter appears in these lines, and if Keats had deliberately set himself to construct the most securely closed poem ever written, he could hardly have bettered them. They are all there: verbal repetitions, monosyllabic diction, metrical regularity, formal parallelism, unqualified absolutes, closural allusions, and the oracular assertion of an utter and ultimate verity. And yet it is an open question whether or not these lines offer a poetically legitimate or effective resolution to the thematic structure of the entire ode. We shall return to the question in the next chapter, for it involves a broader one of considerable interest, namely whether strong closure may not become, in certain styles, a violation of the style itself.

[56] *Poetical Works*, p. 210.

5 *Further Aspects and Problems of Closure*

I Epigram and Epigrammatic

Closure is, of course, a relative matter. A poem may be gently though firmly closed, or slammed shut, locked, and bolted. Also, as the metaphor suggests, the ending of a poem is a gesture of exit, and like all gestures it has expressive value. The manner in which a poem concludes becomes, in effect, the last and frequently the most significant thing it says. The relation between these two aspects of closure, its relative strength and its expressive qualities, will concern us throughout the present chapter. It can be best appreciated in one of its most extreme forms—the epigram.

As an utterance, the epigram seems to be the last word on its subject. This quality can probably be referred to the origins of the form: engraved on tombs, statues, public buildings, or wherever an inscription was wanted to identify or characterize something both briefly and permanently, the epigram would stand, for all time, to all readers, as the ultimately appropriate statement thereupon. Since engraving is laborious and space limited, concision was obviously a physical and perhaps an economic necessity. And since it was impractical to carve, for example, a man's entire biography on his tombstone, the few markings that would remain as his most permanent testament would have to be entirely "to the point." Every word had to pay its way in reference and effect, while the final responsibility was to the truth—or to the sound of it, anyway. What was originally a practical problem apparently became, in time, as aesthetic one, with its own rewards; for concision and economy could be seen not as necessary limits but as expressive means. The strictly literary "art epigram" acknowledges its origins in its self-imposed brevity and in that quality of pointedness that brevity once required but now serves.[1]

The epigram is of particular interest to us here because the characteristics that we associate with it—witty or sententious conclusions, aphoristic formulations, balanced and alliterated repetitions, puns, and antitheses, and, indeed, brevity itself—can all be seen as either arising from or contributing to especially strong closural effects. In fact, the more closely we look, the more evident it becomes that what we usually mean by *epigrammatic* is something like "having maximal closure." As the preceding chapters have suggested, the conditions for maximal closure will arise when the structural principles in a poem predetermine its conclusion most rigorously and when the greatest number or concentration of certain features appear in its terminal lines. In such a poem, every element would be designed to set up or secure the conclusiveness of its conclusion. It would be a pre-eminently teleological poem and in a sense a suicidal one, for all of its energy would be directed toward its own termination.

[1] J. C. Scaliger insisted that pointedness (*argutia*) was the soul of the epigram, brevity an entailed or adventitious property (*Poetics, libri septem* [1561], quoted by James Hutton [see below], p. 62). This, however, was a Renaissance notion, not a classical one. As Hutton points out, the reverse is true of the original Greek inscriptionary epigram: "Its only *differentia* is brevity. Point, in the rhetorical sense, is relatively rare in the Greek epigram. . . . Point, however, is not long separable from brevity. . . ." (*The Greek Anthology in Italy to the Year 1800* [Ithaca, N.Y. 1935], p. 55).

The poem described here does not, I think, exist, but the epigram tends to apprach it in many respects.[2] We may observe, to begin with, that although an epigram is brief and sometimes seems to close almost as soon as it opens, it is nevertheless long enough to have a characteristic structure. Lessing described it as consisting of two parts, which he called *Erwartung* and *Aufschluss*.[3] We might translate this as "expectation" and "resolution" or (so as not to mix causes with effects) as "set-up" and "conclusion." What he had in mind is illustrated in the following epigram:

In Nigellum

If I should choose, yea, for my life,
To be thy hawk, Nigell, or wife,
I would the hawk choose of the one,—
She wears a hood, thy wife wears none.[4]

[2] It is difficult to make general observations on the epigram without engaging in the treacherous sport of definition stalking. The problem of finding for any literary term defining properties that will be both broad enough to accommodate historical usage and specific enough to be interesting is particularly harrassing with regard to the epigram, for the range and diversity of its moods and subjects are enormous. Also, attempts at normative definition must confront the long-standing controversy over the respective claims made for the Greek and Roman epigram as norm or model. (Recent attempts of this kind and reviews of the problem can be found in the following: T. K. Whipple, *Martial and the English Epigram . . .* [Berkeley, 1925]; James Hutton, *The Greek Anthology in Italy to the Year 1800;* H. H. Hudson, *The Epigram in the English Renaissance* [Princeton, 1947].) It may be that as a potential subject for formal definition, "the epigram" must remain an elusive or even chimerical animal. My intention here, however, is not to offer a definition as such, but to explore in terms of the present study what we mean by "epigrammatic" and to attempt to specify the causes and nature of the effects that seem most characteristic of the genre. My illustrations are drawn, therefore, from classical and modern periods, and if I scant the Greeks it is because my Greek is scanty.

[3] *Ammerkungen uber Das Epigramm* (1771), quoted in translation by H. H. Hudson, *The Epigram in the English Renaisssance, pp.* 9–13.

[4] From John Weaver's *Epigrams in the Oldest Cut and Newest Fashion* (1599); text in *Poetry of the English Renaissance,* ed. J. William Hebel and Hoyt H. Hudson (New York, 1957), p. 525.

The dash here marks the turn from set-up to conclusion; it is the point at which the forces for continuation are strongest, where the reader's expectation, in other words, is most acute. The set-up is the part of the epigram that both demands and implies a succeeding completion which, in turn, will be the locus of particularly strong closural forces. Lessing's two-part division is probably not as characteristic as that turn itself. The set-up may be relatively extensive and consist of more than a single movement. It may, for example, involve the title of the epigram or, as in the following poem, be formed by succeeding waves of "anticipation" that reach maximal tension at a certain point (here at the end of the fifth line):

On Gut

Gut eates all day, and lechers all the night,
So all his meate he tasteth over, twise:
And, striving so to double his delight,
He makes himselfe a thorough-fare of vice.
Thus, in his belly, can he change a sin,
Lust it comes out, that gluttony went in.[5]

We may think of the characteristic structure of the epigram, then, not as a division into two parts, but rather as a thematic sequence which reaches a point of maximal instability and then turns to the business of completing itself. Although this structure takes various forms in individual epigrams, it will be found to consist almost always of a highly concentrated or focused example of one of those thematic principles which do imply a definite termination.

Among the most common thematic structures in epigrams are those discussed earlier as "logical and syntactic sequence," that is, where the conventions of discourse condition us to expect an assertion of one form to be followed and completed by its particu-

[5] *Poems of Ben Jonson,* ed. George Burke Johnston (Cambridge, Mass., 1955), p. 61.

lar counterpart. In the following two poems, Lessing's divisions correspond to the obviously effective sequence of question and answer:

> You wonder why *Drab* sells her love for gold?
> To have the means to buy it when she's old.[6]

Of treason

> Treason doth never prosper; what's the reason?
> For if it prosper, none dare call it treason.[7]

Or, as here, the division follows the common syntactic pattern "if . . . (then) . . .":

> All hastens to its end. If life and love
> Seem slow it is their ends we're ignorant of.[8]

It is clear that the turn in this last epigram occurs not at the end of the first sentence, but after the phrase, "If life and love seem slow." The conclusion of the epigram is what completes *that* sequence. The first sentence is, of course, part of the set-up. What it sets up, however, in connection with the first part of the next sentence, is something like a puzzle: "Given that 'All hastens to its end,' why is it that life and love seem slow?" The resolution of the poem is the solution to that problem, and the pun self-validates it, thus securing closure. But closure here is obviously not just a matter of "Oh yes, of course, as you just said—*end, ends,* to be sure." The conclusion is stable, predetermined in form and syntax, reinforced by rhyme—and yet unexpected. It is this combination

[6] J. V. Cunningham, *The Exclusions of a Rhyme* (Denver, 1960), p. 97.

[7] From Sir John Harrington's *Elegant and Witty Epigrams* (1618); text in Hebel and Hudson, *Poetry of the English Renaissance,* p. 522.

[8] Cunningham, *Exclusions,* p. 73. Harrington's epigram on treason, by the way, also involves the use of an "if-then" sequence, and the turn there might properly be located after "For it it prosper."

of surprise and fulfilment that gives the last phrase its wit and the epigram its point.

The following is another example of the puzzle-solution sequence where once again the puzzle is a paradox which the conclusion explains or defends through a pun:

To Pertinax Cob

Cob, thou nor souldier, thiefe, nor fencer art,
Yet by thy weapon liv'st! Th'hast one good part.[9]

But here the puzzle is more explicitly presented as such, while the pun does not so much solve as extend it. The wit is not in the pointedness, but in the point—which the reader must "get" if closure is to be secured.

The same is true of this epigram by Crashaw, where the puzzle and its solution attest to, as well as depend upon, the paradox of the Incarnation:

Matthew 8. *I am not worthy that thou*
should'st come unto my roof.

Thy God was making hast into thy roof,
  Thy humble faith and feare keepes him aloofe:
Hee'l be thy Guest, because he may not be,
  Hee'l come—into thy house? no, into thee.[10]

Here we might notice also that the epigram proper is actually only the last two lines. The scriptural citation and the first two lines set up the set-up, providing (as titles frequently do in epigrams) just enough information and enough of a context to give the point its point.

A final example of the type is this epigram from *The Greek Anthology*, a warrior's dedication of his bow to the god Serapis:

[9] Jonson, *Poems*, p. 33.
[10] *The Poems of Richard Crashaw*, ed. L. C. Martin (Oxford, 1927), p. 90.

O Serapis, thine are the bow of horn and the quiver.
The quiver is empty.
The enemy has my arrows.[11]

As the puzzle is solved (why is the quiver empty, the offering defective?), the apparently apologetic confession turns to and is turned into a coldly proud assertion, touched with contempt (not only for the enemy but for the reader who, it is implied, should have know better) and perhaps with compassion. Although the final line is pointed, we would not think of it as witty. And yet there is a pun—for it is in a special sense that the enemy *has* the arrows.

There is an unmistakable rhythm to each of the epigrams quoted above, a swing that has much more to do with the poem's syntactic structure than with its meter or rhyme (although the latter are also involved), and its effect is almost graphic. In the first ("You wonder . . ."), the opening line seems to haul us up to a peak, while the closing line immediately lowers us, first evenly, but then, at the landing, with a bump. Although the rhythm is characteristic, the kinesthetic image for it is likely to vary with the tones and themes of the particular poem. In certain of Martial's epigrams, the effect might suggest some predatory animal drawing to a position of tense reserve and then lunging for the kill. In the following epigram, the kill is almost literal:

Semper agis causas et res agis, Attale, semper:
est, non est quod agas, Attale, semper agis.
si res et causae desunt, agis, Attale, mulas.
Attale, ne quod agas desit, agas animam. (I. lxxix)

(You are always doing the pleader and always doing the man of business, Attalus; whether there is or is not something to do, Attalus, you are always doing something. If business and plead-

[11] Kallimachos, "Dedication of a bow: to Serapis" (XIII:7); trans. Dudley Fitts, *Poems from the Greek Anthology* (New York, 1956), p. 9.

ings fail you, you do the mule-driver, Attalus. Attalus, that something to do may not fail you, do for yourself.)[12]

We might recall here allusions to the punch, sting, bite, or sense of almost (and perhaps, for the nervous system, actual) physical assault frequently associated with epigrammatic endings. The examples quoted thus far almost all attest to this, but not all epigrams are satiric, nor are their conclusions always mordant. Indeed, they are not even always witty. The structure I have been describing creates the conditions for strong closure, but the affective quality of that closure will be quite different if the epigram is, for example, elegiac, eulogistic, proverbial, or sacred. In other words, the expressive possibilities of an epigrammatic structure are not narrowly confined by its characteristic closural effect. Consider, for example, Jonson's epigram, "On my First Sonne":

Farewell, thou child of my right hand, and joy;
My sinne was too much hope of thee, lov'd boy,
Seven yeares tho' wert lent to me, and I thee pay,
Exacted by thy fate, on the just day.
O, could I loose all father, now. For why
Will man lament the state he should envie?
To have so soone scap'd worlds, and fleshes rage,
And, if no other miserie, yet age?
Rest in soft peace, and, ask'd, say here doth lye
Ben. Jonson his best piece of poetrie.
For whose sake, hence-forth, all his vowes be such,
As what he loves may never like too much.[13]

[12] Text and translation from the Loeb Classical Library edition of Martial's *Epigrams*, trans. Walter C. A. Ker (London, 1960), I, 78–79. As Professor Ker points out in a footnote: "This epigram cannot satisfactorily be translated: it plays on the meanings of *agere*, which means (*inter alia*) 'conduct,' 'do,' or 'drive.' " The point of the final phrase might be better rendered, however, by the colloquial "do yourself in."

[13] *Poems*, p. 23.

If the validity of the opposition be granted, we might say that the occasion of this poem would seem to lend itself more to lyrical than to epigrammatic utterance. This, however, is precisely the source of its power, for the poem ultimately serves not as an expression of emotions but as a containment of them. The measured rhythm and language of tenderness in the opening lines convey a sense of grief just under control. Although emotion breaks out in the fifth line, by the conclusion of the poem it has been securely mastered, and the last lines complete what we understand to have been, in every sense, a last farewell—it will not, and need not, be spoken again. The final couplet is neither ingenious nor witty, and yet the conclusion may certainly be regarded as epigrammatic. The characteristic effects of strong closure have been achieved here through a more subtle and, in this case, morally interesting device, namely ironic understatement. An epigram, as I suggested earlier, tends to define its subject for eternity, to view it *sub specie aeternitatis*. The understatement with which this epigram concludes puts grief into that perspective; it yields emotion, which is not stable, over to wisdom, which is.

I will turn shortly to a further consideration of the expressive possibilities of epigrammatic closure, but first our more general description must be completed. The conditions for maximal closure arise not only when the conclusion of a poem is strongly determined by the entire structure that precedes it, but when it is also reinforced in that particular form by special closural devices—when, in other words, structural completeness coincides with an unusually high degree of nonstructural order or control. This coincidence might be referred to as *hyperdetermination*, and an impressive instance of it occurs in Donne's epigram, "Hero and Leander":

> Both rob'd of aire, we both lye in one ground,
> Both whom one fire had burnt, one water drownd.[14]

[14] *The Poems of John Donne*, ed. H. J. C. Grierson (London, 1957), p. 67. I am indebted for some of the observations that follow to J. V. Cunningham's analysis of this epigram in "The Problem of Form," *The Journal of John Cardan . . .* (Denver, 1964), pp. 14–15.

The final three words here, individually and taken together, are so strongly determined by all that precedes them (including, of course, the title), that one could hardly imagine how the epigram might have been otherwise concluded. In the terms of the communications-engineer, these words are completely "redundant," so predictable that they communicate no "information" whatsoever. And yet to the reader they are surely both necessary and in a way surprising. To appreciate how this apparent contradiction is possible, we might first notice that the four clauses of this epigram—

(A) Both rob'd of aire
(B) we both lye in one ground
(C) Both whom one fire had burnt
(D) one water drownd

—are related to each other as the terms of a ratio: A:B::C:D, and its permutation, A:C::B:D. This mathematical symmetry, which allows the reader to "solve for D" as soon as he knows the values of A, B, and C, arises from the nature of the central conceit and a number of formal and thematic patterns.[15] The conceit is not only finite but restricted to four terms only; thus the sequence *aire, ground* (i.e., earth), *fire* . . . yields only one possible succeeding term—*water.* This term, moreover, completes not only the sequence but also its antithetical subpattern: *aire, ground; fire,* . . . Similarly, syntactic parallelism determines the word order of the final clause (D repeats C as B repeated A), and other patterns of this kind, touching the meaning and form of almost every element in the poem, create a virtuoso-piece of verbal symmetry, economy, and coherence.

For the reader, the existence of these ratios means that by the time he reaches the word "burnt" at the end of the third clause, he will have in his possession all that he needs to write the conclusion himself. The point remains, however, that he will not realize that until he has indeed read to the end; and there he willingly suffers

[15] A comparable ratio, also resulting from a multiple antithesis, is discussed above (p. 169) as it appears in the concluding couplet of one of Spenser's sonnets. The couplet is obviously "epigrammatic."

the "redundancy" of hyperdetermination for the sake of the actual *experience* of the completed pattern. What surpirses him, moreover, is not the novelty of the material but the elegance and economy with which it was deployed. In an imperfect world, perfection is surprising.

Although this epigram is distinguished by its ingenuity, and we may think of it as witty, it is also a moving poem. What is more, we experience its affective quality not in spite of its epigrammatic features but because of them. The economy of language has produced a rather impersonal, dispassionate tone, and crabbed, unidiomatic rhythms. But since these lines are to be read as "spoken" by the dead lovers, these qualities suggest also a kind of oracular or supernatural utterance; and we may sense in it the remote compassion of the now disembodied Hero and Leander for their mortal selves, or an austere pride in their ironically unified destiny. The brevity of the poem is itself expressive: "See in how few words our lives can be defined; so brief as this was our love." The development of the conceit is similarly not only ingenious but resonating: while the inevitable completion of that series reflects the inexorable fate of the unlucky pair against whom all the elements of nature conspired, the formal patterns and symmetries suggest an ultimate justice in it: "Both whom one fire had burnt, one water drownd."

The degree of hyperdetermination in this epigram is, of course, extraordinary. All epigrammatic verse (and utterance) is, however, more or less hyperdetermined; that is, structural and nonstructural forces of closure are so strong that expectation is not only fulfilled but exceeded. This excess, combined with the economy of its means, is probably what we experience as *pointedness*. A hyperdetermined conclusion will have maximal stability and finality; and when these qualities occur in conjunction with unexpected or in some way unstable material (e.g., novel, illogical, or paradoxical statements, puns or hyperboles), the result will be *wit*—which, as many have observed, occurs when expectations are simultaneously surprised and fulfilled. When, on the other hand, the material is itself commonplace, general, or gnomic, hyperdetermination gives its stamp of special validity to that which one is otherwise disposed to find acceptable; the result is *sententiousness*. Proverbs, didactic maxims, household "quotations," and so forth, share with witty epigrams almost all the features we have discussed here and in the previous chapter: the structure of set-up and conclusion, and devices such as formal repetition, alliterated antithesis or parallelism, and unqualified assertion. And epigrams themselves, of course, may be sententious. Pope, aware of the relation between wit and sententiousness, gave an example of the latter while describing it under the name of the former:

> *True Wit* is *Nature* to Advantage drest,
> What oft was *Thought*, but ne'er so well *Exprest*.[16]

Although there are many varieties of pointedness, and the expressive possibilities of epigrammatic verse are not narrowly confined, it remains true that hyperdetermination tends to have a particular affective quality. In speaking of an utterance, poem, or couplet as "epigrammatic," we refer not only to a kind of verbal structure but to an attitude toward experience, a kind of moral temper suggested by that very structure. The epigram seems to offer itself as a last word, an ultimately appropriate comment, a definitive statement. "A poem," writes Yvor Winters, "is what stands/When imperceptive hands,/Feeling, have gone astray./It is what one should say/. . . . The poet's only bliss/Is in cold certitude—. . . ." [17] He speaks, epigrammatically, of epigrams and epigrammatists. Elsewhere, Winters advises the poet:

> Write little; do it well.
> Your knowledge will be such,
> At last, as to dispel
> What moves you overmuch.[18]

[16] "An Essay on Criticism," ll. 297–98, *The Poems of Alexander Pope*, ed. John Butt (New Haven, 1963), p. 153.

[17] "On Teaching the Young," *Collected Poems* (Denver, 1960), p. 90.

[18] "To a Young Writer," *ibid.*, p. 73.

To "dispel" (to undo the spell) or to dismiss is the epigrammatist's characteristic gesture. In love or hate, praise or blame, he is saying something so that he will not have to say it again. He writes a poem not when he is moved, but when he ceases to be. He records the moment of mastery—not the emotion, but the attitude that conquered it.

The epigrammatist is proud: he does not wish to endear or ingratiate himself to the reader. Nor is he intimate. He holds the reader at a distance, addressing him directly, but not inviting him to share experiences. (To a reader who says he does not like an epigram, the epigrammatist is likely to reply, "You are not supposed to.")

What he does to others, he does to his own experiences: he defines them, gives them their right names.[19] To epigrammatize an experience is to strip it down, to cut away irrelevance, to eliminate local, specific, and descriptive detail, to reduce it to and fix it in its most permanent and stable aspect, to sew it up for eternity. The epigrammatist does not have "Negative Capability"; he "irritably search[es] after fact and reason"; he is not "capable of being in uncertainty, Mysteries, doubts"; he is "incapable of remaining content with half knowledge." [20]

The measure of the epigrammatist's success in his art is his control and economy. He cannot afford to falter; he has not the room or time to make up for mistakes. But his miserly way with words affects our impression of his personality. He will seem brusque, cold, uncompromising, arrogant, authoritative, "authori-

[19] The satirical epigrammatist salutes his victim by an appropriately identifying name before impaling him. Cf. Jonson's "To My Lord Ignorant," "On Sir Voluptuous Beast," "To Fine Lady Would-be" (*Poems*, pp. 10, 16, 29), etc.

[20] *The Letters of John Keats*, ed. Hyder Edward Rollins (Cambridge, Mass., 1958), I, 193–94. In this passage, Keats was of course interested in describing not the epigrammatist, but his opposite. In rejecting the epigram as a genre, the Romantic poet was rejecting a style and an attitude more than a form. The point should be remembered when we consider the anti-closural impulses of modern poetry in the last section of this chapter.

tarian." If we are not put off by his manner, however, we will sense, beneath the reserved surface, the pressure of the mastered emotion, the guarded vulnerability. (It is the later that distinguishes Jonson from Martial, who is both more brilliant and more brutal.)

"The greatest poverty," said Wallace Stevens," "is not to live/In a physical world. . . ."[21] The epigrammatist does not live in a physical world. He lives in a moral world. And although he is sceptical and tough-minded, he is a moral traditionalist. The only novelty with which he surprises us is that of conventional truth. Economizing for the sake of pointedness, the epigrammatist uses short, simple sentences or clauses, and omits certain words and expressions that otherwise give to speech a tone of gracious reasonableness. The epigrammatist is not reasonable, for reason is his passion.

The epigram may be distinguished from the *haiku,* of which it seems to be the Western counterpart and to which it is frequently compared. But the intention of the *haiku* is to capture an experience, of the epigram to clinch it. Nor is the epigrammatist "objective" in the same sense as is the *haiku* poet. Whereas the objectivity of the latter is metaphysical and consists in the obliteration or surrender of personality to the object evoked, the objectivity of the former is moral and consists in the obliteration of illusion and the conquest of sentimentality toward the object defined.

I have been characterizing the epigram in an epigrammatic manner: making my assertions in balanced clauses, antithetically and alliteratively, without qualifications or exceptions, and scrupulously eliminating the scholar's scruples, his reservations and tentative "perhaps," "probably" and "tends to." There are, of course, exceptions and qualifications, and what I have been describing here are not characteristics but tendencies. But if in this way I have further illustrated the expressive effects, limits, and risks of epigrammatic utterance, the purpose will have been served.

[21] "Esthétique du Mal," *Collected Poems* (New York, 1961), p. 325.

Neither the occurrence nor the significance of hyperdetermination is confined to the epigram as such. To the extent that any poem is hyperdetermined we will experience it as "epigrammatic" and sense in it the expressive qualities described above. The epigram is a genre, but epigrammatic is a style; and it is as a stylistic possibility, particularly as one to be rejected, that the epigrammatic will concern us in the pages that follow. But before exploring it further in that connection, we shall consider its reverse: closural inadequacy.

II Failures of Closure

The sources of weak poetic closure could be indicated simply enough as the opposite of everything that produces strong closure. Closural effects will tend to be minimal when the structural forces of continuation are not arrested or overcome, when a conclusion is not determined by any thematic principles and no speical devices appear in the terminal lines, when these lines are metrically irregular or deviant and not otherwise formally patterned, when the last allusions are to beginnings or to unstable events, and when concluding assertions are qualified and tentative. Such a catalogue, however, even if it were amplified or refined, would not tell us all we might want to know about the conditions and effects of weak closure. Are all these circumstances, for example, equally significant, and do all closural failures fail in the same way? Is an inadequately closed poem necessarily a bad poem, and is strong closure always desirable? In order to approach answers to such questions, we would want to examine the possible varieties and the affective qualities of closural failure, as well as the general conditions that produce it.

The catalogue given above suggests, however, a procedural difficulty, for the characteristics listed are mostly negative ones, and the risk of question-begging, particularly in the matter of illustration, is thus considerable. It is easier to point to something that exists than to something that does not; and the difficulty here is increased by the fact that, like closure itself, closural failure is an effect, a quality of the reader's experience—and one that is particularly likely to vary among different readers. Since the reasons for this are interesting and involve aspects of closural failure that will continue to concern us, we may begin by considering them.

First of all, we must recall that although success and failure are absolute terms, closure is a relative matter: it is more or less weak or strong.[22] When it is fairly strong, readers may agree that it is successful even though they experience the degree of its strength differently. It is at the far end of the scale, however, that the question of its effective presence arises and that the balance may tip differently for each reader.

Second, when a poem is experienced via a printed text, no matter how weak the forces of closure are, the simple fact that its last line is followed by an expanse of blank paper will inform the reader that it is concluded. And, as I pointed out earlier, we tend to impose closural qualities on events (such as the last chime of a bell) that we know, independently, to be terminal. Consequently, when we "perform" a poem, either vocally or subvocally, we will tend to modify the tempo, pitch, force, duration, and general inflection of the concluding words so as to enhance whatever

[22] By "relative," I do not mean "subjective." The latter term has been debased almost beyond usefulness, and what it could legitimately mean is covered here by the notion of "effect" or "experience" or "response" (as opposed to "cause" or, in psychological terms, "stimulus"). Moreover, it would not be very informative to say that the experience of closural failure varies among readers because it is subjective: the assertion is circular and would take us nowhere. "Relative," however, is a term that refers not to the experience of closure but to its sources. An analogy may clarify this. A tone may be spoken of as more or less—i.e., *relatively*—loud or soft independent of any listener, and the degree of its loudness may be specified in decibels: it is a purely physical parameter. The conditions under which a listener would call a tone "loud" or "soft" of course involve this physical dimension, but different listeners will vary—"subjectively," if you like—in their responses to that same tone.

closural forces are present. Since we do this unconsciously, we may sometimes be unable to distinguish the closural effects we thereby experience from those created by the poem (rather than ourselves); and when closure is weak, the distinction may be crucial in determining its ultimate adequacy for different readers.

Third, the reader's experience of closure both depends upon and affects his interpretation of the poem—not his critical exegesis, but his general impression of, in both senses, its *design:* its intention (tones and motives) and its pattern (most significant generating principles). Again, when closural effects are fairly strong, readers with more or less different interpretations of a poem are likely to agree about the adequacy of its conclusion. But when the effects are weak, the reader's interpretation may become crucial in his experience of closure. Conversely, since this impression of design operates during the reading of the poem as a running hypothesis, the conclusion may be crucial in either confirming it or not. When it is not confirmed, the conclusion may create an instantaneous readjustment of the hypothesis—what I have referred to as "retrospective patterning." But whereas one reader's hypothesis may accommodate the adjustment readily, another reader's may resist it altogether, and the unexpected conclusion that is ultimately gratifying to the first will remain disappointing to the second. One reader's retrospective justification may strike another as retrospective rationalization.

Finally, the fact that the sense of closure is the complex product of so many diverse elements in a poem makes possible something we can call "false closure," where the use of particularly effective devices in the terminal lines of a poem can compensate for or obscure—for some readers more than others—the structural inadequacy of the conclusion.

The variety of ways in which closure may be defective can be better appreciated if we first consider more closely the distinction suggested earlier between surprises and disappointments. In ordinary usage, a surprise is an event that occurs, and a disappointment one that does not occur, both contrary to expectation; and while we often speak of unpleasant surprises, we rarely speak of pleasant disappointments—the value in either case apparently attaching to the quality of the event itself. The distinction can be made, however, on slightly different grounds, and although it may involve a slight strain of usage, it will be more serviceable to us here. With regard to the experience of poetic events, then, and particularly of poetic endings, we will say that both surprises and disappointments are events that occur, but each with a different relation to the reader's expectations, and that the value (pleasant or unpleasant) will attach not to the quality of the event itself but to the nature of that relation. All surprises, by this view, will be pleasant and all disappointments unpleasant. The surprise ending is one which forces and *rewards* a readjustment of the reader's expectations; it justifies itself retrospectively. A disappointing ending, on the other hand, is not accommodated by such a readjustment; it remains unjustified and the reader's expectations remain foiled. Another way to put this is to say that a disappointing conclusion leaves the reader with residual expectations, but the surprise ending does not, or that whereas a surprise ending provides a perspective point from which the reader can now appreciate a significant pattern, principle, or motive not grasped before, a disappointing conclusion reveals nothing about the poem's structure but, on the contrary, only disturbs or unsettles the reader's retrospective experience of it.

This sonnet from Sidney's *Astrophel and Stella* illustrates the surprise ending:

> Who will in fairest booke of Nature know,
>   How Vertue may best lodg'd in beautie be,
>   Let him but learne of *Love* to reade in thee,
> *Stella,* those faire lines, which true goodnesse show.
> There shall he find all vices' overthrow,
>   Not by rude force, but sweetest soveraigntie
>   Of reason, from whose light those night-birds flie;
> That inward sunne in thine eyes shineth so.

And not content to be Perfection's heire
Thy selfe, doest strive all minds that way to move,
Who marke in thee what is in thee most faire.
So while thy beautie drawes the heart to love,
As fast thy Vertue bends that love to good:
'But ah,' Desire still cries, 'give me some food.' [23]

The first thirteen lines develop with perfect logic and consistency a conventional Neo-Platonic statement of the relation between the love of beauty and the inspiration to virtue. Having heard exactly what one expects to hear in a poem of the Petrarchan mode, one will further expect the final line to complete it with a generalization or personal application in the same tradition. The conclusion, however, in a single stroke of magnificent simplicity, both shatters the expectation and modifies the significance and tone of all that precedes it.[24] Astrophel does not offer the poem, as we might have thought, as a testament to the theoretically ennobling power of Stella's beauty; on the contrary, it bears desperate witness to the irrelevance and inadequacy of such a theory, and the lines which had seemed, at first, to have the grace and lucidity of secure conviction now take on a quality of mechanical exposition. This quality does not detract from our pleasure in the poem, however, but is incorporated in our appreciation of the motive now revealed.

It is commonly remarked that in a number of Shakespeare's sonnets, the concluding couplet is the poem's weakest point. These couplets, it is said, are "flat," "limp," "slack," or "tacked-on," and although readers vary in assigning the weakness to "poetic" or "intellectual" failings, they tend to agree that it is characteristic.[25]

[23] *The Poems of Sir Philip Sidney*, ed. William A. Ringler, Jr. (Oxford, 1962), p. 201.

[24] Surprise endings do not always consist of such striking turns. We may be surprised by any number of more or less unexpected elements, from a slight shift in tone to the introduction of a wholly new aspect of psychological realism and a radical reversal of motives, as here.

[25] See e.g., Edward Hubler, *The Sense of Shakespeare's Sonnets* (Princeton, 1952), pp. 24–27; G. Wilson Knight, *The Mutual Flame . . .* (London, 1955), pp. 79 and 81; and Yvor Winters, "Poetic Styles, Old and New," *Four Poets on Poetry*, ed. D. C. Allen (Baltimore, 1959), pp. 48–49.

We may pursue our ends here by considering one of these sonnets and trying to determine more precisely the nature and sources of its closural failings. Sonnet 66, like the poem by Sidney discussed above, concludes with a surprising (or is it disappointing?) turn:

> Tir'd with all these, for restful death I cry:
> As to behold desert a beggar born,
> And needy nothing trimmed in jollity,
> And purest faith unhappily forsworn,
> And gilded honor shamefully misplaced,
> And maiden virtue rudely strumpeted,
> And right perfection wrongfully disgraced,
> And strength by limping sway disablèd,
> And art made tongue-tied by authority,
> And folly, doctor-like, controlling skill,
> And simple truth miscalled simplicity,
> And captive good attending captain ill.
> Tir'd with all these, from these would I be gone,
> Save that, to die, I leave my love alone.

Yvor Winters observes that "this is one of a number of Elizabethan poems dealing with disillusionment with the world," and he mentions Ralegh's "The Lie," discussed above (pages 102–7), as another of the group so defined. But, he suggests, whereas the other poets "offer the best solutions that they can, . . . [Shakespeare] turns aside from the issues he has raised to a kind of despairing sentimentality, and the effect is one of weakness, poetic and personal." Winters goes on to cite other sonnets that, in his view, fail in the same way, that "do not rise to the occasions which they invoke." [26]

This last remark obviously describes what we referred to above as a disappointing conclusion, and although we may argue with Winters' interpretation of the couplet, it is not difficult to see why he would speak of closural weakness here. Read in the company of the other poems he mentions, and identified as one of their

[26] Winters, "Poetic Styles Old and New," p. 49.

number, this sonnet will arouse expectations that the concluding line fails utterly to fulfil; *so read*, the final turn will be both unexpected and ungratifying. And even a reader less familiar with Elizabethan poetry might feel a sense of slackness in the conclusion. Like Ralegh in "The Lie" (and with many of the same devices of relentless repetition and monolithic structure), Shakespeare has hammered out a catalogue of corruption and injustice only too compellingly. The catalogue is introduced and framed, moreover, by the poet's explicit and unqualified desire for death; and even though its modified repetition in line 13 sets up the turn syntactically ("I would . . . [but—]"), the tones and terms of the catalogue itself would seem to call for something other than a renunciation of renuniation. We participate in the poet's stinging recognitions and indictments and are similarly oppressed; but whereas Ralegh arms us all through with a weapon for striking back ("And give them all the lie"), Shakespeare does nothing of the kind. On the contrary, in the sonnet the cumulatively oppressive force of a world so seen is allowed to stand not only unanswered but finally ignored, as the poet turns to—his *love!* What we wait for is a blow *back*; what we get is a gesture of sentimental withdrawal.

Or do we? What I have presented here is a reading of the sonnet that evidently will not accommodate its concluding line. By this view, the turn does not illuminate a retrospective reading, but contaminates it. The bitter power of the catalogue takes on a tone of bravado, like the soldier's drunken shout to his companions: "I can't take another minute of it. The Army is brutal, dehumanizing, and filled with morons. It's time something was done. When I get back to camp, I'll write my mother about it." [27] But the more we press the case, the more uncomfortable we feel with it. *No*, we object, he is not withdrawing; it is not a sentimental gesture of despair; it is a blow back, or something better than that—if we understand it rightly.

[27] I shall return later to the question of why, as an anecdote, this would be humorous.

It was Winters, of course, who put Sonnet 66 in the company of Ralegh's "The Lie," and while the association is reasonable on several counts, the sonnet was originally published in the company of one hundred and fifty-three others, almost all of them love poems. If the reader associates Sonnet 66 with others in this group—especially those such as 29 ("When, in disgrace with Fortune and men's eyes . . .") and 30 ("When to the sessions of sweet silent thought . . ."), dealing not with disillusionment but with the redemptive power of love, the final line here might strike him as less surprising and less disappointing.[28] The line might be experienced, in fact, as fulfilling an expectation suppressed to some degree by the body of the sonnet but nevertheless present. Also, the sonnet may be distinguished from "The Lie" by more than the company it keeps. Ralegh's disillusionment was comprehensive, radical, reductive, and nihilistic:

> Tell men of high condition,
>   that manage the estate,
> Their purpose is ambition
>   their practice onely hate . . .
>
> Tell Arts they have no soundnesse . . .
>
> Tell zeale it wants devotion
>   tell love it is but lust . . .

It evoked a world of fools and knaves. Shakespeare's disillusionment is qualified from the very beginning, however, by an awareness of and compassion for the victims of such a world. In the sonnet, desert, faith, honor, virtue, and so forth, are seen not as essentially corrupt but as corrupted (or betrayed or strangled) from without. "Good" may be captive (line 12), but it remains good—like Lear and Cordelia at the beginning of Act V of the play. Indeed, the sonnet could have been spoken by the king at

[28] Winters mentions 29 and 30 as suffering from the same weaknesses as 66, but one may suspect a temperamental bias here. See n. 29, below.

that point, and the last line would stand, as it does in this poem, as a gesture not of withdrawal but of defiance and protectiveness: "No, I will not die, for to do so would be to leave my love alone and vulnerable in this rotten world." The deferral of this consideration to the very end of the poem could be seen, then, as reflecting not an afterthought or an evasion, but a dramatic representation of the transcendent power of love. For Winters, the final lines "do not rise to the occasion which they invoke." Do they not, however, rise above it?

I have developed these two interpretations of the sonnet in order to illustrate the power and limits of retrospective justification. One would expect that the reader whose interpretation of the poem tended, broadly, to resemble the second one offered here would experience the couplet as a self-justifying surprise, and adequately closed. I would like to suggest now, however, that while the interpretation is compelling, and a good performance of the sonnet could emphasize it and enhance whatever closural forces appear in the couplet (the monosyllables, alliteration and rhyme), nevertheless, even with this interpretation in mind, the ultimate sense of closure here is weak. Nor do I think that this is because we fail to appreciate, in all its power, the notion of redemptive love,[29] but rather that its power has not been realized in this poem. The concluding turn does, to be sure, illuminate a motive that qualifies our retrospective response to the whole sonnet, and we may engage in rereadings thoroughly armed with the expectations that best accommodate this final line—but we will continue to be, to some degree, disappointed.

If the fact is granted, we may ask why it is so. For one thing, the possibility of the first interpretation, however deficient in certain respects, will probably remain potent enough to affect us in any case. Secondly, although there are, as I have just mentioned, certain closural devices in the couplet, their effects are weakened by other anti-closural elements in the lines. The rhyme, for example (*gone-alone*), though possibly a just one in Elizabethan pro-

[29] For Winters, of course, the notion may be inherently sentimental.

nunciation, either strikes the modern reader as false or obliges him to alter his normal pronunciation of one of the two words. In either case, the self-stabilizing and integrating effect of the rhyme is weakened.[30] Also, in modifying the opening line so as to set up the final turn, the poet has sacrificed some of its closural features, and the echo will only emphasize this: "for restful death I cry/ . . . from these would I be gone." The second phrase is not only less vivid but less specific—and it might seem, in contrast to the first, an ambiguous euphemism. One hesitates to rewrite Shakespeare, even for the sake of illustration, but the reader may test this point by imagining how the couplet would sound if the first line were repeated there exactly:

> Tir'd with all these, for restful death I cry,
> Save that, to serve my love, I would not die.

(A change of this kind would not, of course, solve the problem of the couplet's thematic relation to the body of the poem.)

The final alliteration, moreover (*leave . . . love . . . alone*), which might be expected to have closural force, here suffers in a curious way by contrast to the kind of alliteration appearing earlier in the poem. Consider the following: *faith . . . forsworn* (line 4), *right . . . wrongfully* (7), *strength . . . sway* (8), *art . . . authority* (9), *simple . . . simplicity* (11), *captain . . . captive* (12). In each, the alliteration binds together antithetically related words, thus emphasizing the words and their relationship, and reinforcing the indictment of a world where moral contraries are so inevitably linked. Alliteration here has been in the service of meaning, but in the final line it seems to be gratuitous or to serve only euphony. (It probably contributes also to Winters' sense of the "sentimental degeneration of courtly rhetoric" in the couplet.) In

[30] Cf. Helge Kökeritz, *Shakespeare's Pronunciation* (New Haven, 1953), pp. 34, 233–34. In the sonnet discussed above, Sidney also concludes with a rhyme false to our ears (*good-food*), but since closure there is otherwise so effective, the defect is more or less inconsequential.

any case, since the final alliteration is not pointed as it had been earlier, its closural effect seems undermined by the contrast.

Finally, and perhaps most obviously, the force of the terminal allusion to death is not only weakened but becomes anti-closural by virtue of its position in the last line: the syntax, forcing a suspension after "to die," resolves itself anticlimactically.

An inadequately closed poem is not necessarily a bad poem, although it may be bad in that respect. If we allow that there should be a distinction between our response to a poem and our evaluation of it, we can say that whereas the response may be complex, the evaluation may be compound. The sixty-sixth is, I think, among Shakespeare's best sonnets, and although one's experience of it is ultimately defective, one's sense of its greatness is not thereby annihilated; we may always say, "A great poem—with a weak conclusion." Since our experience of a poem is not instantaneous but extensive, there is no reason why we cannot read (and reread) with pleasure a poem that concludes badly; and the notion of the "organic unity" of good poems must confront the fact that some very good poems, such as *The Fairie Queene,* have been left unfinished and that we know *Paradise Lost* is a great poem before we have read a quarter of it.

Two further points must be added here. First, a failure of closure is not always a local defect, confined to the conclusion of a poem. If the total design is ill-wrought, incoherent or self-divided, closure may be not only inadequate but impossible. Some of the glorious fragments that strew the landscape of nineteenth-century poetry—Keats's *Fall of Hyperion,* for example—in all likelihood could not have been, given their present form, finished at all. Second, the success or failure of closure *will* become crucial in our evaluation of a poem when it is truly crucial in our response to it. Nothing is as worthless as a limp epigram, for all of its effects are more or less subordinated to and experienced in terms of the effectiveness of its conclusion. If that fails, there is little else to redeem it.

Failures of Closure

The reverse of this is also true, and perhaps more obviously so: a poem that concludes with secure closure is not necessarily a good poem—and here we may add, *not even in that respect.* Not all the devices and effects of closure are particularly subtle, and even a child who knows nothing but nursery rhymes and songs knows enough about both to construct a closed poem. This one was composed by an eight-year-old:

> If I were an Indian girl
> I would have a reddish-brown face
> And not have to wear any lace.
> I would live in a pretty wigwam
> And wear a belt of wampum.
> I would walk the path that was narrow
> And carry a bow and arrow—
> If I were an Indian girl.[31]

The process can be inferred from the product: having exhausted her impulse or imagination after seven lines, wanting a finished poem and knowing that she did not have one yet, the poet artfully repeated the first line—and was probably no less surprised than delighted to see how effectively it turned the trick. Ungenerously, we may call this cheap closure, and if the poem were not otherwise so beguilingly naïve, we would resist its effect even as we recognized it; for while it successfully exploits our tendency to respond to certain terminal features as stabilizing, we are aware of its spurious relation to the structure of the poem. As we saw in chapter 3, the principles that generate a paratactic structure (such as here) do not yield a termination point, and closure in such a poem is either secured in terms of some other nonparatactic principle also present or depends upon special terminal devices. The latter, however, may be more or less gratuitous with respect to the poem's thematic structure, and the more gratuitous they are, the more we will be inclined to regard as unearned the sense of

[31] B. J. B., unpublished.

closure thus conveyed. Also, although the devices may be to some degree effective, we are likely to be left, once again, with residual expectations; for our expectations of *true* closure will remain unfulfilled—as in the little poem above, where the catalogue seems to demand a summary comment or generalization.

Like many other forms of closural failure or disappointment, cheap closure can be humorous. Related as an anecdote, for example, the terminal collapse of that complaining soldier's vainglorious announcement would be the punch-line. The effect is reversed because, to put it simply, we recognize the anticlimax as intentional, as the "design" of the anecdote. The humorous effect of cheap closure, as well as the fact that such closure always leaves residual expectations, is illustrated in the camp-and-college song that develops from one piece of nonsense to another and concludes, in the middle of a musical phrase, as follows:

> Now, you may think that this is the end;
> Well, it is.

Since the term "anticlimax" is frequently used to signify or describe the effect of closural inadequacy, we might give it some attention here. In the broadest terms, a climax is the "highest" point of an "ascending" series. I have enclosed these two words in quotation marks because they are really figurative, but figurative in an irreducible way. That is, they cannot be translated into anything more literal or objective: each is a metaphor for a quality shared by our responses to many different kinds of phenomena, but the quality cannot be specified without the metaphor.[32] In any

[32] It is impossible to say, for example, what there is in common between the topmost step of a staircase and the highest pitched tone in an ascending scale, without using these very terms to state it. There is nothing *spatially* higher about one tonal frequency compared to another, and although we represent higher notes on the upper part of the musical staff, they could just as well be on the lower. The upperness of high frequencies is a convention that seems to follow the curious transference of spatial order to nonspatial series. Pitch, of course, is a function of higher, that is, more *numerous*, frequencies. But even the notion that numbers are higher or lower reflects the same transference.

case (whether it is a matter of force, number, rapidity, or whatever), when events occurring in temporal succession are also related to each other in such a way as to suggest a scale, the event that defines the uppermost limit of that scale will be continuously and increasingly expected and, when it occurs, will be experienced as climactic. It will provide the expected limit and thus release the tension that accompanied its expectation. Everything that we have said here concerning expectations, especially with regard to sequential series, will suggest how significant this is for closure. We may ask, however, whether the occurrence of any climax in a poem (or play or novel) is necessarily equivalent to successful closure at that point; and I think that, again, much of what we have observed in the preceding chapters will suggest why it is *not.*

In a literary work, the scale of which a particular event is the climax may, of course, constitute one of its most significant thematic principles. When it does, and when the scale is a series with an implicit termination point, the occurrence of this point will be both climactic and closural. These conditions are not always present, however, for the series may very well be only one among several thematic principles, and in that case the completion of the poem will depend upon more than the occurrence of that climax. In Melville's *Billy Budd,* for example, the murder of Claggart is *a* climax, but the story and the reader are concerned with more than the expected consummation of the events leading up to it. This also suggests why it is not always true that everything that follows a climax is necessarily anticlimactic.

Since it is the anticlimactic that interests us in this section, a further distinction should be made. If I were to say to a child, "I'll give you anything your heart desires—a new doll, the biggest lollipop you ever saw, the most expensive dress in the store . . . ," one could feel the cumulative force of the superlatives and abso-

---

One may observe, by the way, that not all languages exhibit this metaphor. In Latin, e.g., *altus* "means" either high or deep, depending on what it refers to, while our word *high* is variously translated as *acutus, amplus, carus, maximus, magnus,* etc., depending, again, on the reference.

lutes as tending toward, and increasingly requiring, a climax and resolution—something like "I will give you the moon," suggesting that I had reached an ultimate limit. However, if I were to complete the series with a different sort of statement, something like "I'll give you a nickel," it would be anticlimactic not in the sense that it followed a climax but that it interrupted an apparent approach to one, displacing it with something that sent us back to the bottom of the scale or off the scale altogether.

The point to be made is that "anticlimactic" may refer to a variety of closural failings and describes not so much the source as the effect of the inadequacy. The more common failing is the one I just described: where the conclusion that appears does not supply the anticipated limit and thus leaves the reader with residual expectations. What we sometimes refer to as "tacked-on" endings are another sort of anticlimax. The reader of a poem should, at its conclusion, be satisfied with nothing but a margin of blank paper. If, however, he has reached this state *before* the end of the poem, he will experience its actual conclusion as defective, as distinctly anticlimactic. (One is tempted to call this a case of *foreclosure.*) In a sonnet, for example, where the formal requirements are fixed, the reader will, at any point, either anticipate formal completion or simply observe that there are so many more lines to the poem; but if the thematic structure has been completely resolved by the end of line 12, let us say, the couplet will seem both anticlimactic and "tacked-on."

What we have considered up to this point are closural failures that arise primarily from a deficient, defective, or spurious relation between the structure of a poem and its conclusion. The assumption in each instance was that some sort of adequate termination was possible but did not appear. As I mentioned earlier, however, there are instances when the poem could not have been well closed, and one of these is where the closural weakness reflects structural weakness. In our experience of such poems, the structural problem is sometimes not recognized until the conclusion, for we may have been juggling our responses all through, entertaining one hypothesis after another in an attempt to locate the poem's significant thematic principles. And as each successive hypothesis is made unviable by unexpected and unaccommodatable turns, we will increasingly look to the conclusion to reveal or clarify an implicit design. If the design is defective, however, even though the conclusion itself may have terminal features that suggest finality, our residual expectations will make them more or less ineffective for the sense of closure.

The problem I have been describing is illustrated in this otherwise engaging poem from Fulke Greville's *Cælica:*

> I with whose colors *Myra* drest her head,
> I, that ware posies of her owne hand making,
> I, that mine owne name in the chimnies read
> By *Myra* finely wrought ere I was waking:
>   Must I looke on, in hope time comming may
>   With change bring backe my turne againe to play?
>
> I, that on Sunday at the Church-stile found,
> A Garland sweet, with true-loue knots in flowers,
> Which I to weare about mine arme was bound,
> That each of vs might know that all was ours:
>   Must I now lead an idle life in wishes?
>   And follow *Cupid* for his loaues, and fishes?
>
> I, that did weare the ring her Mother left,
> I, for whose loue she gloried to be blamed,
> I, with whose eyes her eyes committed theft,
> I, who did make her blush when I was named;
>   Must I lose ring, flowers, blush, theft and go naked,
>   Watching with sighs, till dead loue be awaked?
>
> I, that when drowsie *Argus* fell asleep,
> Like Iealousie o'rewatched with desire,
> Was euen warned modestie to keepe,
> While her breath, speaking, kindled Natures fire:
>   Must I looke on a-cold, while others warme them?
>   Doe *Vulcans* brothers in such fine nets arme them?

Was it for this that I might *Myra* see
Washing the water with her beauties, white?
Yet would she neuer write her loue to me;
Thinks wit of change while thoughts are in delight?
Mad Girles must safely loue, as they may leaue,
No man can print a kisse, lines may deceiue.[33]

The thematic structure of the poem is a bit deceptive, for while the repetitions would suggest that the first four stanzas are parallel, there is a break between the first three and the fourth. Lines 17–18 seem to recapitulate the development of the poem up to that point, and what the reader is likely to expect thereafter is not another allusion to good times past and further questions, but an answer to the questions thus neatly summarized. Since the fourth stanza does not supply the answer or even seem to set one up, the reader will be groping for some clues to the poem's direction at that point. Moreover, however interesting the material of the fourth stanza, the repetitive structure will be somewhat anticlimactic, and the reader will be looking to the conclusion of the poem both to integrate the fourth stanza with the preceding three and to provide the expected answer. The fifth stanza does not quite do either, and although lines 25–26 are among the best in the poem, our delight in them will be mixed with some dismay at an even further loss of direction. Finally, the last four lines are, once again, sparkling (and express as well as any in *Cælica* Greville's ironically bemused view of feminine constancy), but they do not conclude the poem as a whole in an entirely satisfactory manner. It is true that the final turn does, in a sense, answer the questions by suggesting that to ask them at all was foolish: "Come to think of it, she never did anything to commit herself. I suppose I should just forget the whole thing." But even this "answer" is there only by implication, while the force of the final lines is directed to and dissipated by the two wholly new notions of Myra's having been

[33] "Sonnet XXII," *Poems and Dramas of Fulke Greville*, ed. Geoffrey Bullough (New York, 1945), I, 84–85. (The italics are in the text.)

concerned with strategic retreats all along and having refused to commit herself in *writing*. The concluding couplet is quite crisp, but the poem to which it would have provided a fine conclusion is not this one.

The final closural problem that I wish to consider here is somewhat similar to the one discussed above, but is particularly interesting in its implications for the history of style. It is illustrated by Shakespeare's fifty-ninth sonnet:

> If there be nothing new, but that which is
> Hath been before, how are our brains beguiled,
> Which, laboring for invention, bear amiss
> The second burden of a former child!
> O, that record could, with a backward look—
> Ev'n of five hundred courses of the sun—
> Show me your image in some antique book,
> Since mind at first in character was done,
> That I might see what the old world could say
> To this composèd wonder of your frame:
> Whether we are mended, or where better they,
> Or whether revolution be the same. 12
> O sure I am the wits of former days
> To subjects worse have given admiring praise.

There are two impulses in this poem, the primary one being the poet's musings on the cyclical theory of history, the secondary one being his effort to put this notion into the service of a compliment to his friend. Whereas the first is essentially undirected, the second is, or tries to be, directed toward a particular end. The structural problem of the sonnet results from the incompatibility of these two impulses; and it is emphasized rather than resolved in the couplet, for the retrospective reading of the poem that best clarifies the associative relations among the quatrains also makes that couplet most obviously irrelevant. One of the more significant things that such a reading reveals is that the apparently general concern of the first quatrain is really specific: the poet is speculating on what that theory of history would imply about the creation of *poetry*. A rough paraphrase of lines 1–12 will be useful: "If what they say is true, then all our efforts to create novelty are absurd, for what we think of as invention is really duplication. (Specifically, it occurs to me that if you lived before, other poets must have celebrated you in this previous incarnation, and anything we—I and your other contemporary admirers—bring off has already been anticipated by them.)[34] I wish I could see such an original work and compare it to what we are currently writing. I wonder if those ancient poets were more or less skilled than we or if, really, everything was, as they say, just the same then as now." Put together this way, the sonnet—up to the couplet—makes sense, and very interesting sense: not, however, as a conceit that sets up a compliment but as a series of more or less associative musings that, by their very nature, neither require nor admit of resolution.

The meaning or emphasis of the couplet is somewhat ambiguous: either, "But the more I think of it, the more certain I am that what the old poets praised was not a true incarnation of you, but something inferior," or, taking "worse" as a pointed understatement (as in our expression "you could do worse than . . . ," meaning "you could not do better than . . ."), "I'm sure that whatever else they praised, you (in that incarnation) were their best subject." No matter how we interpret it, however, the couplet seems to be closurally weak, either as a new turn of speculation not more final than any of the earlier ones, or simply as a compliment *occasioned* but not justified by the train of thought that preceded it.[35]

[34] What I have parenthesized here is the implicit link that is ultimately seen as relating the first and second quatrains.

[35] It may be worth something to observe in passing that in Sonnet 106 Shakespeare seemed to rework the same material to better advantage structurally; here the speculations give way entirely to the compliment which is itself richer and more complex:

Failures of Closure

The structural problem illustrated by Sonnet 59 was anticipated above in our discussion of associative structure. If, as I suggested there, we recognize that Shakespeare's use of such a structure was unconsciously revolutionary, and that it involved closural problems that he was not aware of or, sensing them, was not always able to solve, we may consider the failure of such a sonnet in an interesting light. In brief, what we have here is a poet who continues to use the closural conventions of a traditional lyric style for a structure that they will no longer serve. The complimentary turn of this couplet was such a convention, but the sonnet itself had been generated in such a way as to make it ineffective for closure.

The point is significant not only with respect to Shakespeare. In more general terms, we might surmise that any major stylistic development will on occasion create the same problem: that is, there will be something comparable to what we speak of as a "cultural lag," where elements of the older style will continue to appear, but now inappropriately, or where poets will attempt to solve the closural problems created by the new style with conventions that are no longer effective.

The controversial conclusion of Keats's "Ode on a Grecian Urn" may be seen as illustrating this possibility.[36] The structure of that

---

When in the chronicle of wasted time
I see descriptions of the fairest wights,
And beauty making beautiful old rhyme
In praise of ladies dead and lovely knights,
Then, in the blazon of sweet beauty's best,
Of hand, of foot, of lip, of eye, of brow,
I see their antique pen would have expressed
Even such beauty as you master now.
So all their praises are but prophecies
Of this our time, all you prefiguring;
And, for they looked but with divining eyes,
They had not skill enough your worth to sing:
For we, which now behold these present days,
Have eyes to wonder, but lack tongues to praise.

[36] The history and bibliography of the controversy are conveniently, if appallingly, summarized in *Keats' Well-Read Urn: An Introduction to Liter-*

poem was certainly revelutionary, and perhaps more so than Keats himself recognized. As James Ralston Caldwell suggests most persuasively, this ode, like the Nightingale Ode and other earlier works (notably "Sleep and Poetry"), is offered as the poetic report of a train of associations evoked by the poet's response to a specific object, and develops in accord with Keats's notion of the sequence of psychological events in a "bardic trance." [37] The source of this notion need not concern us here, but its details are significant. Caldwell describes it as follows:

> In moments of creative ecstasy, the mind of the poet is passive to the procession of visions moving across it. Conscious intellection, guidance of the course of images, what we call "thought," have no apparent place in the event. The impact of the physical beauties of nature [or a work of art] starts the poet on a spontaneous and inconsequent mental process which gathers emotional momentum as it goes forward, and which carries him to heights of speculation, to insights valid in some profound sense [from which he must inevitably descend, returning to "reality"].[38]

As Caldwell makes clear, Keats apparently seized upon the idea "that poetry might consist in representations, purporting to be literal," of such experiences (p. 25).

What distinguishes the "Ode on a Grecian Urn" from other poems of similar structure and intention, however, is that the "insights valid in some profound sense" are not incorporated here

---

ary Method, ed. Harvey T. Lyon (New York, 1958), in which are reprinted interpretations of, and comments on, the ode by various hands (about eighty of them) from 1828 to 1957. More recent contributions of note include Walter Jackson Bate's *John Keats* (Cambridge, Mass., 1963), pp. 510–20, and Aileen Ward's *John Keats: The Making of a Poet* (New York, 1963), pp. 281–83.

[37] *John Keats' Fancy: The Effect on Keats of the Psychology of his Day* (Ithaca, N.Y., 1945).

[38] *Ibid.*, p. 12. (The bracketed additions paraphrase points made elsewhere in Caldwell's study.)

into the representation of the imaginative experience itself, but are offered as a sententious memento of it:

> When old age shall this generation waste,
> Thou shalt remain, in midst of other woe
> Than ours, a friend to man, to whom thou say'st,
> 'Beauty is truth, truth beauty,'—that is all
> Ye know on earth, and all ye need to know.[39]

It is, of course, impossible to say whether these last two lines, and those which introduce them, were actually composed or even designed last. It seems probable enough, however, that at the end of the fourth stanza, where the poet's revery was represented as having drawn him from speculations about the urn's inhabitants to the purely extrapolated little town left desolate by them, the imaginative experience evoked by the urn was so attenuated that the inevitable return to "reality" was the only possible sequence. It was just this sort of extrapolation (from clowns and emperors to "faery lands forlorn"), "teas[ing] us out of thought as doth eternity," that, in the Nightingale Ode, precipitated the poet "back from thee to my sole self." In that ode, however, the poet returns to a reality made ambiguous by the vividness and intensity of the experience just sustained, and his allegiance as well as his consciousness remains divided. The poem concludes with a question, and it is not a rhetorical one:

> Was it a vision or a waking dream?
> Fled is that music—Do I wake or sleep? [40]

In the "Grecian Urn," however, the poet returns with a didactic motto.

[39] *The Poetical Works of John Keats,* ed. H. W. Garrod (London, 1961), p. 210. The controversy over the punctuation of these lines—the question of whether the quotation marks should embrace only the motto or the whole of the last two lines—need not occupy us here. I am assuming that the whole of the lines is to be understood as the urn's message to man, and accepted as such, though not explicitly endorsed, by the poet.

[40] *Ibid.,* p. 209.

Many readers have commented on the complexity of attitudes revealed in the ode, particularly the attitudes toward mutability. If there was an insight profoundly valid, this, we might feel, was its focus: the unresolved paradox of the inevitable loss of perfection reflected in human experience and the trap of permanence reflected in works of art. This is an insight, however, not an aphorism. What I am suggesting here, then, is that Keats, perhaps not trusting the sufficiency of the insight so *implied*, or not recognizing himself how central it had become in the structure of the poem, sensed the need for a stabilizing or resolving conclusion and provided one more resolutely conclusive than the poem as a whole could justify.[41] What unsettles us, I think, is not so much the oracular motto itself as the almost accusatory tone of the absolute pronouncement that follows it: "Beauty is truth, truth beauty" —well, that is something to meditate upon, but how can it be all one knows, and so forth, if one is not sure (and the poem as a whole has not made one sure) that one knows it at all?

My point here has been that, in addition to its tenuous and perhaps spurious relation to the ode's structure, this conclusion, in being so epigrammatic, will convey expressive effects that may be felt as incongruous in such a poem. In other words, even the reader who sees the final lines as reflecting an insight justified by the ode's thematic development may be alienated by the "cold certitude" with which that "Cold Pastoral" delivers it. He might have been better satisfied than Keats knew with something far less authoritatively conclusive; he might have been satisfied, in fact, with relatively weak closure.

[41] Perhaps I should mention that while I find these lines endlessly intriguing and recognize their relation to Keats's own concerns elsewhere in his poems and letters, I have also found attempts to reconcile their terms with the reader's experience of the concerns of the ode unconvincing. (This, by the way, would be an instance of what I referred to earlier as one reader's retrospective justification striking another as retrospective rationalization.) Also, I do believe that however interesting these lines may be for students of Keats's mind and development, one should not confuse one's interests as a student with one's experience as a reader.

The possibility thus raised is one that will concern us throughout the following section: namely, whether, in certain styles, relatively weak closure may not be the most successful kind of closure. That the question is not contradictory will, I think, become evident; but we may recall, in any case, what was observed above regarding the humorous possibilities of weak closure: the fact that the ultimate effect of an anticlimax, let us say, will depend upon the reader's sense of how it fits the author's design. If, for one reason or another, we are confident that the closural weakness is part of that design (again, in the two meanings of structure and intention), it will be successfully incorporated into our total experience of the poem. Indeed, whatever it was that made us confident of such a design—so that to some extent what we *expected* was weak closure—would leave us dissatisfied with anything else. Our assumption, of course, will be that the term "weak" is descriptive rather than evaluative. And since the implication is that it was so designed, we may call any instance of it "anti-closure." It will be precisely the reverse of epigrammatic closure, and its most significant effects will be those that result from the expressive quality of that final "gesture" I spoke of earlier.[42]

Thus, whereas the epigrammatic conclusion will convey authority, secure conviction, emotional containment, and brusque dismissal, the open-ended or anti-closural conclusion will convey doubt, tentativeness, an inability or refusal to make absolute and unqualified assertions. It will affirm its own irresolution and compel the reader to participate in it. As the description suggests, the expressive qualities of anti-closure, like those of epigrammatic closure, may imply moral and epistemological attitudes that reach beyond the specific concerns of the poem. They ask, "What do we know? How can we be sure we know it?" They question the

[42] There is, of course, a wide range of expressive effects, counterparts to the range of closural force, between epigrammatic and open-ended conclusions. At the upper end of the scale, not all secure closure is epigrammatic: there can be repose rather than snap, gentle cadence rather than lethal fall, stability rather than fixity. So, also, at the lower end of the scale; openness is as relative as closure.

validity and even the possibility of unassailable verities, the moral or intellectual legitimacy of final words. But we are evidently speaking here of modern poetry, and it is to this that we shall turn for our closing words on closure.

III Closure and Anti-Closure in Modern Poetry

I suggested in chapter 1 that a study of poetic closure could probably be made on historical lines, in which one traced the styles of poem endings from one age to another and considered such matters as closural traditions, conventions, and revolutions. The broad outlines of such a study have been to some extent implied here, and we have on occasion touched upon some fairly specific historical points. Thus (although it was not my intention), the preponderance of examples drawn from sixteenth- and seventeenth-century poetry might have suggested that Renaissance closure was (or was being considered) normative, while the discussions of associative structure and free verse were obviously tending toward generalizations about closure in Romantic and post-Romantic poetry. If we add that epigrammatic closure, in both its techniques and its expressive effects, would naturally be associated with neoclassical verse, we can see what those broad outlines might come to: closure in Renaissance poetry tended to be strong and secure, in Augustan poetry to be maximal, in Romantic poetry to be weak, and in modern poetry it has become minimal. This formulation is neat, but the moment we have thus explicitly constructed it, we know it must crumble under the weight of all the exceptions and qualifications we should have to add. How does one delimit Renaissance poetry? What does one do with Milton? Are there not important distinctions to be made among genres in any age? Are Pope's satires and epistles really so well closed? Is Wordsworth like Keats in this respect? And is it possible to generalize at all about modern poetry?

It is because of such questions and all that would be required to answer them that the present study cannot be regarded as even a crude approach to a historical survey; nor is it offered as such. I recognize that the title of this section, especially since it is the last one of the study, may suggest that an implicit historical line here reaches its natural termination. But examples from modern poetry have appeared throughout the preceding chapters and without special comment on the fact. Indeed, one of my major points has been that whereas certain forms and devices of closure are more appropriate to, and effective for, particular styles and structures, their appearance is not otherwise confined to any particular period. This last section has, to be sure, a certain strategic propriety, but modern poetry is thus set apart primarily because certain stylistic and structural possibilities have been fully realized only or most notably in the poetry of this century, and some of these possibilities involve special forms or devices of closure, or unusual variations on and departures from those considered earlier. These innovations and variations are, moreover, quite radical in certain respects, and reflect developments common to all the arts, and developments in cultural and intellectual history as well. For these reasons it is revealing to consider the closural modes of modern poetry as such.

The term "modern poetry" is a literary historian's nightmare, not only because dates always imply definitions (and vice versa), but because the most striking characteristic of the poetry of our time is its stylistic multiplicity. Not only are the forms widely various, but also the modes and mannerisms, the implied aesthetics, and the allegiances—or what we should ordinarily call the "traditions." The latter term is almost meaningless, however, in an era such as the present one, when almost every poetic tradition that has ever existed—native or foreign, Western or Oriental, classical or medieval—is to some extent viable, and the most characteristic feature of our poetic activity, broadly considered, is the apparent absence of any principle of *rejection*. It is an era in which we not only have free verse and syllabic verse, "Beat" poems and "academic" poems, poems inspired by drugs and poems created by electronic computers, but in which sonnets (a genre that both Pope and Whitman deplored) are printed side by side with epigrams (a genre that Keats would have regarded as subpoetical).

As this catalogue indicates, however, even if it is true that everything that has gone before still, in a way, goes, and that stylistic pluralism is more characteristic of twentieth-century poetry than any or all of its stylistic innovations, it is also true that some things now go in a very revolutionary way—and both facts are significant in an appreciation of closure in modern poetry.

First, we must recognize that modern poems exhibiting traditional formal and thematic structures are neither rare nor obviously anachronistic. We may observe, in fact, that contemporary poetry (of the past twenty years, let us say) is distinguished from contemporary music and art in just this respect. Although free verse, imagism, symbolism, and other stylistic developments have made their mark, none of them has created a break between modern and traditional poetry as radical as the break between nonobjective and representational painting, or between atonal and traditional music. Moreover, in art and music, *avant-garde* movements continue to occupy a significant and even dominant place, whereas in poetry, the very phrase "*avant-garde*" seems already dated. The point to be emphasized is that a large and entirely respectable part of contemporary poetry is simply indistinguishable from traditional poetry *in the ways that would affect closure*; and consequently, for much modern poetry there is little to add here—aside from that fact—that has not already been considered in earlier chapters.

Indeed, far from being revolutionary in this respect, much of the poetry that seems most characteristic of our time has struck several observers as being reactionary (commendably or not, as their positions incline them). John Press, for example, in a study subtitled "Trends in British Poetry Since the Second World War," writes:

> All these poets [he alludes to a large group including Elizabeth Jennings, Donald Davie, Philip Larkin, and A. Alvarez], mistrusting or ignoring the legacy of the Romantics . . . , are trying to bring back into the currency of the language the precision, the snap, the gravity, the decisive, clinching finality which have been lost since the late Augustan age.[43]

And Karl Shapiro, from a quite different point of view, complains as follows:

> A poem, according to [William Carlos] Williams, should not be that closed, should not click like a box. . . . The "closed" poem—the poem that clicks like a box—is the type of poem which has lately become a standard in the twentieth century. . . .[44]

The semiscriptural allusion to William Carlos Williams is, however, as "standard" as the alleged click, and the clear implication that strong closure is undesirable brings us to the second point.

In much modern poetry and in modern poems otherwise quite dissimilar in style, one may readily observe an apparent tendency toward anti-closure. To a considerable extent, this tendency reflects the proliferation and dominance of forms and modes such as free verse and interior monologue in which the structural resources of closure are minimal. More significantly, it seems to reflect a general preference for, and deliberate cultivation of, the *expressive* qualities of weak closure: even when the poem is firmly closed, it is not usually slammed shut—the lock may be secure, but the "click" has been muffled. Causality in these matters is, however, impossible to determine, for the forms and preferences not only reflect each other, but both reflect more general developments in literary history and ultimately in cultural history. Moreover, anti-closure is a recognizable impulse in all contemporary art, and at its furthest

[43] *Rule and Energy* (London, 1963), pp. 45–46.
[44] *In Defense of Ignorance* (New York, 1960), p. 161.

reaches it reflects changing presumptions concerning the nature of art itself.

I shall turn below to some of the broader considerations that may be involved in poetic anti-closure, but a relatively specific one will illustrate some of the points just raised. As we observed in chapter 1, one of the functions or effects of poetic form is to "frame" the poetic utterance: to maintain its identity as distinct from that of ordinary discourse, to draw an enclosing line, in other words, that marks the boundary between "art" and "reality." Now, it is clear that to the extent that the propriety of that boundary line itself is questioned, so also will be the propriety of its closural effects. What one may think of here are certain current (though by no means exclusively modern) conceptions of poetry and art that value the "natural" or the illusion of naturalness while disdaining the artful, the obviously conventional or artificial. Anti-closure in modern poetry, then, may be referred to some extent to this effort toward poetic realism, where structural or other features that mark the work as a verbal artifact—rather than a direct transcription of personal utterance—are avoided. Free verse itself, of course, is often hailed as being closer than more fixed meters to the natural rhythms of speech, and other closurally weak forms of poetry—thematically diffuse and deliberately "unfinished" fragments, for example—might be cultivated for corresponding reasons. The conception of poetry referred to here should not, however, be consigned too quickly to literary history, viewed merely as a legacy of Romanticism or an extension of realism. For the challenge it delivers to traditional notions concerning the functions and effects of poetry, and the very nature of art, is not itself narrowly confined.

Some of the broader aspects and implications of anti-closure have been suggested by Leonard B. Meyer in an article published in 1963 in which he distinguishes traditional and contemporary music as, respectively, "teleological" and "anti-teleological."[45] The

[45] "The End of the Renaissance? Notes on the Radical Empiricism of the Avant-garde," *Hudson Review* 16 (Summer, 1963): 169–85.

latter, he writes, "directs us toward no points of culmination—establishes no goals toward which to move. It arouses no expectations, except presumably that it will stop" (p. 174). He suggests that anti-teleological art embraces not only the serial music of Stockhausen and John Cage's composition by random operations, but also the paintings of Tobey, Rothko, and Mathieu, and the writings of Beckett, Robbe-Grillet, and Jackson Mac Low. His major point, however, as the title of his article indicates, is that "underlying this new aesthetic is a conception of man and the universe, which is almost the opposite of the view that has dominated Western thought since its beginnings" (p. 175).[46] Meyer associates this new conception, which he calls "radical empiricism," with Oriental philosophy and, to a lesser extent, with Existentialism and the philosophy of modern physics; but he points out that it is not so much a matter of the influence on one side as of the receptivity on the other.

The anti-teleological character of contemporary art has been observed by others and is, by one name or another, proclaimed by the spokesmen and leaders of *avant-garde* movements in painting, music, and fiction. The art critic, Doré Ashton, writes: "The feeling in much contemporary music that there is no beginning and no end but only 'aggregate units' corresponds to the feeling in certain abstractions [i.e., abstract paintings] that the heaving rhythms come to no formal conclusion but resume constantly. . . ."[47] As for fiction, Meyer's observations are echoed by a reviewer in a recent issue of the *Times Literary Supplement*. Speaking of the French novelists, Nathalie Sarraute, Claude Simon, Michel Butor, and, again, Alain Robbe-Grillet, he writes:

[46] The philosophy of the new aesthetics is summarized by Meyer as follows: "The denial of the reality of relationships and the relevance of purpose, the belief that only individual sensations and not the connection between them are real, and the assertion that predictions and goals depend not upon an order existing in nature, but upon the accumulated habits and preconceptions of men—all these rest upon a less explicit but even more fundamental denial: a denial of the reality of cause and effect" (*ibid.*, p. 178).

[47] *The Unknown Shore: A View of Contemporary Art* (Boston, 1962), p. 209.

> Two other features of the "New Novel" [i.e., in addition to the attempt to obliterate temporality] reinforce the sensation of unresolved movement in an abstract present where nothing is certain: the frequent recourse to labyrinthine patterns leading nowhere, and the use of detective-story suspense which remains suspended, or fizzles out in a non-solution.[48]

This reviewer sees an obvious relation between the techniques of the new French novelists and the Existentialist theory of the "absurd." Meyer had made a similar connection between anti-teleological art and modern philosophy, while Miss Ashton remarked that one motive for "openness" in modern painting was part of a general reaction against the European tradition: "The general opinion that European art was too 'finished' led American artists to rationalize their own lack of finish. A positive value was placed on the 'unfinished' look."[49] "Openness," the "anti-teleological," the positive value placed on the unfinished look or sound—anti-closure, in other words, is evidently a sign of the times in contemporary art; and whether one refers it specifically to a revolution in philosophy or in art history, one suspects that it is ultimately related to even more general developments and crises.

I do not propose to offer here a short history of modern times, nor do I think it necessary. The developments and crises I speak of are the commonplaces of our literature, sermons, political speeches, and lives. The stylistic pluralism of contemporary poetry reflects a broader pluralism of values in an age that is the heir to perhaps too many revolutions, what Nathalie Sarraute has called "the age of suspicion."[50] We know too much and are sceptical of all that we know, feel, and say. All traditions are equally viable partly because all are equally suspect. Where conviction is seen as

[48] "A Fiction Outside Time," anonymous review, *TLS*, January 21, 1965, p. 45.

[49] *The Unknown Shore*, p. 28.

[50] *The Age of Suspicion: Essays on the Novel* (New York, 1963); originally published in France under the title *L'Ere du Soupçon* (1956).

self-delusion and all last words are lies, the only resolution may be in the affirmation of irresolution, and conclusiveness may be seen as not only less honest but *less stable* than inconclusiveness.

What is particularly significant for poetry, as opposed here to art and music, is the suspicion of language. It is an age where linguistics is a branch of almost every discipline and almost every discipline is a branch of linguistics. Language is the badge of our suspect reason and humanity. It is the lethal trap sprung for truth; it is the reliquary of the mortmain of the past; it categorizes and codifies, obliterating the complexities, subtleties, and ambiguities of experience. Language is always making us mean more or less than what we want to mean. We look back upon our own self-betraying assertions not as the expressions of knowledge or conviction, but only as "a way of putting it," and upon the assertions of the past as "bequeathing us merely a receipt for deceit." [51]

Eliot's poem not only expresses the problem I speak of, but also embodies the paradox it entails. Language is what fails us and

[51] T. S. Eliot, "East Coker," *Four Quartets*, in *The Complete Poems and Plays* (New York, 1952), p. 125. The entire passage is relevant and revealing:

> That was a way of putting it—not very satisfactory:
> A periphrastic study in a worn-out poetical fashion,
> Leaving one still with the intolerable wrestle
> With words and meanings. The poetry does not matter.
> It was not (to start again) what one had expected.
> What was to be the value of the long looked forward to,
> Long hoped for calm, the autumnal serenity
> And the wisdom of age? Had they deceived us
> Or deceived themselves, the quiet-voiced elders,
> Bequeathing us merely a receipt for deceit?
> The serenity only a deliberate hebetude,
> The wisdom only the knowledge of dead secrets
> Useless in the darkness into which they peered
> Or from which they turned their eyes. There is, it seems to us,
> At best, only a limited value
> In the knowledge derived from experience.
> The knowledge imposes a pattern, and falsifies,
> For the pattern is new in every moment
> And every moment is a new and shocking
> Valuation of all we have been. . . .

what fails between us; but language is also the material of poetry. In the poem, "On Teaching the Young," referred to in connection with epigrammatic style (see p. 207, above), Yvor Winters wrote:

> A poem is what stands
> When imperceptive hands,
> Feeling, have gone astray.
> It is what one should say. . . .
> The poet's only bliss
> Is in cold certitude—. . . .

But what if the poet's problem is precisely that he does not know what one *should* say? What if silence and certitude are equally impossible? One answer was given by Yeats, who wrote, "Unlike the rhetoricians, who get a confident voice from remembering the crowd they have won or may win, we sing amid our uncertainty. . . ." [52] Although this could stand as an epigraph to the present section, Winters' lines are not therefore irrelevant for contemporary poetry. On the contrary, the demand for certitude reflects, to a large extent, the same cultural situation as the affirmation of uncertainty. When certitude can be assumed, it need not be announced; and, as intellectual history reveals, in an age when beliefs are crumbling, militant fideism will be as characteristic as desperate scepticism. It is not surprising, then, that the same generation of poets that developed the song of uncertainty also gave new life and power to the oracular epigram, for if the one is naturally anti-closural, perhaps we might best see the other as anti-anti-closural.

The song of uncertainty in modern poetry expresses the temper (or distemper) of our times thematically; it also reflects it in its very structure. The relation between structure and closure is of considerable importance here, for "anti-closure" in all the arts is a matter not only of how the works terminate but how and whether

[52] W. B. Yeats, *Essays* (New York, 1924), p. 492.

they are organized throughout. The "openness" and "unfinished" look and sound of *avant-garde* poetry and music is not a quality of their endings only, but affect the audience's entire experience of such works.[53] Also, when Charles Olson speaks of the new "OPEN verse" as opposed to the " 'closed' verse . . . which is pretty much what we have had, in English & American, and have still got, despite the work of Pound & Williams," [54] one gathers (though the openness of his rhetoric is often incoherent) that he refers to the over-all structure of both kinds of poetry. Whereas the weak closure of much modern poetry can be understood partly as the result of the prevalence of formal and thematic structures that offer minimal resources for closure, the reverse is also likely: the prevalence of free verse, for example, probably reflects, in part, the impulse to anti-closure, the reaction against poems that "click like a box." Thus, although a survey of the modifications of formal and thematic structure in modern poetry would take us far afield from our specific concerns here, it must be emphasized that anti-closure cannot be seen solely as a radical conception of how poems should *end.*

The relation of anti-structure to anti-closure is also important in view of the apparent backwardness of poetry in both respects as compared to modern painting and music. Although the *avant-gardism* to which Meyer was alluding is significant in these arts, it represents only a minor and tangential aspect of contemporary poetic activity. But if the anti-teleology of the modern poet is not so thoroughgoing as that of the painter or composer, it may be due more to the conservatism of the material of his art than to the conservatism of the poet himself. While he may share the general impulse to "radical empiricism," he is confined by the fact that if his empiricism is too radical, his art loses both its identity and, more important, the sources of its characteristic effects. For the

[53] In painting, of course, one does not speak of endings in any case, but see p. 36, above, for the idea of closure in spatial art.

[54] "PROJECTIVE VERSE . . . vs. The NON-Projective," in *The New American Poetry, 1945–1960*, ed. Donald M. Adams (New York, 1960), p. 386.

material of poetry is not words, but *language*—a system of conventions previously determined and continuously mediated by usage in a community—and if the poem divorces itself utterly from the structure of discourse, it ceases to be poetry and ceases to affect us as such. Although traditional *formal* structures may yield to deliberate dissolution, the design of a poem is never wholly formal and a considerable degree of organization is built into it by virtue of its fundamental relation to the structure of discourse. Consequently, to the extent that anti-closure is a matter of anti-structure, the poet cannot go all the way.

Indeed, what we find as we look more closely at individual poems is that, while anti-closure in modern poetry is a recognizable tendency with interesting consequences, it is rarely realized as the total absence of closural effects. The tendency reveals itself primarily in what might be called "hidden closure," where the poet will avoid the expressive qualities of strong closure while securing, in various ways, the reader's sense of the poem's integrity.

The techniques of anti-closure and hidden closure are far too numerous and various to be adequately represented here, either in discussion or illustration. Some of the more significant possibilities can be considered, however, and we may begin by observing that any of the terminal features mentioned earlier as sources of weak closure can, of course, become anti-closural devices. Thus, even if a poem is otherwise well closed in terms of its structure, unwanted finality effects in the concluding lines can be weakened or obscured by metrical deviations, self-qualifying expressions, allusions to unstable events, and so forth. Also, some of the most interesting developments in modern modes of closure arise not so much from radical departures as from subtly effective variations upon traditional ones. Although the poems of Wallace Stevens, for example, frequently contain absolute pronouncements and epigrammatic aphorisms, they also illustrate extremely delicate kinds of terminal suspension, usually through a combination of strong and weak closural features. Thus, in the lines from "Sunday Morning" cited earlier as an example of closural allusion, we may also notice that the ultimate effect is far from a click, and more complex than even a settling:

> And, in the isolation of the sky,
> At evening, casual flocks of pigeons make
> Ambiguous undulations as they sink,
> Downward to darkness, on extended wings.[55]

Frequently, as here, the sense of a lingering suspension results partly from the rhythm of the syntax, as a fairly long sequence of unresolved clauses is brought to syntactic completion, but concluded with a final qualification. The same sense of combined continuity and stability is achieved in different ways in the final stanza of "Thirteen Ways of Looking at a Blackbird":

> It was evening all afternoon.
> It was snowing
> And it was going to snow.
> The blackbird sat
> In the cedar limbs.[56]

and in the concluding lines of "Debris of Life and Mind":

> . . . she will listen
> And feel that her color is a meditation,
>
> The most gay and yet not so gay as it was.
> Stay here. Speak of familiar things a while.[57]

Another effective variation upon traditional modes of closure is illustrated in several of Yeats's poems in which traditional formal structures yield closural forces of the kind discussed in chapter 2.

[55] *The Collected Poems of Wallace Stevens* (New York, 1961), p. 70.
[56] *Ibid.*, p. 95.
[57] *Ibid.*, p. 338.

Yeats not only exploited traditional forms for ironic and parodic (and sentimental) effects, but also turned them to anti-closural ends. We might consider here only one example of this poetic sabotage, his frequent use of stanzaic refrains in pseudo-ballads. As we observed earlier, a refrain tends to function as a force for continuation unless it is modified in the last verse. Yeats, however, usually carries a single refrain throughout—and the refrain itself is often a question, a paradox, or some similarly unsettling utterance. In "The O'Rahilly," for example, each of the four stanzas concludes, irrelevantly enough each time, with the refrain, "*How goes the weather?*", and its anti-closural effect in the final stanza is obvious:

> What remains to sing about
> But of the death he met
> Stretched out under a doorway
> Somewhere off Henry Street;
> They that found him found upon
> the door above his head
> 'Here died the O'Rahilly
> R.I.P.' writ in blood.
> *How goes the weather?* [58]

Sometimes, of course, the continued iteration of a refrain can have a cumulative force, so that its final occurrence is climactic or self-reinforcing: yes, that's the way it is, there is no other way.[59] But in many of these poems, the repeated refrain often has an expressive effect that we shall encounter several times in the following pages: a refusal to comment, to "draw conclusions."

[58] *The Collected Poems of W. B. Yeats* (New York, 1951), pp. 305–6. (Italics in text.)

[59] See, e.g., "Three Things," with its refrain, "*A bone wave-whitened and dried in the wind,*" and "The Apparitions," ("*Fifteen apparitions have I seen;/The worst a coat upon a coat-hanger.*"), *ibid.*, pp. 258 and 332. (Italics in text.)

The simplest way in which a poet can suggest a state of instability is to represent it directly—and here we approach one of the most interesting aspects of modern closure. As I remarked earlier, until the development of the Romantic lyric, a poem was likely to represent a dialectic process only when it could also be represented as ultimately resolved. In much modern poetry, however, the occasion for a poem is more likely to be the existence of an ultimately unresolvable process, and the conclusion is more likely to be a question than an answer. The following poem by Robert Graves is characteristic in this respect:

The Straw

Peace, the wild valley streaked with torrents,
A hoopoe perched on his warm rock. Then why
This tremor of the straw between my fingers?

What should I fear? Have I not testimony
In her own hand, signed with her own name
That my love fell as lightning on her heart?

These questions, bird, are not rhetorical.
Watch how the straw twitches and leaps
As though the earth quaked at a distance.

Requited love; but better unrequited
If this chance instrument gives warning
Of cataclysmic anguish far away.

Were she at ease, warmed by the thought of me
Would not my hand stay steady as this rock?
Have I undone her by my vehemence? [60]

The questions are, indeed, not rhetorical, which is why they evade stability. Nevertheless, although closure here is not strong, it is secure; for if the central question remains unanswered, it has been,

[60] *Collected Poems: 1955* (New York, 1955), p. 275.

by the conclusion of the poem, explicitly *defined*—and we do know then why the straw trembles and what the speaker fears. The poem has developed toward a moment of self-recognition; although for the speaker it takes the form of self-doubt, for the reader it is transformed into a stable enough revelation of character and circumstance. The expressive effect of the concluding question is, again, that sense of a lingering suspension so typical of modern closure. But closure it is.

While it would be impossible to determine the specific origins of this particular closural mode, one of its most significant and probably influential realizations was in T. S. Eliot's early dramatic monologues. In these poems, Eliot depicted in a memorable style what would eventually become the most familiar representative *persona* of twentieth-century poetry and fiction. We encountered him earlier, with all his characteristic hesitations, qualifications, self-doubts, and self-questionings, in our discussion of "The Love Song of J. Alfred Prufrock," and, as we observed there (pp. 145–48), the representation of such a consciousness made irresolution the most and perhaps the only dramatically appropriate conclusion. In "Portrait of a Lady," Prufrock or another version of him once again enacts his internal dialectics and once again concludes in a quandary. His questions ring throughout the poem and, in one form or another, throughout the years that follow, unanswered and unanswerable: "Are these ideas right or wrong?" and, in the concluding passage:

> Well! and what if she should die some afternoon,
> Afternoon grey and smoky, evening yellow and rose;
> Should die and leave me sitting pen in hand
> With the smoke coming down above the housetops;
> Doubtful, for a while
> Not knowing what to feel or if I understand
> Or whether wise or foolish, tardy or too soon . . .
> Would she not have the advantage after all?
> This music is successful with a "dying fall"

> Now that we talk of dying—
> And should I have the right to smile?[61]

The music that has accompanied the external and internal scenes ("attenuated tones of violins/Mingled with remote cornets," and "inside my brain a dull tom-tom . . ./Absurdly hammering a prelude of its own") concludes, as does the poem itself, with a "dying fall"—just as, in "The Hollow Men," the poem ends in the same way the world does. The whimper, the question, the dying fall: with these, Eliot established a tone and style of poetic closure that has become as familiar and representative as the personality of Prufrock. What we must add, however, is that in "Portrait of a Lady," as in "Prufrock," "Gerontion," and "The Hollow Men," the inconclusiveness is only a thematic element, and that all these poems are, in terms of their respective structures, successfully closed. In "Portrait," for example, the concluding questions are not only appropriate to the consciousness that evolves them, but the passage in which they appear is clearly terminal: it is a retrospective summary, an evocation of death, of afternoon and evening "with the smoke coming down"—and the music is, indeed, "successful with a 'dying fall.' "

Eliot was not the only modern poet for whom unanswerable questions became a stylistic signature, nor was he the first for whom thematic irresolution was a characteristic closural mode. Several of Yeats's well-known poems conclude with equally well-known questions:

> . . . And what rough beast, its hour come round at last,
> Slouches towards Bethlehem to be born?[62]

[61] *Complete Poems and Plays*, p. 11. (Ellipsis marks in text.)

[62] "The Second Coming," *Collected Poems*, p. 185. I alluded a bit earlier to metrical deviation as one of the anti-closural resources of modern poetry. In form and effect, it is the exact reverse of the terminal "return to the norm" discussed in chapter 2. In his recently published study of modern prosody, Harvey Gross points out this particular anti-closural effect (though not quite as such—neither closure nor anti-closure is his concern) in "The Second Com-

Being so caught up,
So mastered by the brute blood of the air,
Did she put on his knowledge with his power
Before the indifferent beak could let her drop? [63]

O chestnut-tree, great-rooted blossomer,
Are you the leaf, the blossom or the bole?
O body swayed to music, O brightening glance,
How can we know the dancer from the dance? [64]

In each of these poems, as in those by Eliot cited above, the questions convey the expressive qualities of weak closure—a sense of open-endedness, a refusal to speak the unspeakable, solve the unsolvable, resolve the unresolvable—but they also secure adequate closure. Even without commenting on the general structural forces that give these lines closural strength, we may observe that terminal features, such as those discussed in the last chapter, are evident in all of them: the conclusion of "Among School Children" is epigrammatic in several obvious respects, "Leda and the Swan" concludes with a "drop," and the rough beast's hour has "come round at last."

If Eliot sends us back to Yeats, then Yeats send us back, here as elsewhere, to Blake. One of the most common sources of anti-closure in modern poetry is the simple articulation of antinomies, a possibility illustrated in the following poem as throughout the *Songs of Innocence and of Experience:*

---

ing": "Since the penultimate line is regular, . . . the last lines of the poem show symmetry and asymmetry in sharp rhythmical contrast. There can be no comfortable scansion of the last line. . . . However conceived in scansion, the line is rhythmically unresolved. The poem ends taut with expectancy; prosodic energy does not diminish but reaches out into the surrounding darkness" (*Sound and Form in Modern Poetry: A Study of Prosody from Thomas Hardy to Robert Lowell* [Ann Arbor, Mich., 1964], p. 50).

[63] "Leda and the Swan," *Collected Poems*, p. 212.

[64] "Among School Children," *ibid.*, p. 214.

The Clod and the Pebble

'Love seeketh not itself to please,
Nor for itself hath any care,
But for another gives its ease,
And builds a Heaven in Hell's despair.'

So sung a little Clod of Clay,
Trodden with the cattle's feet,
But a Pebble of the brook
Warbled out these metres meet:

'Love seeketh only Self to please,
To bind another to its delight,
Joys in another's loss of ease,
And builds a Hell in Heaven's despite.' [65]

We could hardly speak here of a closural failure, and yet the stark representation of an absolute contradiction—with no final assessment, no comforting integration—is clearly a special mode of closure. The implicit "conclusion" here that, in the absence of any other, forces itself upon the reader is, in Gloucester's words, "And that's true, too." We might also recognize that there is a stability of deadlock as well as a stability of repose.

There are numerous contemporary counterparts to Blake's poem, not only in the articulation of antinomies but, more generally, in thematic structures that seem to call for some final comment that is, however, not given. The effect, as here, is to compel the reader to "draw his own conclusions"—and we may think, perhaps, of Leonard B. Meyer's "radical empiricist" as, in one guise, the poet who merely presents the data. He may in various ways call attention to the fact that he is standing off, offering no final words; he may, for example, conclude with an apparently irrelevant observation. A recent poem by Robert Lowell presents a

[65] *The Poetical Works of William Blake,* ed. John Sampson (London, 1961), p. 92.

sort of documentary picture of a man trying to drink away his domestic griefs:

> This man is killing time—there's nothing else.
> No help now from the fifth of Bourbon
> chucked helter-skelter into the river,
> even its cork sucked under.
>
> Stubbed before-breakfast cigarettes
> burn bull's-eyes on the bedside table;
> a plastic tumbler of alka seltzer
> champagnes in the bathroom.[66]

Six stanzas follow, in which the intractable disorder of his emotions and situation is further represented both metaphorically and graphically. The poem concludes:

> The chcese wilts in the rat-trap,
> The milk turns to junket in the cornflakes bowl,
> car keys and razor blades
> shine in an ashtray.
>
> Is he killing time? Out on the street,
> Two cops on horseback clop through April rain
> to check the parking meter violations—
> their oilskins yellow as forsythia.

The assertion with which the poem had opened ("This man is killing time")—ambiguous, ironic, and therefore unstable in any case—now becomes a question, no less ambiguous, ironic, or unstable. Having posed it, or perhaps hearing it posed, the speaker does not answer, but instead turns to glance outside the window—and changes the subject. The concluding observation, however, is perhaps not entirely irrelevant after all; for what he discovers in the

[66] "The Drinker," *For the Union Dead* (New York, 1964), pp. 36–37.

scene outside are images of his own concern, mirrors "of insidious intent," which, like the streets in "Prufrock," "lead you to an overwhelming question." Rain falls, the cops clop, and parking meters click. The answer is unspoken, but the answer may be there; time is being killed, but time, as on the clocks of those parking meters, is running out.

In the discussion of the "narrative lyric" (pp. 122–26) we observed that poems of this sort usually secure closure through the poet's more or less clear statement, at the end, of the *significance* of the events so reported—as when, in everyday conversation, someone tells an anecdote and then explains the point: "Well, that goes to show. . . ." Modern poetry, however, is filled with what we should otherwise call "pointless anecdotes," or anecdotes of which the only point could be, "This is a kind of thing that happens." [67] In such poems, closure will depend upon and be secured primarily through the reader's sense of the implied integrity rather than the announced significance of the events related—though, as in the following poem, closure will frequently be strengthened by the natural stopping places of time:

My Papa's Waltz

The whiskey on your breath
Could make a small boy dizzy;
But I hung on like death:
Such waltzing was not easy.

We romped until the pans
Slid from the kitchen shelf;
My mother's countenance
Could not unfrown itself.

[67] There is clearly a relation between this narrative mode in poetry and the current emphasis in fiction or criticism on the objective, invisible, in a sense inaudible, nonmoralizing narrator who "shows" rather than "tells" his tale—and who does not, of course, draw conclusions. The history and rationale of this emphasis are discussed extensively by Wayne C. Booth in *The Rhetoric of Fiction* (Chicago, 1961).

The hand that held my wrist
Was battered on one knuckle;
At every step you missed
My right ear scraped a buckle.

You beat time on my head
With a palm caked hard by dirt,
Then waltzed me off to bed
Still clinging to your shirt.[68]

The refusal to make final comments is only one aspect of a more general refusal—that is, to make assertions. The irony and ambiguity which we noted above in Robert Lowell's poem and which, as we all know, have become axioms of contemporary poetic criticism can be seen as refusals of just this kind. Both irony and ambiguity are "pluralistic" ways of speaking, evasions of committed speech. If, as I suggested earlier, we recognize that the suspicion of language itself is a significant aspect of the contemporary malaise, one may see the development of a poetry of nonstatement as a possible consequence of this. If the traitor, language, is not to be exiled, one may disarm him and make him a prisoner of war. But first, one must force him to renounce his major claim to glory and the mainspring of his treachery: the power to assert. For only a statement, not a word, can lie or delude. Poetry must be language and it must have some relation to discourse, but it need not be "discourse of reason."

The retreat from formal discourse took two directions in modern poetry—toward subjectivity and toward objectivity. I alluded to the first of these in chapter 3, in the discussion of associative structure and the poetic representation of interior speech. The second was the self-consciously proclaimed empiricism of the early Imagists, who insisted that in a poem one should *present* the object rather than talk about it. The poems that resulted were often, though not always, nonstatements:

[68] Theodore Roethke, *Words for the Wind* (New York, 1958), p. 53.

In a Station of the Metro

The apparition of these faces in the crowd;
Petals on a wet, black bough.[69]

Closure in the "pure" imagist poem was usually weak, but that was part of its intended effect. The image itself, the presentation of the raw data, the sensory experience of the poet recreated in the reader—that was the object of the objectivity. If it was successful, presumably the recreated experience would be sufficient and stable enough—but in the way any sense impression would be, with a lingering "after-image." Like the *haiku* by which it was influenced, the imagist poem did not assert the speaker's motives or personality except in what has been described as "a tone of melancholy and restrained plaintiveness."[70] And it usually did not assert anything else either.

I shall return later to the poetry of nonstatement, particularly as it appears in the work of William Carlos Williams. First, however, I would like to consider some of the more immediately striking departures from the conventions of discourse in the poetry of E. E. Cummings. In general, Cummings' familiar uses and abuses of grammar, punctuation, typography, lineation, and space conceal fairly conventional thematic structures and—what concerns us here—modes of closure. By placing ordinarily terminal punctuation at the *beginning* of a concluding line, by ending a poem with a comma or semicolon, by disarranging normal word order or just by leaving sentences and phrases syntactically incomplete, Cummings can avoid the unwanted expressive qualities of strong closure. At the same time, however, through occasional rhyme or systematic half-rhyme, through repetition, closural allusions, and absolute assertions, he usually secures an adequate sense of stability and finality.

One poem, for example, opens as follows:

[69] Ezra Pound, *Personae* (New York, 1926), p. 109.

[70] Earl Miner, "Pound, *Haiku*, and the Image," *Hudson Review*, 9 (Winter, 1956–57): 580.

> i was sitting in mcsorley's.   outside it was New
> York and beautifully snowing.
>
> Inside snug and evil. [. . .] [71]

As the poem develops (in "lines" ranging from four to one hundred words with no perceptible principle of formal order or limitation), the evil is eventually incarnated as a monstrous drunk sitting beside the speaker. The poem concludes:

> gone Darkness   it was so near to me, i ask of shad-
> ow won't you have a drink?
>
> (the eternal perpetual question)
>
> Inside snugandevil.   i was sitting in mcsorley's
> It, did not answer.
>
> outside.(it was New York and beautifully,snowing. . . .

In circling back to its own opening, the poem appropriates one of the simplest and most effective closural devices. By concluding, however, with the "eternal perpetual question" unanswered, with four dots and an open parenthesis, Cummings is also able to convey the expressive qualities of anti-closure.

Even where Cummings' violations of linquistic propriety and poetic tradition are apparently most radical—that is, in his typographic picture-poems—closure can still be seen as arising from such conventional sources as syntactic structure. It is true, for example, that the celebrated grasshopper poem cannot be performed, vocally or subvocally, as an utterance of consecutive words, and that it must be seen to have its effect: [72]

[71] *Poems: 1923–1954* (New York, 1954), pp. 78–79. (I have bracketed my own ellipsis marks to distinguish them from those in the text.)
[72] *Ibid.*, p. 286.

r-p-o-p-h-e-s-s-a-g-r
who
a)s w(e loo)k
upnowgath
PPEGORHRASS
eringint(o-
aThe):l
eA
!p:
S a
(r
rIvInG .gRrEaPsPhOs)
to
rea(be)rran(com)gi(e)ngly
,grasshopper;

Nevertheless, the poem is not an entirely visual event. Indeed, as a visual design, it is of only minimal interest and hardly self-sufficient. If, however, it is read as a verbal sequence (scrambled, to be sure), the final line is obviously closural; for it not only correctly assembles the anagrams of "grasshopper," but it brings to syntactic completion a fragmented and disarranged, but otherwise conventional, sentence.

In certain respects, the poetry of William Carlos Williams is more radical in its intentions and possibilities than that of Cummings and, in the one respect to be discussed below, more interesting and significant for the concerns of this study. Consider, to begin with, the following poem, which returns us to the poetry of nonstatement:

BETWEEN WALLS

The back wings
of the

hospital where
nothing

will grow lie
cinders

in which shine
the broken

pieces of a green
bottle.[73]

These lines are not, of course, without significance, and if we supply from the title the otherwise lacking preposition, they will form a grammatically complete sentence. The structure of this sentence involves a series of syntactic suspensions emphasized by enjambment, so that, while the short lines hold down his pace, the reader is nevertheless propelled forward at every point save line 6, which allows a slight resolution, and line 10, when the sentence is completed. Although the lineation and spacing here create an obvious visual structure, the formal sources of closure are otherwise quite minimal. Reading this poem, in fact, is like watching someone in the process of sketching a landscape visible only to him. We know it is finished because he stops, and at that point we are invited to observe what we now understand to be a completed drawing. What is most interesting about this form of closure is that little supports it aside from the grammatical resolution and the fact that nothing follows. By stopping, however, the poem announces its own sufficiency, and, in compelling the reader to accept that sufficiency, gives a retrospective emphasis more or less to every element in it. It is as if the poet were saying, "What? did you expect more? Look again, it's all there."

The paradoxical effect of the nonassertive conclusion, then, is to heighten the apparent significance of everything else in the poem. The effect can be seen even more clearly, perhaps, in the following:

[73] *The Collected Earlier Poems of William Carlos Williams* (Norfolk, Conn., 1951), p. 343.

THIS IS JUST TO SAY

I have eaten
the plums
that were in
the icebox

and which
you were probably
saving
for breakfast

Forgive me
they were delicious
so sweet
and so cold [74]

We might regard a poem like this as, in effect, the literary counterpart of what is called in contemporary art, *"l'objet trouvé"*: that is, a work of art created by the isolation, framing, and labeling of an otherwise ordinary object—a bottle-cap, a used razor blade, a bird feather, and so forth. In poetry, "les paroles trouvées" are otherwise ordinary utterances isolated from the context of ordinary affairs, framed by the margin of a page, and labeled by the title; and, just as the ordinary object may be further aestheticized by a coat of paint or shellac, or simply by being turned upside down, so the utterance may be made fictive by meter or at least a lineation that obliges one to pace one's reading somewhat "unnaturally." [75]

[74] *Ibid.*, p. 354.

[75] This paragraph was written before the appearance of Ronald Gross's *Pop Poems* (New York, 1967). What Gross offers therein and refers to as "found poetry" apparently corresponds to my description, but is not what I had in mind here. Williams' poems *are* poems: noncontextual, ahistorical *representations* of ordinary utterances, and composed as such by the poet himself. Gross, on the other hand, creates pseudo-verse by imposing his own lineation on actual news items, advertisements, etc. Cf. the discussion of Seldon Rodman's transcription of Vanzetti's "Last Speech to the Court," above, pp. 22–23.

Closure here, as in the poem discussed above, is strengthened by formal features as well as syntactic resolution. Once again, however, it also depends upon the reader's tendency or willingness to respond to the implicit closure as such: to grant that the utterance has, as an *artful* structure, justified its own integrity, stability, and sufficiency. The poem's status and effect as art, and the reader's sense of its closural adequacy, are, then, mutually reinforcing and to some extent mutually dependent. The possibility and significance of precisely that relationship between closure and art comprise, perhaps, the major burden of our argument throughout these pages.

IV Coda: Beyond Closure

It would be possible to conclude this study in either a closural or anti-closural manner, bearing witness thereby to the nature of its subject or the weight of the moment in which it was written. We have, in a sense, come full circle here; and we may choose between remaining within that circle—within the mutually reinforcing confines of our initial definitions of poetry and subsequent considerations of closure—and stepping outside it into the swirl of history, all unstable, incoherent, and open-ended as it is. The circle has its psychological comforts as well as its aesthetic charms, but once we have felt the tugs and seen the perimeter grow faint and troubled, the security it otherwise offers has, in any case, been compromised. The circle, it seems, is broken; one might as well walk over to the rim and take a look at what lies beyond it.

There is hardly an observation or assumption made in this study concerning the nature of poetry and the relation between art and closure that has not been challenged by some development in contemporary artistic activity or theory. Not only has the initial proposition that the sense of closure is a valued quality in most experiences been implicitly questioned by the "anti-teleological" structures of *avant-garde* paintings and musical compositions, but long-standing conceptions of the very nature of art have, implicitly or explicitly, become subject to radical revision. In the poetry considered in the previous section, anti-closure was repeatedly seen as an impulse, not a reality, and none of these poems qualified the validity of principles evolved earlier in the study. Works—whether or not to call them works of poetry or even of art is precisely the problem—have been produced, however, that do upset our categories and put knots into the thread of our argument. It is true that the "radical empiricism" of contemporary art is represented by only a fugitive fraction of current poetic activity, and, for reasons outlined above, there appears to be a fundamental conservatism built into the very nature of literature. Nevertheless, it is becoming increasingly evident that the techniques of *avant-garde* music and painting may have counterparts in poetry, and that certain radical theories concerning art in general may have applications to literary art.

Central to our arguments here have been notions regarding the perception and general experience of art that apparently require modification in the light of contemporary theories and techniques involving *chance*. These theories and techniques have been most notable in musical composition, but have recently been extended to the theater, the cinema, and other more or less literary forms of art. Although, for example, the techniques of serial music and John Cage's composition by "random generation" are in many ways directly opposed to each other, both involve conceptions of the relation of art to determinacy and indeterminacy which, in turn, play some havoc with our assumptions regarding the place of expectation, determination, and predictability in the perception of structure and closure. Some of the thinking that attends this sort of activity appears in an article by Ernst Krenek, a composer who uses serial procedures (that is, mathematical rules of generation) to determine every tonal and rhythmic parameter of his works:

> Generally and traditionally "inspiration" is held in great respect as the most distinguished source of the creative process in art. It should be remembered that inspiration by definition is closely

> related to chance, for it is the very thing that cannot be controlled, manufactured, or premeditated in any way. . . . Actually the composer has come to distrust his inspiration because it is not really as innocent as it was supposed to be, but rather conditioned by a tremendous body of recollection, tradition, training, and experience. In order to avoid the dictations of such ghosts, he prefers to set up an impersonal mechanism which will furnish, according to premeditated patterns, unpredictable situations. . . . The unexpected happens by necessity. The surprise is built in.[76]

It might be observed, however, that the unexpected, the surprise, had always been built into the work of art. What is different here is that the artist is not less surprised than his audience; and, given certain traditional conceptions of art, this may be supposed to make all the difference. We remarked in chapter 1, for example, that games and works of art have much in common: in both, the sequence of events is confined according to predetermined principles; both thus create "enclosures" within the ground of ordinary, more or less fortuitously determined, experience. However, whereas in games we "play" with chance, it might be thought that in art we *control* chance; whereas in games we hedge in the randomness of events by arbitrary rules, in art all events are ultimately put to the service of the artists's design—the effects, that is, which he designs his work to have on an audience. As long as one regards this as a crucial distinction, then works created by the artist's deliberate abdication of sovereignty are not works of art, but games (often, to be sure, requiring much intellectual skill of the players and yielding corresponding rewards). What is lacking is precisely what has been eliminated: not predetermined events (for as Krenek, Cage, and others would insist, the events are most scrupulously determined by certain operations) but *designed effects.*

In serial music and randomly generated musical, verbal, or

[76] "Extents and Limits of Serial Techniques," in *Problems of Modern Music,* ed. Paul Henry Lang (New York, 1960), pp. 90–91.

theatrical "happenings," effects on the audience do, of course, occur; but they only "happen" to occur. One could say of a traditional work of art that it was to a large extent caused by its own effects—that most of its features, that is, were determined (whether "consciously" or "unconsciously" is beside the point) by the artist's continuous adjustment of his design to accord with his estimation of its potential effectiveness upon its potential audience, using himself and his own responses as a measure. Here, however, once the machinery that generates them has been set up, the nature of those features presumably cannot or should not be modified by the artist's sense of their interest, expressive power, or other effects on the perceptions or emotions of an audience—himself or any other. It is true, of course, as Krenek points out, that chance is always involved in the creative process in the sense that numerous aspects and elements of the work of art seem to be given to the artist or to occur to him "spontaneously." As Krenek also suggests, however, these elements are not really given by raw chance (if there is such a thing), but are themselves determined by the artist's personal history and his experiences in a particular culture. At every level of determination, then, the work of art, as traditionally conceived, reflects the humanity of the artist: not necessarily his individual "personality," but his peculiarly human psychological organization, his sensations, perceptions, emotions, and experiences. It might be thought that herein lay the characteristic interest and value of art, and that to the extent that the artist rejects the pressures of his own humanity in favor of the dictates an "impersonal mechanism," to that extent he has ceased to function as an artist, and what he creates thereby—whatever it is and however it affects us—is not and does not affect us as "art."

As all my qualifications indicate, I am aware of the fact that the distinctions I am making here do indeed depend upon certain traditional notions of the nature of art. And, as one soon learns, no sane man or woman willingly engages for long in arguments regarding the proper definition of art. The definitions will change to accommodate the practices, and it is quite possible that, as Meyer seems to suggest, we are about to enter an era in which art, as it has been understood since classical times, will no longer be practiced. That closure, too, will no longer be of interest or value is suggested by the following comments made by a French critic writing sympathetically of serial music:

> For the univocal trajectory of the work of the past, with its ineluctable termination, predictable and reassuring, is substituted now the aleatory—a musical time open to a thousand possibilities. . . . [Serial music] has become a form of thought, a manner of living time in its discontinuity and its absence of finality. . . .[77]

Less radical in their implications than works that blur the line between art and other experiences—and oblige us, therefore, either to revise our definitions of art or ungraciously deny those works the status they claim—are those that blur the line between traditionally distinct art forms, such as painting and poetry. The latter, however, are of even more direct interest to us, and it will be appropriate to conclude this study with a brief consideration of them.

It was suggested earlier that unless a poem retains a particular characteristic relation to the conventional structure of discursive language, it is not poetry, or at least is not affecting us as such. This implicit definition is challenged, however, by the existence of what might be called "nonrepresentational poetry": poems which involve a use of language that is more or less divorced from the conventions of discourse. Nonrepresentational poetry takes many directions—that is, directions away from what we usually think of as poetry. Indeed, much of it seems to have been influenced more by the techniques and aesthetic theories of *avant-garde* music and painting than by any development in even the most radical *literary* movements of the century. The variety with which I am most concerned here, however, commonly referred to as "concrete poetry," has a long tradition in literary history and will recall such

[77] André Boucourechliev, "Qu'est-ce la musique sérielle?," *France Observateur*, August 31, 1961; quoted by Ashton, *The Unknown Shore*, p. 211.

ancient forms as anagrams, acrostics, and palindromes, as well as the picture-poems of E. E. Cummings and, in certain respects, the verse of William Carlos Williams.

We have already noted that the structure of much free verse relies to a significant extent upon visual clues to form, and that certain contemporary poems may resist vocal performance altogether. It is certainly true that as poetry has increasingly become a form of art encountered primarily as print upon a page, the visual properties of language-as-text have become increasingly important and interesting to both the reader and the poet. Whether or not they "click like a box," poems are getting to *look* much less like boxes, and free-verse poets in particular are evidently more concerned now with what was heretofore a quite marginal source of formal possibilities and expressive effects, namely the spatial design of their works.

While the formal aspects of much contemporary poetry may, then, appeal to the eye as well as to the ear, there remains a significant difference between reading a poem and looking at one. When one reads, one is responding to a text as a symbolic notation, and even though we learn to interpret the notation without the point-for-point mediation of a vocal or subvocal translation into speech-sounds, we nevertheless interpret it through a conventional system of symbol translation. In concrete poetry, however, this system may become only a marginal factor in the reader's appropriate response to the work. Graphic as well as typographic techniques are used to anchor words, letters, fragments of letters, or punctuation marks firmly to the page as more or less purely visual events, as elements of a spatial design that insist upon their *physical* identity and, to that extent, resist conventional translation. A concrete poem may, for example, consist of a group of orthographically similar words (e.g. *black, block, lack, look*) repeated and arranged on the page so as to create a visual design out of corresponding and contrasting letter shapes. Although the words frequently have thematic connections as well, so that visual "puns" are produced, the spatial arrangements discourage syntactic interpretation; there are sometimes brief phrases, but rarely sentences and even more rarely groupings that could be understood as references or assertions.

The concrete poem resists reading not only because symbol translation becomes an inappropriate or unrewarding response, but also because the observer's perception of linguistic elements is organized spatially rather than temporally. Normally, when we read a text our experience is controlled and modified by the sequential order in which the symbolic elements are arranged and perceived. We can read sequences of words that are printed along vertical or oblique as well as the conventional horizontal lines, and we can even (though with strain) read from bottom to top or right to left; we always, however, read the symbols in linear order, one after the other. "One after the other" implies, furthermore, a specifically temporal ordering of experiences. Reading is a process in which events occur and affect us in a strictly determined temporal sequence and over a distinct period of time. It takes time, of course, to look at a concrete poem or any work of spatial art, but there is usually nothing in the work itself that either determines the temporal sequence or controls the duration of our perceptions. Concrete poems, in other words, have tops, sides, and bottoms, but not necessarily beginnings, middles, and ends.

The question of closure in concrete poetry may thus seem to remove itself conveniently from concern here, for presumably the closural as well as structural aspects of such works are the province of the art critic proper. We may, that is, simply refuse to regard them as poems, noting merely that the traitor, language, has here been brought to his knees and not only disarmed but beheaded. The question re-asserts itself, however, when we consider certain of these works more closely; for it becomes evident that, although the poems remain "nonrepresentational" in that they do not represent utterances, nevertheless the structure and effect of many of them do depend significantly upon the reader's responses to the symbolic properties of language and, therefore, upon the conventions of discourse.

Before turning to a specific example, one further general point should be added here. It might be thought that when we look at a concrete poem, every tendency we carry over from our ordinary experiences with language is met with an obstacle, a barrier on which hangs a sign with the intimidating message, "All linguistic baggage must be deposited at this point." And this, indeed, is often the effect desired by the concrete poet, whose rebellion against the tyranny of words may be a central motive of his theory and practice. My generalizations here, however, have not attempted to embrace all the varieties of *avant-garde* experiments with language, and even what I have referred to specifically as "concrete poetry" takes many forms, not all of them equally radical or equally remote from traditional verse. Furthermore, although the emphasis on the irreducibly visual nature and sufficiency of concrete verse inevitably counteracts our tendency to interpret and respond to the linguistic elements in a conventional manner, nevertheless the effectiveness of much of this poetry lies precisely in the tension thereby created; for our tendencies to respond to linguistic structures in a certain manner are continuously being reinforced by all our nonaesthetic experiences with language, and are not so readily counteracted. The concrete poet may exploit our conditioned responses to language only in order to reveal their limitations, futility, or irrelevance, but he may also do so in order to engage our interest or emotions and to take advantage of hitherto untapped resources of wit and even of expressiveness. What he "expresses" may seem minimal enough compared with what is or has been possible in traditional poetry, but perhaps that is not the most relevant area of comparison.

The concrete poem that will furnish the final illustration of closure to appear in this study was composed by Ian Hamilton Finlay, one of the more prominent among a group of Scottish and English poets who are energetically committed to the linguistic enterprises I have been describing.[78] Finlay's poem (see p. 268) is

[78] An adequate bibliography of concrete poetry is difficult to compile, since most of the poets are European or South American and most of their works have appeared in fugitive publications not readily available in the United States. Among the other poets significantly involved in the movement are Dom Sylvester Houédard, Edwin Morgan and John Sharkey in Britain, Augusto de

a a a a a
c c c c
r r r r r
o o o o
b b b b b
a a a a
t t t t t
s s s s
t t t t t
a a a a
b b b b b
o o o o
r r r r r
c c c c
a a a a a

composed of multiple acrostics of the word *acrobat* deployed in such a manner as to create a symmetrical visual pattern. It is evident that while any other selection of eight letters, so arranged, would produce a similar pattern, the reader's experience of both the structure and closural force of the piece depends to a significant extent upon the thematic (that is, symbolic and conventional) properties of that particular selection. Most obviously, of course, the conventional meaning of the word is relevant here, for it titles and reflects the very process by which we respond to the poem's structure: the reader's eye, in tracing the work through all its realizations, performs or perceives something like acrobatic somersaults and pyramids. More significant, however, than the particular thematic reference of the word is simply its thematic *integrity*: the fact that it *is* a word and that the letters, when "read" in certain linear sequences, will satisfy the reader's inevitable search for linguistic coherence.[79]

When the piece is viewed simply as a spatial design, closure of

Campos in Brazil, Eugen Gomringer in Switzerland, and Diter Rot in Iceland. An exhibition entitled "Between Poetry and Painting" was given by the Institute of Contemporary Arts in London, Oct. 22 to Nov. 27, 1965, for which a catalogue was printed, including a useful but not too readable "Chronology" of the movement compiled by Houédard. An article, "Concrete Poetry," by Mike Weaver, appeared in *The Lugano Review* 1 (Summer, 1966): 100–125, and some observations and further bibliographic notes by Jonathan Williams may be found in his article, "Parsons Weems and Vachel Lindsay . . . ; or Travails in America Deserta," in *Arts in Society* 3, no. 3 (1965): 371–88. A recent issue of the *Beloit Poetry Journal*, 17 (Fall, 1966) is devoted to the movement and contains a number of representative concrete poems.

The version of Finlay's poem, "Acrobats," printed here was designed and executed in letterpress by Ann Stevenson at the Bath Academy of Art.

[79] Finlay has acknowledged and described his intention here as follows: ". . . I used the principle that the eye—that is the mind, through the eye—will always try to make simple sense of a constellation of letters; by reflex it will attempt to string them into words; so that you can actually create patterns within a constellation, obtaining a basic pattern of letters, plus additional patterns that occur when the words start to form, as they will, even if the viewer is quite passive in front of the poem." (Letter to the author, March 5, 1965.)

the most basic kind is achieved here through the formal symmetry of the arrangement of letter shapes. When it is "read," however, closure of another kind is achieved by the multiple formations of the word *acrobat*. This is, indeed, a highly closed poem, a visual epigram. Nevertheless, it must be added that the two sources of closure are mutually incompatible and that the poem is, therefore, in a certain sense thoroughly anti-closural. The sort of tension mentioned earlier is created here by the fact that one's tendency and ability to *read* the letters in various sequences conflict directly with one's tendency and ability to *look at* the symmetrical and stable spatial pattern; one can, in fact, experience the tension as an optical strain if one tries to do both simultaneously. We may, in order to serve and further substantiate the principles of this study, wish to emphasize the fact that insofar as Finlay's piece *is* a "poem"—that is, insofar as it affects us not merely as a visual design—both its structure and closure depend upon an exploitation of linguistic convention. Nevertheless, we must also recognize that the exploitation results in a structure that is experienced as both spatial and temporal, stable and unstable, finite and infinite, closed and open.

We conclude, then, à la mode, with paradoxes. As we look over the rim of the circle, we apparently find ourselves confronted by a situation that demands either a total revaluation of all we have said or, at the least, our recognition that we have been speaking only of "special cases," that our observations are dependent, throughout, upon definitions of art and poetry and assumptions concerning the experience of both that have only limited validity. We could, of course, also meet the situation by refusing to modify the definitions or assumptions, by refusing to regard the recalcitrant "works of art" as art or the "poems" as poetry. But it is hard to say what would be gained thereby. Definitions must accommodate usage, assumptions must accommodate evidence. Not only do all art forms have a history—ends as well as beginnings—but so also does art itself, along with all human institutions. It may be suspected, however, that what we should now have to call "traditional" poetry is not without a sustaining vitality continuously fed and renewed by its relation to the rather formidable institution of language itself—and that as long as we continue to speak at all, no matter what new uses are made of language, there will remain revelations and delights to be found in the old uses. Poetry ends in many ways, but poetry, I think, has not yet ended.

BIBLIOGRAPHY

A. GENERAL WORKS CITED

Allport, Floyd H. *Theories of Perception and the Concept of Structure.* New York, 1955.

Ashton, Doré. *The Unknown Shore: A View of Contemporary Art.* Boston, 1962.

Bate, Walter Jackson. *John Keats.* Cambridge, Mass., 1963.

Beloit Poetry Journal 17 (Fall, 1966).

Between Poetry and Painting. Catalogue of the exhibition given by the Institute of Contemporary Arts. London, Oct. 22–Nov. 27, 1965.

Blanchard, Brand. *Reason and Analysis.* La Salle, Ill., 1962.

Booth, Wayne C. *The Rhetoric of Fiction.* Chicago, 1961.

Bowra, C. M. *Primitive Song.* Cleveland, 1962.

Brower, Reuben. *The Poetry of Robert Frost.* New York, 1963.

Browne, Sir Thomas. *The Works of Sir Thomas Browne.* Edited by Geoffrey Keynes. 4 vols. Chicago, 1964.

Burke, Kenneth. *Counter-Statement.* Chicago, 1931.

———. "On Musicality in Verse," in *The Philosophy of Literary Form.* New York, 1957.

Caldwell, James Ralston. *John Keats' Fancy: The Effect on Keats of the Psychology of His Day.* Ithaca, N.Y., 1945.

Cherry, Colin. *On Human Communication.* Cambridge, Mass., 1957.

Coleridge, Samuel Taylor. *Biographia Literaria.* Edited by J. Shawcross. 2 vols. Oxford, 1965.

Cunningham, J. V. *Tradition and Poetic Structure.* Denver, 1960.

———. *The Journal of John Cardan: Together with The Quest of the Opal and The Problem of Form.* Denver, 1964.

Farnsworth, Paul R. *The Social Psychology of Music.* New York, 1958.

"A Fiction Outside Time." Anonymous review. *Times Literary Supplement,* Jan. 21, 1965, p. 45.

Gombrich, E. H. J. *Art and Illusion.* New York, 1960.

Greenberg, Joseph H., ed. *Universals of Language.* Cambridge, Mass., 1963.

Gross, Harvey. *Sound and Form in Modern Poetry: A Study of Prosody from Thomas Hardy to Robert Lowell.* Ann Arbor, Mich., 1964.

Gross, Ronald. *Pop Poems*. New York, 1967.
Hebb, D. O. *The Organization of Behavior*. New York, 1949.
Henderson, Harold G. *An Introduction to Haiku*. New York, 1958.
Herbert, T. Walter. "Sound and Sense in Two Shakespeare Sonnets." *Tennessee Studies in English*, 1958. Pp. 43–52.
Hough, Graham. "Free Verse," in *Image and Experience: Reflections on a Literary Revolution*. Lincoln, Neb., 1960.
Hubler, Edward. *The Sense of Shakespeare's Sonnets*. Princeton, 1952.
Hudson, H. H. *The Epigram in the English Renaissance*. Princeton, 1947.
Hutton, James. *The Greek Anthology in Italy to the Year 1800*. Ithaca, N.Y., 1935.
Hymes, Dell H. "Phonological Aspects of Style: Some English Sonnets." In *Style and Language*, edited by Thomas A. Sebeok. New York, 1960.
Johnson, Edgar. *Charles Dickens: His Tragedy and Triumph*. 2 vols. New York, 1952.
Johnson, Samuel. *The Idler and The Adventurer*. Edited by W. J. Bate, John M. Bullitt, and L. F. Powell. The Yale Edition of the Works of Samuel Johnson, vol. 2. New York and London, 1963.
Jonson, Ben. "Timber: or, Discoveries." In *Ben Jonson*, edited by C. H. Herford, Percy and Evelyn Simpson. Vol. 8. Oxford, 1954.
Keats, John. *The Letters of John Keats*. Edited by Hyder Edward Rollins. 2 vols. Cambridge, Mass., 1958.
Knight, G. Wilson. *The Mutual Flame: On Shakespeare's Sonnets and The Phoenix and the Turtle*. London, 1955.
Koffka, Kurt. *Principles of Gestalt Psychology*. New York, 1935.
Kökeritz, Helge. *Shakespeare's Pronunciation*. New Haven, 1953.
Krenek, Ernst. "Extents and Limits of Serial Techniques." In *Problems of Modern Music*, edited by Paul Henry Lang. New York, 1960.
Langbaum, Robert. *The Poetry of Experience: The Dramatic Monologue in Modern Literary Tradition*. New York, 1957.
Lanier, Sidney. *The Science of English Verse*. New York, 1907.
Lanz, Henry. *The Physical Basis of Rime*. London, 1931.
Leichentritt, Hugo. *Musical Form*. Cambridge, Mass., 1951.
Lundin, Robert W. *An Objective Psychology of Music*. New York, 1953.
Lyon, Harvey T., ed. *Keats' Well-Read Urn: An Introduction to Literary Method*. New York, 1958.
Martz, Louis. *The Poetry of Meditation*. New Haven, 1962.
Masson, David I. "Free Phonetic Patterns in Shakespeare's Sonnets." *Neophilologus* 38 (1954): 277–89.
Meyer, Leonard B. *Emotion and Meaning in Music*. Chicago, 1956.
———. "The End of the Renaissance? Notes on the Radical Empiricism of the Avant-garde." *Hudson Review* 16 (Summer, 1963): 169–85.
Meyerhoff, Hans. *Time in Literature*. Berkeley, 1955.
Miller, George A. *Language and Communication*. New York, 1951.
Miner, Earl. "Pound, *Haiku*, and the Image." *Hudson Review* 9 (Winter, 1956–57): 570–84.

Mizener, Arthur. "The Structure of Figurative Language in Shakespeare's Sonnets." *Southern Review* 5 (1940): 730–47.
Ness, Frederick W. *The Use of Rhyme in Shakespeare's Plays.* New Haven, 1941.
Olson, Charles. "PROJECTIVE VERSE . . . vs. The NON-Projective." In *The New American Poetry, 1945–1960*, edited by Donald M. Adams. New York, 1960.
Osgood, Charles E. *Method and Theory in Experimental Psychology.* New York, 1953.
Parry, C. Hubert H. "Coda." In *Grove's Dictionary of Music and Musicians*, edited by Eric Blom. Vol. 2. London, 1954.
Pattison, Bruce. *Music and Poetry of the English Renaissance.* London, 1948.
Press, John. *Rule and Energy: Trends in British Poetry Since the Second World War.* London, 1963.
Prince, F. T. *The Italian Element in Milton's Verse.* Oxford, 1954.
Richards, I. A. *Principles of Literary Criticism.* New York, 1930.
———. "How Does a Poem Know When It is Finished?" In *Parts and Wholes*, edited by Daniel Lerner. New York, 1963.
Richmond, H. M. *The School of Love: The Evolution of the Stuart Love Lyric.* Princeton, 1964.
Sarraute, Nathalie. *The Age of Suspicion: Essays on the Novel.* Translated by Maria Jolas. New York, 1963.
Shapiro, Karl. *In Defense of Ignorance.* New York, 1960.
Sidney, Sir Philip. "An Apologie for Poetrie." In *Elizabethan Critical Essays*, edited by G. Gregory Smith. Vol. 1. London, 1950.
Skinner, B. F. *Verbal Behavior.* New York, 1957.
Smith, William George, comp. *The Oxford Dictionary of English Proverbs.* Oxford, 1935.
Souriau, Etienne. "Time in the Plastic Arts." *Journal of Aesthetics and Art Criticism* 7 (1949): 294–307.
Stewart, George R. *The Technique of English Verse.* New York, 1930.
Tillyard, E. M. W. *Milton.* New York, 1930.
Valéry, Paul. "On Speaking Verse." In *The Art of Poetry*, translated by Denise Folliot. *The Collected Works of Paul Valéry*, vol. 7. Bollingen Series, no. 45. New York, 1961.
Vygotsky, L. S. *Thought and Language.* Edited and translated by Eugenia Hanfmann and Gertrude Vakar. Cambridge, Mass., 1962.
Ward, Aileen. *John Keats: The Making of a Poet.* New York, 1963.
Weaver, Mike. "Concrete Poetry." *Lugano Review* 1 (Summer, 1966): 100–125.
Wellek, Albert. "The Relationship between Music and Poetry." *Journal of Aesthetics and Art Criticism* 21 (Winter, 1962): 149–56.
Wellek, René, and Warren, Austin. *Theory of Literature.* New York, 1949.
Wertheimer, Max. "Laws of Organization in Perceptual Forms." In *A Source Book of Gestalt Psychology*, edited by Willis D. Ellis. New York, 1939.

Whaler, James. *Counterpoint and Symbol: An Inquiry into the Rhythm of Milton's Epic Style*. Angelistica, vol. 6. Copenhagen, 1956.
Whipple, T. K. *Martial and the English Epigram from Wyatt to Jonson.* Berkeley, 1925.
Williams, Jonathan. "Parsons Weems and Vachel Lindsay . . . ; or Travails in America Deserta," *Arts in Society* 3, no. 3 (1965): 371–88.
Wilson, John Dover. *An Introduction to the Sonnets of Shakespeare for the Use of Historians and Others*. New York, 1964.
Wimsatt, W. K., Jr. *The Prose Style of Samuel Johnson*. New Haven, 1941.
Winters, Yvor. *In Defense of Reason*. Denver, 1943.
———. "Poetic Styles, Old and New." In *Four Poets on Poetry*, edited by D. C. Allen. Baltimore, 1959.
Yeats, William Butler. *Essays*. New York, 1924.

B. EDITIONS OF POEMS CITED

Arnold, Matthew. *Poetical Works of Matthew Arnold*. London, 1913.
Blake, William. *The Poetical Works of William Blake*. Edited by John Sampson. Oxford, 1961.
Browning, Robert. *The Poetical Works of Robert Browning*. London, 1957.
Bullett, Gerald, ed. *Silver Poets of the Sixteenth Century*. London, 1960.
Campion, Thomas. *The Works of Thomas Campion*. Edited by Percival Vivian. Oxford, 1909.
Carew, Thomas. See Howarth, *Minor Poets.*
Carroll, Lewis. *Logical Nonsense: The Works of Lewis Carroll.* Edited by Philip C. Blackburn and Lionel White. New York, 1934.
Crashaw, Richard. *The Poems of Richard Crashaw*. Edited by L. C. Martin. Oxford, 1927.
Cummings, E. E. *Poems: 1923–54*. New York, 1954.
Cunningham, J. V. *The Exclusions of a Rhyme*. Denver, 1960.
Daniel, Samuel. See Hebel and Hudson, *Poetry of the English Renaissance.*
Dickinson, Emily. *The Complete Poems of Emily Dickinson*. Edited by Thomas H. Johnson. Boston, 1960.
Donne, John. *The Poems of John Donne*. Edited by H. J. C. Grierson. London, 1957.
Eliot, T. S. *The Complete Poems and Plays*. New York, 1952.
Empson, William. *Collected Poems*. New York, 1949.
Finlay, Ian Hamilton. "Acrobats" in letterpress version executed by Ann Stevenson at Bath Academy of Art.
Fitts, Dudley, trans. *Poems from the Greek Anthology*. New York, 1956.
Frost, Robert. *The Complete Poems of Robert Frost*. New York, 1964.
Gascoigne, George. See Hebel and Hudson, *Poetry of the English Renaissance.*
Graves, Robert. *Collected Poems: 1955*. New York, 1955.
Greville, Fulke, Lord Brooke. *Poems and Dramas of Fulke Greville*. Edited by Geoffrey Bullough. 2 vols. New York, 1945.
Hardy, Thomas. *Collected Poems*. New York, 1931.

Harrington, Sir John. See Hebel and Hudson, *Poetry of the English Renaissance.*

Hebel, J. William, and Hudson, Hoyt H., eds. *Poetry of the English Renaissance*. New York, 1957.

Herbert, George. *The Works of George Herbert.* Edited by F. E. Hutchinson. Oxford, 1959.

Herrick, Robert. *The Complete Poetry of Robert Herrick.* Edited by J. Max Patrick. Garden City, N.Y., 1963.

Hoskins, John. See Hebel and Hudson, *Poetry of the English Renaissance.*

Howarth, R. G., ed. *Minor Poets of the Seventeenth Century.* London, 1959.

Jonson, Ben. *Poems of Ben Jonson.* Edited by George Burke Johnston. Cambridge, Mass., 1955.

Kallimachos. See Fitts, *Poems from the Greek Anthology.*

Keats, John. *The Poetical Works of John Keats.* Edited by H. W. Garrod. London, 1961.

Kunitz, Stanley. *Selected Poems: 1928–1958.* Boston, 1958.

Landor, Walter Savage. *Poems.* Selected and introduced by Geoffrey Grigson. Carbondale, Ill., 1965.

Levertov, Denise. *O Taste and See.* New York, 1964.

Lomax, John A., and Lomax, Alan, comps. *American Ballads and Folk Songs.* New York, 1934.

Lowell, Robert. *For the Union Dead.* New York, 1964.

Martial. *Epigrams.* Translated by Walter C. A. Ker. Loeb Classical Library. 2 vols. London, 1960.

Marvell, Andrew. *The Poems and Letters of Andrew Marvell.* Edited by H. M. Margoliouth. 2 vols. Oxford, 1952.

Milton, John. *John Milton: Complete Poems and Major Prose.* Edited by Merritt Y. Hughes. New York, 1957.

Opie, Iona, and Opie, Peter, eds. *The Oxford Dictionary of Nursery Rhymes.* Oxford, 1951.

Owen, Wilfred. *Collected Poems.* Edited by C. Day Lewis. Norfolk, Conn., 1964.

Pope, Alexander. *The Poems of Alexander Pope.* Edited by John Butt. New Haven, 1963.

Pound, Ezra. *Personae.* New York, 1926.

Ralegh, Sir Walter. *The Poems of Sir Walter Ralegh.* Edited by Agnes M. C. Latham. Cambridge, Mass., 1962.

Richards, I. A. *Screens and Other Poems.* New York, 1959.

Robinson, Edward Arlington. *Collected Poems.* New York, 1937.

Rodman, Seldon, ed. *A New Anthology of Modern Verse.* New York, 1938.

Roethke, Theodore. *Words for the Wind.* New York, 1958.

Shakespeare, William. *Sonnets.* Edited by Barbara Herrnstein Smith. To be published, 1968.

———. *The Complete Works of Shakespeare.* Edited by George Lyman Kittredge. Boston, 1936.

Shelley, Percy Bysshe. *The Complete Poetical Works of Percy Bysshe Shelley.* Edited by Thomas Hutchinson. London, 1960.

Shirley, James. See Hebel and Hudson, *Poetry of the English Renaissance.*

Sidney, Sir Philip. *The Poems of Sir Philip Sidney.* Edited by William A. Ringler, Jr. Oxford, 1962.

Skelton, John. *The Complete Poems of John Skelton.* Edited by Philip Henderson. London, 1931.

Smart, Christopher. *The Collected Poems of Christopher Smart.* Edited by Norman Callan. 2 vols. Cambridge, Mass., 1949.

Spenser, Edmund. *The Poetical Works of Edmund Spenser.* Edited by J. C. Smith and E. de Selincourt. London, 1957.

Stevens, Wallace. *The Collected Poems.* New York, 1961.

Suckling, Sir John. See Howarth, *Minor Poets.*

Surrey, Henry Howard, Earl of. See Bullett, *Silver Poets.*

Thomas, Dylan. *Collected Poems.* New York, 1953.

Vanzetti, Bartolomeo. See Rodman, *A New Anthology.*

Vaughan, Henry. *The Works of Henry Vaughan.* Edited by L. C. Martin. 2 vols. Oxford, 1914.

Vaux, Thomas, Lord. See Hebel and Hudson, *Poetry of the English Renaissance.*

Weever, John. See Hebel and Hudson, *Poetry of the English Renaissance.*

Whitman, Walt. *Leaves of Grass: Comprehensive Reader's Edition.* Edited by Harold W. Blodgett and Sculley Bradley. *The Collected Writings of Walt Whitman,* Vol. 9. New York, 1965.

Williams, William Carlos. *The Collected Earlier Poems.* Norfolk, Conn., 1951.

———. *The Collected Later Poems.* Norfolk, Conn., 1963.

Winters, Yvor. *Collected Poems.* Denver, 1960.

Wordsworth, William. *The Poetical Works of William Wordsworth.* Edited by Thomas Hutchinson; revised edition by Ernest de Selincourt. London, 1961.

Wyatt, Sir Thomas. *Collected Poems of Sir Thomas Wyatt.* Edited by Kenneth Muir. Cambridge, Mass., 1960.

Yeats, William Butler. *The Collected Poems of W. B. Yeats.* New York, 1951.

INDEX

Index

Index